Beyond the Palio

Note from the Series Editor

This volume marks the fourth publication in the occasional series of essay collections published for the Society for Renaissance Studies by Blackwell Publishing. These collections make available in book form selected special numbers of the Society's journal, *Renaissance Studies*. The volumes are all guest edited, and all the material appearing will also have been peer-reviewed in the normal way, and approved by the journal's editorial board.

John E. Law,
Series Editor

Previous books in the series:
Daniel Carey, Editor, *Asian Travel in the Renaissance* (2004)
Ceri Davies and John E. Law, Editors, *The Renaissance and the Celtic Countries* (2004)
Roberta J. M. Olson, Patricia L. Reilly and Rupert Shepherd, Editors, *The Biography of the Object in Late Medieval and Renaissance Italy* (2006)

Beyond the Palio

Urbanism and Ritual in Renaissance Siena

Edited by

Philippa Jackson and
Fabrizio Nevola

Neroccio di Bartolomeo de'Landi, *San Bernardino Preaching on the Campo*, c. 1468, Museo Civico, Palazzo Pubblico, Siena (Photo: Museo Civico, Siena)

Published on behalf of the Society for Renaissance Studies

Blackwell Publishing

BLACKWELL PUBLISHING
350 Main Street, Malden, MA 02148-5020, USA
9600 Garsington Road, Oxford, OX4 2DQ, UK
550 Swanston Street, Carlton, Victoria 3053, Australia

The right of Philippa Jackson and Fabrizio Nevola to be identified as the Authors of the Editorial Material in this Work has been asserted in accordance with the UK Copyright, Designs, and Patents Act 1988.

First published 2006 by Blackwell Publishing Ltd

Library of Congress Cataloging-in-Publication Data has been applied for

ISBN: 1-4051-5572-8
ISBN 13: 978-1-4051-5572-4

A catalogue record for this title is available from the British Library

Set in 10/12pt New Baskerville by Graphicraft Limited, Hong Kong

For further information on
Blackwell Publishing, visit our website:
www.blackwellpublishing.com

FSC
www.fsc.org
MIX
Paper from
responsible sources
FSC® C013604

Contents

Acknowledgements

PHILIPPA JACKSON AND FABRIZIO NEVOLA

The essays in this collection were originally presented in two study days, entitled 'Ritual in Siena: Comparative Disciplinary Approaches' held respectively at the University of Warwick and the Università degli Studi di Siena on 16 May and 12 June 2003. Firstly, we would like to thank all those who contributed stimulating papers and participated in making both days a success. We are particularly grateful to Julian Gardner, Director of AHRB Centre for the Study of Renaissance Elites and Court Cultures, for supporting the conference in Warwick. Our special thanks go to Gioachino Chiarini, Dean of the Facoltà di Lettere e Filosofia of the Università degli Studi di Siena, who, as Director of the Centro Warburg Italia, provided a venue for the Siena day, which included an on-site seminar in the city's churches and streets. The latter involved both speakers, and other participants, and we would like to thank in particular Matthias Quast, Gabriele Fattorini, Ludwin Paardekooper, Monika Butzek and Christa Gardner von Teuffel for their contributions. Friends and colleagues have provided encouragement, support and helpful criticism, and we should like to mention particularly: David Chambers, Diana Norman, Georgia Clarke, Jonathan Davies, Kate Lowe and Guido Rebecchini. All scholars working on Sienese history owe a great debt to the directors and staff of the Archivio di Stato di Siena and the Biblioteca Comunale, and we should like to thank them collectively here. Financial support for the conference was provided by the AHRB, the Centro Warburg Italia and the Fondazione Monte dei Paschi di Siena. Finally of course, John Law has been an enthusiastic supporter of this project, and we thank him for welcoming this collection as a special issue of *Renaissance Studies*.

Foreword

It gives me great pleasure to introduce this collection of essays, the result of successful collaboration between the Centre for Renaissance Studies at the University of Warwick, the Facoltà di Lettere e Filosofia of the Università degli Studi di Siena and the Centro Warburg Italia of Siena, over the past few years. The fruits of this collaboration are also to be seen in the two international conferences on the political, economic and cultural history of Siena in the Renaissance period, which were attended by a large group of international scholars, the proceedings of which are to be published this year (*Siena nel Rinascimento: l'ultimo secolo della repubblica. I: Cultura e arte*, Acts of the International Conference, Siena (28–30 Sept. 2003 and 16–18 Sept. 2004), ed. Gianni Mazzoni and Fabrizio Nevola Florence [edizioni Cadmo] 2006 and *Siena nel Rinascimento: l'ultimo secolo della repubblica. II: Storia*, Acts of the International Conference, Siena (28–30 Sept. 2003 and 16–18 Sept. 2004), ed. Mario Ascheri and Fabrizio Nevola, Siena [Accademia Senese degli Intronati] 2006).

Siena is well known for the *palio* horse race that the title of this volume evokes, but as the editors suggest in their introduction and the essays in the collection show, the city's ritual calendar was far richer and more varied than this strongly felt bi-annual event, and indeed studies of the *palio* are in part responsible for the lack of attention given to other urban rituals. As Director of the Centro Warburg Italia, a cultural research centre that encourages interdisciplinary studies, the theme of this collection is also significant to our own research objectives. Consideration of the ritual use of public space requires skills and interests that go beyond the disciplinary boundaries of political history or the history of art and architecture, but require instead a combination of these, as well as conscious engagement with methods and themes borrowed from the social sciences. The quality of the studies that are presented here provides clear evidence of the innovative research that can result from such a varied approach. The Centro Warburg Italia's support for the publication of this volume in the *Renaissance Studies Special Issue* series again confirms our interdisciplinary mission and international focus. In conclusion, I would also like to thank the editors for the energy and enthusiasm that has brought this publication to completion, as also the contributors for their fine essays.

Gioachino Chiarini,
Preside della Facoltà di Lettere e Filosofia
Università degli Studi di Siena
and Director of the Centro Warburg Italia

Notes on Contributors

Machtelt Israëls received her Ph.D. in art history from the University of Amsterdam and is an independent scholar based in Amsterdam and Siena. During 2004–2005 she was a fellow at the Villa I Tatti, The Harvard University Center for Italian Renaissance Studies in Florence. She has published on painting in Quattrocento Siena and is currently preparing a monograph on Sassetta.

Mauro Mussolin received his Ph.D. in the History of Architecture at the Istituto Universitario di Architettura di Venezia and currently teaches at New York University in Florence. He was Research Fellow at Villa I Tatti, The Harvard University Center for Italian Renaissance Studies in Florence in 2002–3. His research focusses on the relationship between liturgy and architecture and the process of sanctifying sacred spaces. His publications include several studies of Sienese and Florentine religious communities and their buildings. Mussolin's forthcoming book is on Michelangelo's Reliquary Balcony built for Clement VII in the church of San Lorenzo, Florence.

Fabrizio Nevola teaches at the Università degli Studi di Siena. He has held fellowships at the Canadian Centre for Architecture (Montreal) and Villa I Tatti, The Harvard University Center for Italian Renaissance Studies (Florence) and was AHRB Research Fellow at the University of Warwick (2001–4). His research focus is on the architectural and urban history of Renaissance Siena. He has published numerous articles (e.g. *Art Bulletin*, 2000 and *Renaissance Studies*, 2003) and has a book forthcoming entitled *Architecture and Government in Renaissance Siena: Fashioning Urban Experience* with Yale University Press *(1400–1555)*.

Diana Norman is Senior Lecturer in the History of Art at The Open University. She is the author of *Siena and the Virgin. Art and Politics in a Late Medieval City State* (1999) and *Late Medieval and Renaissance Painting in Siena, 1250–1555* (2003), both published by Yale University Press. She is also the academic editor of the two volume series: *Siena, Florence and Padua. Art, Religion and Society 1260–1400* (1995), published by Yale University Press and The Open University, and has written numerous articles on late medieval and renaissance Italian art.

Philippa Jackson is completing research at the Warburg Institute in London on the patronage of Pandolfo Petrucci, the leading citizen of the Sienese republic at the beginning of the sixteenth century. She has written on the cult of Mary Magdalen under his regime and is currently preparing a book entitled *Pandolfo Petrucci: Politics and Patronage in Renaissance Siena*. Her major interests are in Renaissance cultural history and cardinals of the late fifteenth and early sixteenth centuries.

Christine Shaw is a Senior Research Associate at the Faculty of History of the University of Cambridge; she has previously been a research fellow at the London School of Economics and the University of Warwick. Her research has focused on the political society of Italy in the fifteenth and sixteenth centuries. Among her publications are *Julius II: The Warrior Pope* (1993); *The Politics of Exile in Renaissance Italy* (2000); and *Popular Government and Oligarchy in Renaissance Italy* (2006).

Gerrit Jasper Schenk studied in Germany and Italy and took a doctorate in Medieval History at the University of Stuttgart in 2001. After being visiting research fellow at the University of Heidelberg and the Academy of Science Heidelberg in 2000/2001, he lectures Medieval History at the University of Essen and since 2003 at the University of Stuttgart. His publications are on late-medieval urban history, ceremony, ritual, and politics in Italy and Germany, and the perception of Mount Athos in the West, and include *Zeremoniell und Politik. Herrschereinzüge im spätmittelalterlichen Reich*, Köln/ Weimar/ Wien (Böhlau Verlag) 2003.

1

Introduction

Beyond the Palio: urbanism and ritual in Renaissance Siena

PHILIPPA JACKSON AND FABRIZIO NEVOLA

To this day Siena is renowned for the *Palio*, a dramatic horse race staged on the city's central square, whose complex social and anthropological significance has received the attention of numerous scholars.[1] The word 'palio' derives from the Latin word 'pallium' meaning a rectangular length of cloth; it also describes the banner that constitutes the prize for the victor, and gives its name to the race itself. In the past, the term also had the meaning of baldachin or canopy, such as that used for ceremonial processions and entries.[2] The *Palio* then brings together these meanings in a highly ritualized contest that is played out in the city's streets and central square, the Piazza del Campo.

Interest in the *Palio*, and its historical development, has nonetheless deflected attention from Siena's other ritual practices, which have been neglected by comparison to those of other centres.[3] This is surprising, as

[1] Analysis of Siena's ritual calendar has remained largely divided between method-driven studies of the social anthropology of the contemporary phenomenon of the Palio and more empirical accounts of the history of the race and the *contrade* that define the urban competition. See, W. Heywood, *Our Lady of August and the Palio of Siena* (Siena, 1899); idem, *Palio and Ponte* (London, 1904); G. Cecchini and D. Neri, *The Palio of Siena*, trans. E. Mann Borghese (Siena, 1958); A. Dundes and A. Falassi, *La Terra in Piazza. An Interpretation of the Palio of Siena* (Berkeley and Los Angeles, 1975); M. A. Ceppari *et al.* (eds.), *L'immagine del Palio: Storia, cultura e rappresentazione del rito di Siena* (Siena, 2001), which includes an extensive bibliography, 560–72; G. Parsons, *Siena, Civil Religion and the Sienese*, (Aldershot and Burlington, 2004).

[2] An example of this triple meaning of baldachin, race and banner can be seen in the chronicle of Matteo Villani (iii.84) and (iii.85). The first passage describes the cardinal legate being received in Florence in 1353 with great honour 'con un ricco palio di seta e d'oro sopra capo portato da nobili popolani'; a second discusses the horse race in honour of St Reparata 'perchè per antico costume in cotal dì s'è corso il palio' and is followed by a reference to 'un palio di braccia otto': F. Gherardi Dragomanni (ed.), *Cronica di Matteo Villani* (2 vols., Florence, 1846), I, 275–7. See too the comments of Diana Norman in this collection.

[3] Entry points to a vast bibliography are: B. Mitchell, *Italian Civic Pageantry in the High Renaissance. A Descriptive Bibliography of the Triumphal Entries and Selected Other Festivals for State Occasions* (Florence 1979); B. Wisch and S. Munshower (eds.), *"All the World's a Stage . . ." Art and Pageantry in the Renaissance and Baroque* (University Park, PA, 1990), vol. 2; H. Watanabe O'Kelly and A. Simon (eds.), *Festivals and Ceremonies. A Bibliography of Works Relating to Court Civic and Religious Festivals in Europe, 1500–1800* (London and New York, 2000); J. R. Mulryne, H. Watanabe O'Kelly and M. Shewring, *Europa Triumphans: Court and Civic Festivals in Early Modern Europe*, 2 vols. (Aldershot, 2004).

one of the more fertile areas of Renaissance historiography of the last two decades of the twentieth century saw the application of the methods and findings of social anthropologists to the analysis of the rituals of the past.[4] Following on the groundbreaking studies of Richard Trexler and Edward Muir, scholars from various disciplines have shown the active role of urban rituals in defining the identity of every Italian city, both on an internal level, and in their self-promotion to outsiders and visitors.[5]

As is widely recognized, despite its proximity to Florence, Siena's urban identity and mode of cultural expression, was unique, and differed considerably from that of its neighbour.[6] The means by which that civic image was projected and circulated included ceremonial practices that were inextricably bound to the city's urban fabric. Nonetheless, with rare exceptions, the potential for interdisciplinary research often associated with the history of urban rituals, has largely been ignored for Siena.[7] The studies that do so, unsurprisingly reveal the importance of religious celebration and the civic importance of the saints associated with the city, in particular the Virgin, whose feast-day of the Assumption was never eclipsed by any other feast during the Renaissance period.[8]

The urban rituals and processions that are considered in this collection were staged ephemeral events, in which the organising authorities created a temporary interpretation of the city fabric and the social body of the citizens, that reflected positively upon them: these ceremonies altered the city, adjusting the focus onto a guild, a saint, or an honoured guest, in a way that could not be achieved in a permanent manner.[9] They were orchestrated events, whereby streets were commandeered, the façades of buildings altered with hangings and painted symbols, and the occasion made memorable by various visual and sensory stimuli. Moreover, the success of urban rituals rested on the balance between the repetition of standard patterns, such as processional routes through the city streets, and breaks from the norm, that signalled

---

[4] R. Trexler, *Public Life in Renaissance Florence* (New York-London, 1980); R. Strong, *Art and Power: Renaissance Festivals, 1450–1650* (Berkeley, 1984); E. Muir, *Ritual in Early Modern Europe* (London, 1997).

[5] Trexler, *Public Life*; E. Muir, *Civic Ritual in Renaissance Venice* (Princeton, 1981).

[6] For a recent statement of Siena's unique civic identity, see S. J. Campbell and S. J. Milner, 'Art, Identity and Cultural Translation in Renaissance Italy,' in S. J. Campbell and S. J. Milner (eds.), *Artistic Exchange and Cultural Translation in the Italian Renaissance City* (Cambridge, 2004), 5.

[7] Some exceptions are: D. Webb, *Patrons and Defenders. The Saints in the Italian City-States* (London and New York, 1996), 251–316; F. A. D'Accone, *The Civic Muse. Music and Musicians in Siena During the Middle Ages and the Renaissance* (Chicago, 1997).

[8] F. Glenisson-Delanée, 'Fête et société: l'Assomption à Sienne et son évolution au cours du XVI siècle', in F. Croisette and M. Plaisance (eds.), *Les fêtes urbaines en Italie à l'époque de la Renaissance: Vérone, Florence, Sienne, Naples* (Paris, 1993) 65–129; D. Arasse, '*Fervebat Pietate Populus*: Art, dévotion et société autour de la glorification de Saint Bernardin de Sienne', *Mélanges de l'Ecole Française de Rome*, 89 (1977) 189–263; A. M. Testaverde. 'Il "Paradiso" sul Campo di Siena. Tradizione e rapporti con l'arte del visuale', *Quaderni di Teatro*, 25 (1984), 20–30; D. Norman, *Siena and the Virgin: Art and Politics in a Late Medieval City* (New Haven and London 1999), 1–20.

[9] On the promotional aspects of such ceremonies, see R. Trexler, *Public Life*, 279–90.

distinctions precipitated by political or social factors. In the Renaissance, a city's legitimacy depended in part on its image-making and self-presentation, whether through its permanent landmarks or its temporary celebrations, a means for a constant negotiation of its relationship with its citizens and foreigners, with friends and foes alike.[10]

As a growing body of scholarly literature is revealing, architectural space in the Renaissance city operated on multiple levels, forming the setting for everyday life, and the backdrop for numerous religious, civic and also private functions.[11] During such events, ceremonial routes through the city assigned meaning to significant sites, which often benefited from temporary architectural improvements in the form of ephemeral structures and other decorative features.[12]

This collection of essays takes as its focus the urban sites in which various civic rites unfolded. In considering both the visits of eminent outsiders and other habitual public spectacles largely addressed to a local audience, a pattern emerges: the choice of points of departure and arrival, such as the gates, the Palazzo Pubblico and the cathedral, as well as the routes chosen between them, are moulded to each set of particular historical circumstances, but taken together a clear picture arises of Siena's ritual geography.[13] These settings modulated the action from the static celebratory moments focussing around individual monuments, through the dynamic action of procession, which diffused the ritual event along the course of the city's main streets, bringing together the social and architectural fabric.[14] Each *festa* developed specific characteristics and routes, and their repetition reinforced parts of the city's foundation myth, history and religious allegiances.[15] Processions, however, were not always city-wide, thus social groupings, such as confraternities, guilds, religious communities or parishes, were each able to assert

[10] P. Brown, 'The Self-Definition of the Venetian Republic', in A. Molho *et al.* (eds.), *City States in Classical Antiquity and Medieval Italy* (Ann Arbor, Michigan, 1991), 511–48.

[11] On the usage and significance of urban space, see Z. Celik *et al.* (eds.), *Streets. Critical Perspectives on Public Space* (Berkeley, 1994); R. Ingersoll, *Ritual Use of Public Space in Renaissance Rome*, Ph.D. thesis, University of California, Berkeley, 1985; D. Howard, 'Ritual Space in Renaissance Venice', *Scroope*, 5, 1993–4, 4–11; H. de Mare and A. Vos (eds.), *Rituals in Italy and the Netherlands. Historical Contrasts in the Use of Public Space, Architecture and the Urban Environment* (Assen, 1993).

[12] B. Chabrowe, 'On the significance of temporary architecture', *The Burlington Magazine*, 116 (1974), 385–91; M. Fagiolo and M. L. Madonna, 'Il revival del trionfo classico', in M. Fagiolo (ed.), *La festa a Roma* (Rome, 1997), I, 34–41. See now also, M. A. Zaho, '*Imago triumphalis* : the function and significance of triumphal imagery for Italian Renaissance rulers* (New York, 2003).

[13] See the maps detailing the ritual routes used in the events described in this group of essays and G. Piccini, 'Modelli di organizzazione dello spazio urbano dei ceti dominanti del Tre e Quattrocento. Considerazioni sul caso senese', in *I ceti dirigenti nella Toscana tardo comunale*, D. Rugiadini (ed.) (Florence, 1983), 221–236.

[14] This is clearly brought out too in the case of Venice: see D. Howard. 'Ritual Space in Renaissance Venice', 6.

[15] On repetition as a vital part of ritual behaviour, see R. Trexler, *Public Life*, 215–79; for some comments on processional usage of Siena, see F. Nevola, 'Cerimoniali per santi e feste a Siena a metà Quattrocento. Documenti dallo Statuto di Siena 39', in M. Ascheri (ed.), *Siena e il suo territorio nel Rinascimento/Renaissance Siena and its Territory* (Siena, 2001), 171–84.

their worth and traditions upon the public stage of the urban fabric.[16] On occasion, as Machtelt Israëls shows in her essay on the Corpus Christi feast, such was the power of these events, that they were taken over by the government authorities; thus a feast that began as a guild and monastic festivity, took on civic functions, articulated by means of a city-wide procession.[17]

Ceremonies alternated static and kinetic moments, adjusting the focus from specific sites to shared spaces, from monumental buildings such as gates and churches, to streets and piazzas. The symbolic meaning and formal functions of the cathedral, town hall, gates and other civic monuments, were reinforced by the public space that surrounded them and were activated at specific ritual moments.[18] Thus, for example, the city gates marked a legal and military boundary between the *civitas* and the *contado*, but were also a symbolic threshold for citizenship, authority and a host of other values associated with membership of the urban community.[19] They were the point of entry to the centre of the city-state, the heart of its territory, and were the first architectural element of the city with which a visitor engaged. Their appearance was a fundamental part of the image of the city, unifying two different spatial realities, the urban fabric and its surrounding *contado*. Sites immediately outside the gates such as the 'prato di Camollia' which was used to fight duels and to welcome guests, were places of intermediate status, not quite within the city realm but intimately part of it. It was around these liminal spaces outside the gates, that the entry of important guests was ritually negotiated.[20] Thus, for example, the Emperor Frederick III's arrival in Siena on 7 February 1452, was described as having taken place with 'great

[16] Little work has been done on Sienese confraternities. See now M. Ascheri and P. Turrini (eds.), *La Misericordia di Siena attraverso i secoli : dalla Domus Misericordiae all'Arciconfraternita di Misericordia* (Siena, 2004). For an overview of lay religious entities see P. Turrini, 'Religiosità e spirito caritativo a Siena agli inizi della Reggenza Lorenese: luoghi pii laicali, contrade e arti', *Istituto Storico Diocesano Siena*, Annuario (1996–97), 145–293; (2002–2003), 1–234; M. A. Ceppari Ridolfi and P. Turrini, 'Il movimento associativo e devozionale dei laici nella chiesa senese (secc.xiii-xix)' in A. Mirizio & P Nardi (eds.), *Chiesa e vita religiosa a Siena dalle origini al grande giubileo* (Siena, 2002), 247–303.

[17] See Machtelt Israëls' essay below, and her earlier, 'Sassetta's Arte della Lana Altar-piece and the Cult of Corpus Domini in Siena', *The Burlington Magazine*, CXLIII (2001), 532–43. See also, K. Christiansen, 'Sassetta', in *Painting in Renaissance Siena, 1420–1500*, (ed.) K. Christiansen, L. B. Kanter and C. B. Strehlke (New York, 1988), 64–65 and F. Nevola, 'Cerimoniali per santi e feste', 171–84.

[18] On the distinction between passive and active symbolic meaning, see J. Shearman, *Only Connect . . . Art and the Spectator in the Italian Renaissance* (Princeton N. J., 1992); G. Johnson, 'Activating the Effigy: Donatello's Pecci tomb in Siena Cathedral', *Art Bulletin*, 77 (1995), 445–59.

[19] There was a clear division but symbiotic relationship between the city and its surrounding territory. On the contado see G. Chittolini, 'The Italian City-State and its Territory', in A. Molho (ed.), *City States in Classical Antiquity and Medieval Italy* (Stuttgart, 1991), 589–602; and, more specifically on Siena, O. Redon, *L'Espace d'une cité. Sienne et le pays siennois (xiiie- xive siècles)* (Rome, 1994); W. M. Bowsky 'City and Contado: Military Relationships and Communal Bonds in Fourteenth Century Siena', in A. Molho and J. A. Tedeschi (eds.), *Renaissance Studies in Honor of Hans Baron* (Florence, 1971) 75–98. On gates, see N. Adams and S. Pepper, *Firearms and Fortification: Military Architecture and Siege Warfare in Sixteenth Century Siena* (Chicago 1986), 32–7.

[20] R. Trexler, *Public Life*, 306–15; the example of Frederick III's entry is discussed in F. Nevola, 'Lieto e trionphante per la città: experiencing a mid-fifteenth-century imperial triumph along Siena's Strada Romana', *Renaissance Studies* 17 (2003), 581–606, 603–6.

glory, splendour and in peace', resulting from the delicate counterpoint which saw the civic authorities grant the keys of the city gates to the emperor, who subsequently returned them.[21] Passage through the city gates thus formally and ritually controlled the entry of distinguished visitors in two ways, on the one hand providing a dignified reception, while on the other clearly marking boundaries of authority and independence and, where possible, deflecting the visitor's prestige upon the government and the city as a whole.[22]

Like the gates, the other 'static' poles of urban ritual had both formal and symbolic levels of meaning. The city's governors (*Signori*) resided in the Palazzo Pubblico throughout the term of their appointment, and were only allowed to leave its confines on designated 'giorni nei quali la signoria esce dal palazzo'.[23] While in residence, their unity and inviolable authority was physically represented by the palace on the Campo; in turn, this stability was transposed onto the streets and squares of the city through strict ceremonial rules, which governed all their formal excursions. The sixteenth-century 'Libro delle Precedenze', a compendium of statutes and additional decisions pertaining to civic ceremonial, confirms that such exits from the palace took place exclusively on established feast-days, for state funerals, the reception of foreign dignitaries and for the investiture of the rector of the Spedale della Scala.[24] On such occasions, a rigorous hierarchy was observed by participating civic officials, representatives of the city guilds and confraternities, as well as the religious community involved in the celebrations. As occurred in ceremonies enacted in other Renaissance cities, this ceremonial order established and reaffirmed the socio-political structure of the dominant regime.[25]

The streets, which linked the civic and religious centres, were vital components of the kinetic part of the rituals, places of adornment and display, whose decoration was an essential part of the event. Joseph Rykwert perceptively wrote that, a 'street is human movement institutionalized.'[26] It is consequently not at all surprising to find that the city government lavished considerable attention on the main thoroughfares, whose collective façade

---

[21] Archivio di Stato di Siena (hereafter ASS), *Concistoro*, 1673 (copialettere), fol. 27 [7 February 1451/2], 'cum maxima pace, Gloria et triunfo'.

[22] R. Trexler, *Public Life*, 290–306; P. Fortini Brown, 'Measured Friendship, Calculated Pomp: The Ceremonial Welcomes of the Venetian Republic', in *Triumphal Celebrations and the Rituals of Statecraft, (Papers in Art History from the Pennsylvania State University, VI, Part 1)* (Pennsylvania, 1990), 136–187.

[23] *Il Costituto del comune di Siena*, I, II, 539–41 (dist. VI, rubr. 12); ASS *Concistoro* 2357, fol. 2.

[24] ASS *Concistoro* 2357, fol. 2v: 'Ala morte di qualche capitano del popolo o signore al visito. Nella venuta alla città di personaggi. Nel dare il possesso allo spedalingo.'

[25] See, for example, M. Rubin, *Corpus Christi: The Eucharist in Late Medieval Culture* (Cambridge, 1992) 243–71; C. Zika, 'Hosts, Processions and Pilgrimages: Controlling the Sacred in Fifteenth Century Germany', *Past and Present*, 118 (1988), 25–64.

[26] J. Rykwert, 'The Street: The Use of its History', in S. Anderson (ed.), *On Streets*, (Cambridge Mass., 1978), 15; more generally, K. Ashley and W. Husken (eds.), *Moving Subjects. Processional Performance in the Middle Ages and the Renaissance* (Amsterdam/Atlanta, 2001).

amounted to the setting for much of the city's ceremonial life.[27] Siena's main street, the Strada Romana that cuts north-south through the city from the Porta Romana to the Porta Camollia, was reordered during the fifteenth century through publicly-sponsored interventions that made its collective façade better suited to the public functions it performed in processions. As was stated in the preparations for the papal court of Pius II Piccolomini in 1459, such improvements were made specifically as 'it would be a good and honourable thing, particularly on account of the imminent visit of the Papal court'.[28]

In this respect, it is clear that the ceremonial considerations influenced the development of the fifteenth-century city, as it was along the privileged processional pathways that urban improvements were first made, spreading out from the central squares of the Piazza del Campo and Piazza Duomo, which had been the focus of thirteenth and fourteenth-century planning measures.[29] The ceremonial functions of buildings were also, in part, cast in stone; Siena's city gates, of which the most important were the Porta Camollia and the Porta Romana which led out towards Florence and Rome respectively, articulated the civic devotion to the Virgin Mary by means of frescoes which showed, for example, images of the 'Assumption' or 'Coronation of the Virgin,' using artistic formulas drawn from the local tradition, but also from the ceremonial practice of *sacre rappresentazioni*.[30] When Pius II visited Siena in 1460, he was met outside the Porta Camollia, where an elaborate *tableau vivant* re-enacted the Assumption miracle, with the Virgin Mary offering the pope the city keys, in lieu of proffering her girdle to St Thomas.[31] Following this reception outside the gates, the pope reports in his

[27] The Sienese government appointed special deputies to oversee these: see the first statute applying to these 'viarii' in D. Ciampoli and T. Szabó (eds.), *Lo Statuto dei viari di Siena (1290–1299)* (Siena, 1992) and on the most important ritual street of Siena, F. Nevola, '"Ornato della città": Siena's Strada Romana as focus of fifteenth-century urban renewal', *Art Bulletin*, 82 (2000), 26–50.

[28] ASS, *Concistoro* 2125, fol. 10 (quoted from P. Pertici, *La città magnificata. Interventi edilizi a Siena* (Siena, 1995) 71) 'sarebbe bene e honorevole cosa, et maxime havendoci ad venire la corte romana [. . .]'; discussed further in Fabrizio Nevola's essay.

[29] W. Braunfels, *Mittelalterliche Stadtbaukunst in der Toskana* (Berlin 1951); D. Balestracci and G. Piccinni, *Siena nel Trecento. Assetto urbano e prassi edilizia* (Florence 1977). For the squares, see M. Tuliani, 'Il Campo di Siena. Un mercato cittadino in età comunale', *Quaderni Medievali*, 46 (1998), 59–100 and R. Parenti, 'Una parte per il tutto. Le vicende costruttive della facciata dello Spedale e della piazza antistante', in E. Boldrini and R. Parenti (eds.), *Santa Maria della Scala: archeologia e edilizia sulla piazza dello Spedale* (Florence, 1991), 20–96.

[30] These *sacre rappresentazioni* are discussed in many sources, summarized in W. Heywood, *Our Lady of August and the Palio of Siena* (Siena, 1899). Among numerous cross-overs between ritual practice and painted images, see Allegretto Allegretti's description of Pius II's entry to Siena in January 1460, which closely parallels Vecchietta's 'Assumption' composition in Pienza cathedral, A. Allegretti, 'Ephemerides Senenses ab anno MCCCCL usque ad MCCCCXCVI italico sermone scriptae', in L. Muratori (ed.), *Rerum Italicarum Scriptores*, vol. 23, (Milan, 1733), 767–860, 769 (31 January 1460). Such themes are developed by J. Gardner, 'An introduction to the iconography of the Medieval Italian city gate', *Dumbarton Oaks Papers*, 41 (1987), 199–213; M. Israëls, 'New documents for Sassetta and Sano di Pietro at the Porta Romana, Siena', *The Burlington Magazine*, 140 (1998), 436–443.

[31] Described by A. Allegretti, 'Ephemerides Senenses,' 770 (31 January 1460).

autobiographic *Commentarii* that his entry resembled a triumph, that the processional route through the city had been embellished with greenery, and that he was escorted to the cathedral beneath a canopy or baldachin.[32]

The historical circumstances, and the ritual events, surrounding the entries of foreign monarchs who had to be both impressed and appeased, and whose high standing required the commissioning of expensive festive decorations and costly materials to make their entrance baldachins, is the subject of the articles by Diana Norman and Gerrit Schenk. The former not only considers the entries of Angevin royalty in Siena, but also analyses Simone Martini's Maestà in the Palazzo Pubblico in the light of contemporary ritual, to explain the rather unusual appearance of the Angevin heraldry on this important government commission. She argues that the imagery used by Simone Martini was influenced by such rituals and considers the importance of the baldachin as a sign of majesty for the depiction of the Virgin as the Queen of Heaven. Schenk employs the tools of the anthropologist in his analysis of the ritual spoliation that occurred on the entrance of an emperor. He compares the two different entries of Charles IV in 1355 and in 1368; the former *ingressus* was marked by a ritual spoliation, a violent attack on the flags and baldachins of the visiting monarch, a ceremony that also applied to other Sienese entries up to that of Charles V in 1536.[33]

In contrast, Christine Shaw examines peace-making rituals in Siena, of particular importance in the strife-ridden decades of the latter fifteenth century.[34] Her account shows the regular recourse to such ceremonies during this time of discord despite the pessimistic views of many contemporary observers, as well as the harnessing of religious sites to be mechanisms of civic control.[35] Her detailed archival research has also enabled her to reconsider the *Biccherna* panel of 1483, which she convincingly argues is a conflation of two ceremonies, one the peace-making ritual which is the focus of her essay, and the other the dedication of the city to the Virgin.[36] This shows the importance of the historical evidence in interpreting these panels, as they cannot be truly understood unless in the context of contemporary events.

The importance of the city's streets is brought out particularly in the articles by Machtelt Israëls and Fabrizio Nevola. The former takes as her starting

---

[32] A van Heck (ed.), *Pii Commentarii rerum memorabilium que temporibus suis contigerunt* (2 vols., Vatican City, 1984), I, 249–50; For the expenses for cloth, ASS, *Concistoro* 2478, fol. 12v–16v (January–February 1459/60).

[33] G. A. Pecci, *Memorie storico-critiche della città di Siena*, (2 vols., Siena, 1755–60), II 87; and for earlier examples note 40 of Gerrit Shenk's article 'Charles IV and Siena between Politics, Diplomacy and Ritual (1355 and 1368)' in this volume.

[34] Examined in C. Shaw, 'Politics and Institutional Innovation in Siena (1480–98)', (1) in *Bulletino Senese di Storia Patria* (hereafter *BSSP*), 103 (1996), 9–102, and (2) in *BSSP*, 104 (1997), 194–307.

[35] On these rituals more generally see K. Petkov, *The Kiss of Peace. Ritual, Self and Society in the High and Late Medieval West* (Leiden and Boston, 2003).

[36] On the latter see A. Toti, *Atti di votazione della città di Siena e del senese alla SS Vergine madre di G.C.* (Siena, 1870), 24–32.

point the *Biccherna* panel of 1367 for an analysis of the important Corpus Christi celebrations in Siena, promoted by the wool guild and the Carmelites.[37] The separate but complimentary aims of these two bodies combined to make this one of the most important of Sienese annual festivities, reflected in the guild's commissioning of an impressive altarpiece to be used solely on this occasion, which also served as a permanent visual record of the cult. The culmination of the feast was the decorated piazza of San Pellegrino where an open-air altar transformed the square into a sacred place.[38] The conversion of ordinary space into the extraordinary is also the concern of the latter essay, which examines the housing of the papal court of Pius II during his visits to Siena in 1459 and 1460, and the use of various properties in order to do so. These were an important catalyst in the process of urban renewal and beautification, which created patterns of usage along new privileged pathways between the clerical dignitaries, which imprinted the court's ritual geography upon the city.

Philippa Jackson uses the funeral obsequies of the tyrant Pandolfo Petrucci to consider what constituted a public funeral in Renaissance Siena. Although various similarities applied, the role of the testament, family, parish and burial place could add a significant alteration to the general pattern of behaviour even for civic death rites. A consideration of the accounts for wax and banners for state funerals, ephemeral signs of tribute brought out in many of the other essays discussed in this volume, show the wealth of materials and symbols displayed, as well as their use in Pandolfo's case to promote the legitimacy of his regime.

The work of Mauro Mussolin considers the new civic ritual of the Immaculate Conception introduced to Siena in the 1520s. He examines the relationship of the cult to the victory of the battle of Camollia in 1526, its promotion by the government, and the role of the Dominicans in trying to prevent it. He discusses in particular the visual depictions of the Madonna in relation to the Camollia gate, a ritual area consistently portrayed during the sixteenth century. In fact, the depiction of her hovering over this sacralized space was to become the most popular civic image of the Virgin, even appearing on Siena's coinage. The government's adoption of this scene, which links the Madonna to the urban landscape she protects, not only represents the complex relationship between state, saint, and space but records in a concrete form the civic ceremony giving rise to it.

In this respect, urban rituals can fruitfully be considered in the same light as another unique example of Siena's cultural heritage, the *Biccherne*, the small painted panels that were produced to adorn the covers of the city's

---

[37] M. Rubin, *Corpus Christi: The Eucharist in Late Medieval Culture* (Cambridge, 1991).

[38] E. Muir, 'The Virgin on the Street Corner: The Place of the Sacred in Italian Cities', in S. Ozment (ed.), *Religion and Culture in the Renaissance and Reformation* (Kirksville, Missouri 1987), 24–40; E. Muir and R. Weissman, 'Social and Symbolic Places in Renaissance Venice and Florence' in J. Agnew and J. Duncan (eds.), *The Power of the Place* (Syracuse, 1988), 81–103.

tax registers and other financial books.[39] While a number of the paintings remain unattributed, their significance surely lies in their content rather than their authorship.[40] Many earlier panels in the *Biccherna* series are illustrated with simple scenes that show the various monetary and bureaucratic functions of the city tax office, and this has led to a general characterization of these works as objects relating 'art and finance'.[41] It could equally be argued, however, that the *Biccherne* constitute one of the richest visual sources for the ritual life of the city, for an overwhelming number of the images (particularly from the fifteenth century onwards) represent extraordinary events that took place in the year of their production. As William Heywood remarked, they are 'a pictorial chronicle of the Commune'.[42] Thus important events are recorded, such as the theatrical apparatus for the canonization of St Bernardino of Siena, the coronation of Pius II, and the return to Siena of the *Noveschi* in 1487.[43] In other instances, the panels show allegorical compositions that employ the canon of civic imagery and altered these to contemporary events, such as the Virgin Mary steering the ship of government to safe waters which invoked the stability provided by the new *Noveschi* regime.[44] As Ubaldo Morandi acutely noted, a defining characteristic of the *Biccherne* is the number of depictions of the city, often within her walls and protected by the Virgin.[45]

Just as civic ritual in the second half of the fifteenth century usually celebrated extraordinary occasions, so the *Biccherne* commemorated them for posterity, and it is consequently unsurprising to find that many of the essays in this collection are illustrated with them. It is, in fact, rare to find contemporary illustrations of ritual events for the fourteenth or fifteenth centuries, so that most studies of public rituals in Renaissance Rome, Florence or Venice rely on sixteenth-century visual evidence, or turn to depictions of 'fictional' images from such artefacts as *cassoni* and *spalliere*. By contrast, the *Biccherne* are images which record a particular moment for the civic memory; in a sense they are to be seen as civic monuments, invested with a specific meaning that interpreted events within a framework established by the political authority of the day.[46]

[39] See L. Borgia *et al.* (eds.), *Le Biccherne. Tavole dipinte delle magistrature senesi (Secoli XIII–XVIII)* (Rome, 1984) and A. Tomei (ed.), *Le Biccherne di Siena. Arte e Finanza all'alba dell'economia moderna*, (Azzano San Paulo (Bergamo)/Rome, 2002).

[40] Nonetheless, most discussion is over authorship and not identification of the subject matter. This has led to a number of errors of interpretation analysed in Christine Shaw's essay below.

[41] *Le Biccherne* (2002) 35.

[42] Heywood, *Palio and Ponte*, 44.

[43] *Le Biccherne* (1984) 192–93.

[44] *Le Biccherne* (1984), 191.

[45] *Le Biccherne* (1984) 15–17.

[46] The function of the monument as a polarizing element for an interpreted memory is proposed, with later examples, by F. Choay, *The Invention of the Historic Monument* (Cambridge, 2001); in March 1452 a column was erected to commemorate the meeting a month earlier of Leonora of Portugal and Frederick III outside the Porta Camollia, for which see F. Nevola, 'Lieto e trionphante per la città: cited n. 20, 603–6.

Any consideration of the impact and significance of public rituals in the Renaissance city must be founded in a consideration of the area in which they took place and in an interdisciplinary approach which views political and social conditions not merely as the 'context' for artistic, musical, processional or architectural production, but as inseparable aspects of a single phenomenon. The essays that make up this collection do not present an exhaustive analysis of Siena's ritual life, but rather they provide a series of rich case studies that highlight a number of themes and issues that can be fruitfully compared with evidence from other Italian cities. Moreover, the unifying theme that emerges from the essays is the active role of the urban fabric in fashioning civic identity.

London
Università degli Studi di Siena

2

'Sotto uno baldachino trionfale': the ritual significance of the painted canopy in Simone Martini's Maestà

DIANA NORMAN

The recent restoration of Simone Martini's *Maestà* in the Sala del Mappamondo of the Palazzo Pubblico in Siena – undertaken between 1988 and 1994 – has revealed that the edges of the canopy over the throne of the Virgin and Christ Child are embellished with a precise sequence of heraldic shields (Fig. 1). Not only are the two coats of arms of the Sienese Commune on display – as befits the painting's situation within what was then the principal council hall of the city – but also the coats of arms of the kingdoms of both France and Naples (Fig. 2).[1] Although a number of scholars have offered suggestions as to the contemporary meaning and significance of the canopy within the painting, very few have explored, in any detail, the reasons for including the Angevin heraldry in so prominent a fashion.[2] In a discussion of the *Maestà* within the context of a larger study of the Palazzo Pubblico, Gabriele Borghini briefly alludes to the possible relevance of a visit to Siena, in December 1315, by Philip, Prince of Taranto and brother to the reigning king of Naples, Robert of Anjou.[3] More recently, Hayden Maginnis has

---

[1] These are (in the order they appear on the canopy): the golden lilies on a blue field, symbol of the kingdom of France; the black and white *balzana*, symbol of the Sienese Commune; the golden lilies on a blue field with a red horizontal bar with five pendants, symbol of the Angevin kingdom of Naples or southern Italy; and the lion on a red field, symbol of the Sienese Popolo. While adhering scrupulously to the correct heraldic colours and symbols, all these coats-of-arms were once more eye-catching due to their further decoration in gold and silver leaf. For example, the simple black and white design of the *balzana* was once made more elaborate by intricate patterns of silver. Traces of *balzana* shields also survive on the poles that support the canopy. For the identification and description of these details, see A. Bagnoli, *La Maestà di Simone Martini* (Milan, 1999), 17, 24, 155.

[2] Andrew Martindale, *Simone Martini* (Oxford, 1988), 24, n.15, offers the suggestion that 'from its heraldry, it would seem that the canopy has been provided by the city of Siena and the King of Naples'. To these hypothetical donors, C. Jean Campbell, 'The lady in the council chamber: diplomacy and poetry in Simone Martini's *La Maestà*', *Word and Image* 14 (1998), 371–86 (372), adds the *Capitano del Popolo*, whilst Bagnoli, *La Maestà*, 17, interprets the Angevin heraldry more broadly as 'segnali della fede guelfa del Comune e delle sue alleanze . . .'.

[3] G. Borghini, 'La sequenza decorativa documentario-simbolica del piano nobile' in, *Palazzo Pubblico di Siena. Vicende costruttive e decorazione*, ed. C. Brandi (Milan, 1983), 268. Borghini's reference to Philip of Taranto's visit is part of a general discussion of the political situation in Siena in 1315, the year that the painter received his first known payment for the *Maestà*.

Fig. 1   Simone Martini, *The Maestà*, c.1315–21, fresco. Siena, Palazzo Pubblico, Sala del Mappamondo (photo: LENSINI Siena)

elaborated upon this, drawing attention to a sequence of Angevin royal visits to the city that took place between 1310 and 1327 and linking these explicitly to payments in the city accounts for the production of baldachins for these events.[4] As he succinctly observes 'one such baldachin is depicted in Simone's Palazzo Pubblico *Maestà*'.

The first of the payments identified by Maginnis is that for 43 *lire* and 14 *soldi* on 31 October 1310 to the painter Masarello and his assistants for painting two canopies (*pagli*). Payments to other craftsmen confirm that these were for Robert of Anjou and his queen.[5] From entries in two fourteenth-century Sienese chronicles, it appears that the king, en route to Naples from his

[4] H. Maginnis, *The World of the Early Sienese Painter* (University Park, Pennsylvania, 2001), 65–6.

[5] Archivio di Stato di Siena (hereafter ASS), *Biccherna*, 124, fol. 231v (modern re-numbering). See also Maginnis, *The Early Sienese Painter*, 66, 262. Although *pagli* could refer to banners, a further payment to another craftsman for eight poles clearly indicates that these items were canopies. Apart from the payment to Masarello, there is also a payment of 147 *lire*, 16 *soldi*, 2 *denari*, to the goldsmith Maestro Bernardino for two silver cups, covered in gold, and a further payment of 2,687 *lire*, 10 *soldi*, for the 800 gold florins and the 200 gold florins to be placed in the king's and queen's cup, respectively. These items provide evidence of the high cost of these state visits.

Fig. 2   Simone Martini, detail of *The Maestà* showing the painted canopy (photo: LENSINI Siena)

coronation by the Pope in Avignon, was met with 'very great honour' by all the civic corporations of Siena with their banners and that he was housed in the house of Granello Tolomei and entertained to tournaments, dances, games, and displays of fireworks 'as was customary for a man like him'. The Commune further honoured the royal couple by presenting both the king and the queen with gold cups filled with gold florins.[6] The deliberations of the meeting of Siena's principal legislative council, the Consiglio della Campana, for 15 and 27 October 1310 likewise confirm that King Robert

[6] See the broadly similar accounts of the 1310 visit in the 'Cronaca senese dall'anno 1202 al 1362, con aggiunte posteriori fino al 1391 di autore anonimo della metà del secolo XIV' and the 'Cronaca senese di Agnolo di Tura del Grasso' in *Cronache senesi*, eds A. Lisini and F. Iacometti, n.s. *Rerum Italicarum Scriptores* (Bologna, 1931–5), XV, pt 6, 89, 311.

visited the city in October of that year, was given a traditional reception, and that both he and his queen received gifts of money from the Commune on this occasion.[7]

Just under four years later, Robert of Anjou's youngest brother, the eighteen-year-old Peter, Count of Eboli, arrived in the city on his way to Florence to take command of the forces of the Guelph league in Tuscany. Entries in four local chronicles relate that on 14 August 1314, the eve of the feast of the Assumption, the Count of Eboli, together with his escort of baronial counsellors and 300 cavalry, was met by the Sienese civic and military authorities outside the city gate at the hospital of San Lazzaro. He then entered the city under a ceremonial canopy and was escorted to his lodgings in the Palazzo Squarcialupi. Once again, his visit was marked by games, dances and firework displays. On the following morning he knighted Niccolò di Ser Bandino and was presented with a generous amount of money and a gold cup filled with 500 gold florins. Two days after his arrival, he left Siena for Florence.[8] On 20 August, the Council debated the expenses incurred for this visit. These were precisely specified as 63 *lire*, 10 *soldi* for a gold cup, 500 gold florins to be placed inside the cup, and 119 *lire* and 12 *soldi* for the canopy (*palio*) under which the prince entered the city. As customary for his role as the city's syndic, Francesco da Bologna, recommended that the council not endorse these expenses. Despite this, the Council voted to do so, by 206 votes to 3.[9]

Masarello, the painter paid for the canopies for the 1310 visit of Robert of Anjou and his queen, was again reimbursed for similar work in 1315. On this occasion, he was paid 22 *lire* and 10 *soldi* and his son, Tavena, was paid 20 *lire* and 12 *soldi*, for two *pagli* as gifts to Philip, Prince of Taranto and his son and another for the feast of the Assumption.[10] Entries in four chronicle accounts succinctly describe how King Robert's brother, Philip of Taranto, entered Siena on 26 July 1315 on his way to Florence. Accompanying Philip was his young son, Charles, and a substantial military escort of cavalry. Once again, he was received with 'great honour' and presented with gifts by the Sienese

---

[7] ASS, *Consiglio Generale* 77, fols. 56r–57v, 58r–59v (modern re-numbering), deliberations of 15 October 1310, where it was decided that three men, one from each *terzo*, elected and instructed by the magistracy of the Nine, should organize the reception (*adventus*) of the king according to the custom and practice of the city and *contado* of Siena. ASS, Consiglio Generale, 77, fols. 64r–65r (modern re-numbering), deliberations of 27 October 1310, which record the debate and decision by the Council to approve the money spent on gifts for the king and queen. The motion was carried by 208 votes to 15. See also R. Caggese, *Roberto d'Angiò e i suoi tempi*, 2 vols. (Florence, 1922–30), I, 116, n.5.

[8] See the accounts of Peter of Eboli's 1314 visit to Siena given in: the 'Cronaca senese di autore anonimo' (where the prince is described as entering the city 'sotto uno baldachino trionfale'); the 'Frammento di cronaca senese di anonimo (1313–1320)', where he came into the city 'soto el palio'; the 'Cronaca senese conosciuta sotto il nome di Paolo di Tommaso Montauri'; and the 'Cronica di Agnolo di Tura', where he is described as entering the city 'sotto uno palio, cioè, baldacchino'. See *Cronache senesi*, 103, 167, 250, 345–6.

[9] ASS, *Consiglio Generale* 84, fols. 57v–58v. The reference to the cost of the canopy occurs on folio 57v. See also Caggese, *Roberto d'Angiò*, I, 207, n.2; Maginnis, *The Early Sienese Painter*, 66.

[10] ASS, *Biccherna* 377, fol. 115r. This entry occurs in the city accounts for September and October. See also Maginnis, *The Early Sienese Painter*, 66, 262, 272.

Commune.[11] Two days before the Prince of Taranto's entry into the city, the Council agreed to lift the ban on Sienese exiles in order to allow them to join the Guelph army,[12] which was to be led by Philip of Taranto against Uguccione della Faggiuola, *signore* of Ghibelline Pisa. On 1 August, during the Prince's brief stay in Siena, the Council gave formal permission to Siena's current *Capitano del Popolo* to leave the city and district of Siena in order to take part in this military campaign.[13] Philip of Taranto left for Florence on 4 August at the head of his own troops and those of Siena. A single entry in the chronicle attributed to the fourteenth-century Sienese civil servant, Agnolo di Tura, records his brief return to Siena, between 5 and 22 December, before travelling onwards to Naples,[14] a sick man grieving for his son, Charles, and brother, Peter of Eboli, both of whom had been killed on 29 August during the decisive defeat of the Guelph army at the battle of Montecatini.

Finally, Maginnis also cites the well-known payment of 53 *lire* and 4 *soldi* on 31 December 1327 to Simone Martini for work on two *palii* for King Robert's eldest son, Charles, duke of Calabria, and his wife, Margaret of Valois.[15] Although well after the date of the completion of the *Maestà*,[16] the itemised detail of 720 painted double lilies, sixteen pairs of lions of the Popolo, silver fringes and twenty poles, confirms that these were once large and lavishly decorated objects.[17] In terms of their decoration, these canopies appear, therefore, to mirror closely the Simone's painted version of a ceremonial canopy in the *Maestà*.[18]

THE POLITICAL AND RITUAL SIGNIFICANCE OF ANGEVIN ENTRIES

In the brief descriptions of the four entries of Angevin princes into the city of Siena in the chronicle accounts, it is striking how similar these ceremonial events were in terms of programme and protocol. The royal visitors were met outside the city by Siena's leading citizens and members of its principal civic

[11] See the brief, but closely comparable, accounts of Philip of Taranto's 1315 visit to Siena given in the 'Cronaca senese di autore anonimo', the 'Frammento di cronaca', the 'Cronaca di Paolo di Tommaso Montauri', and the 'Cronaca di Agnolo di Tura', in *Cronache Senesi*, 106, 169, 251, 351. Presumably, one of the gifts was the two *palii* painted by Masarello and his son.

[12] ASS, *Consiglio Generale* 86, fols. 36r–40r. See also Caggese, *Roberto d'Angiò*, I, 220, n.1.

[13] ASS, *Consiglio Generale* 86, fols. 45v–46v. See also Caggese, *ibid.*, I, 220, n.2.

[14] 'Cronaca di Agnolo di Tura', in *Cronache senesi*, 356.

[15] ASS, *Biccherna* 392 fol. 125r (modern renumbering), published in P. Leone de Castris, *Simone Martini* (Milan, 2003), 367. See also Maginnis, *The Early Sienese Painter*, 66.

[16] For the various campaigns of work on the *Maestà* and their dates, the reconstruction of which rely on: a fragmentary text referring to 1315 on the painting itself; payments in the city accounts between 7 June 1315 and 17 June 1322; various kinds of technical and stylistic evidence, see Bagnoli, *La Maestà, passim*, but especially 17–20, 52–66, 78–9, 88–95, 158, 160–1.

[17] Although the payment (cited in note 15 above) describes the *palii* as having been sent to the duke and his wife, chronicle accounts of the ceremonial entry of the Duke and Duchess of Calabria into Siena on 30 December 1327 describe the royal couple entering the city, each under a large canopy. See the 'Cronaca senese di autore anonimo' (where both are described as entering the city 'sotto grandi pali') and the 'Cronaca di Agnolo di Tura' (where they are similarly described as making their entry 'sotto grandi pagli'). See *Cronache Senesi*, 135, 464.

[18] Leone de Castris, *Simone Martini*, 249–50.

and military organisations, specified variously as the *magiori di Siena*, the *principali cittadini e cavalieri di Siena*, and the *compagnie* with their standards. The honoured guests entered the city in procession and under canopies – referred to either as *palii*, *pagli* or *baldacchini*. Although the route through the city is not described in the chronicle accounts, the visitors were often provided with accommodation in one of the city's major palaces. In the case of Peter, Count of Eboli, and Charles, Duke of Calabria, both were housed in buildings close to the cathedral. It seems likely, therefore, that – like later ceremonial visits of this kind in the mid-fourteenth and fifteenth centuries – the civic procession culminated at the cathedral and was followed by the celebration of mass at the high altar.[19] The early fourteenth-century Angevin visits were also marked by public festivities and other ritual events, such as the knighting of a member of a leading Sienese family or the presentation of gifts by the Commune to the royal visitors. These gifts usually consisted of either gold cups filled with specific sums of money (carefully calculated to denote the status of the recipient) or of ceremonial canopies. It is significant that, in all the chronicle accounts of the Angevin visits, the standard refrain is that the illustrious visitors are being afforded great honour (*grandissimo onore*) as befits someone of their rank and status.

The relatively sparse – but highly consistent – picture given in the chronicle accounts of the royal entries into Siena corresponds closely to those recorded by the chroniclers of other Italian and European cities during this period. According to the Florentine chronicler, Giovanni Villani, in 1310, Florence, like its close neighbour, Siena, also celebrated King Robert's visit by the presentation of gifts and the staging of jousts, whilst in 1314 the Florentines received his brother, the Count of Eboli, 'like their lord'.[20] Several decades later, the chronicler's brother, Matteo Villani, described in greater detail the form that such a reception might take, referring specifically to the way in which the current cardinal of Ostia was welcomed by the citizens with great honour and escorted into the city under a silk canopy.[21] Other local chroniclers similarly record the way in which, between 1310 and 1312, the progress of the German prince, Henry of Luxemburg, towards Rome and his coronation was punctuated by ceremonial entries into those Italian cities that were willing to acknowledge him as emperor designate.[22] Over fifty years

---

[19] See the essays by Gerrit Schenk and Fabrizio Nevola in this collection.

[20] Giovanni Villani, *Cronica*, bk. 9, chs. 8 and 61, ed. F. G. Dragomanni, 4 vols. (Florence, 1845), II, 150, 184–5. Villani, bk. 9, ch. 70, also describes Philip of Taranto's arrival in Florence in 1315 but makes no comment on the style of reception he received. See *ibid.*, II, 190.

[21] Matteo Villani, *Cronica*, bk. 5, ch. 23, ed. F. G. Dragomanni, 2 vols. (Florence, 1846), I, 416. According to the chronicler, this ceremonial entry took place on 6 May 1355.

[22] See for example, the entries into Asti, 11 November 1310; Milan, 23 December 1310; Genoa, 21 October 1311; and Pisa, 6 March 1312. For which see, W. M. Bowsky, *Henry VII In Italy: The Conflict of Empire and City-State, 1310–1313* (Lincoln, Nebraska, 1960), 61, 78, 132, 153, citing published contemporary sources, such as Giovanni da Cermenate, *Historia Iohannis de Cermenate notarii mediolensis de situ ambrosiane urbis*, ed. L. A. Ferrai (Fonti per la storia d'Italia , II, Rome, 1889), and Ferreto de'Ferreti, *Historia rerum in Italia gestarum*, ed. C. Cipolla, 3 vols. (Fonti per la storia d'Italia, XLII–XLIII, Rome, 1908–20).

earlier in 1252, Conrad IV and his brother Manfred, Robert of Anjou's predecessors as rulers of southern Italy, had also been welcomed into the coastal ports of their kingdom under ceremonial canopies.[23]

Noël Coulet's detailed study of royal entries in fourteenth-century Provence similarly indicates that these events followed a prescribed and highly ritualized form. The custom and practice of entries in this part of Europe is of particular relevance because the Angevin rulers of Naples were also the counts of Provence. As Coulet relates, such ceremonies began with the arrival of the royal visitor being signalled by messengers and by the ringing of the town bells. Representatives of the government and its principal social organisations, both religious and lay, processed out of the city to the location of the formal meeting between the two parties. As in the meeting between the Sienese authorities and Peter, Count of Eboli, in 1314, such receptions frequently took place at a hospice for lepers outside the city walls. At this point, the civic authorities would make a gesture of homage – such as presenting the keys of the city to the royal visitor. At the gates of the city itself the honoured guest would then be presented with a ceremonial canopy under which he or she entered the city. The procession then took a carefully chosen route through the city – which would have been lavishly decorated with hangings and foliage – passing major civic buildings. The procession would usually end at one of the city's principal churches, where a religious ceremony would take place – commonly the celebration of a solemn mass.[24]

It is striking how closely Coulet's reconstruction of these ceremonial events mirrors the descriptions given by local chroniclers of the Angevin entries into Siena during the first two decades of the fourteenth century. It seems, therefore, that the Sienese ceremonies belonged to a well-established pattern of social conventions that were customary, not merely locally in Tuscany, but also internationally. The Angevin princes, in turn, undoubtedly expected to be given such receptions, accustomed as they were to the ceremonies characteristic of their own territories in southern Italy and Provençal France.

A key feature of the ceremonial entries that took place within fourteenth-century Provence was the provision of a canopy under which the royal visitor would enter the city and process through its streets.[25] When, in 1319, in anticipation of his visit to the city to attend the ceremony of the translation of the relics of his recently sanctified brother, Louis of Toulouse, the city councillors of Marseilles decided to stage a formal entry for Robert of Anjou, they resolved to present him and his queen with *palii* which would be carried

---

[23] N. Coulet, 'Les entrées solonnelles en Provence au XIVe siècle', *Ethnologie française*, 8 (1977), 63–82 (76, 77), citing Nicolas de Jamsilla, *Historia antea edita sub inscriptione Anonymi de rebus gestis Frederici II imperatoris* in *Rerum Italicarum Scriptores*, ed. L. Muratori (Milan, 1726), VIII, 505.

[24] Coulet, 'Les entrées solonnelles', 64–9. See also the closely comparable account given by Bernard Guenée of royal entries in the kingdom of France between 1328 and 1515 in B. Guenée and F. Lehoux, *Les entrées royales françaises de 1328 a 1515* (Paris, 1968) 22–3.

[25] Coulet, *ibid.*, 68: 'Ce dais est un élément fondamental du cérémonial d'entrée'.

over them during their procession through the city.[26] Twenty-eight years later, Robert's grand-daughter, Queen Joanna of Naples, was accorded the same honour when she entered the city of Avignon.[27] Variously described in French sources as a '*paile*', '*paly*', '*pavillon*', '*poêle*', or '*ciel*', and in Italian sources as a '*paglio*', '*palio*' or '*baldacchino*', this type of ceremonial object was of simple construction, comprising a framework of wood over which was draped costly material, such as velvet, silk, taffeta, damask or cloth-of-gold. In order to give weight and substance to the canopy, the material would invariably be lined, frequently with an alternative type of precious material. The canopy was also often edged with gold or silver fringes and embellished with painted or woven heraldic ornament. The entire edifice was supported by painted poles, which could vary between four and ten in number.[28] It was, therefore, an object that was highly valued in material terms. In addition, because it had become a central part of an established civic ritual, it possessed great symbolic and ritual significance, both for the donors and for the recipients.

SIMONE MARTINI'S PAINTED CANOPY

Simone Martini's *Maestà* is an impressive rendition of what had become – in Siena, at least – a much favoured and iconic religious subject (Fig. 1). Reprising the subject and figurative composition of the front face of Duccio's altarpiece for the high altar of Siena Cathedral, it offers a monumental and majestic image of the Virgin seated upon an ornate throne and supporting her infant son standing upon her knee. The Christ Child, shown in the act of blessing, also displays a scroll upon which is written (in Latin) the well-known opening verse of the Book of Wisdom: 'Love justice, you who rule the earth'.[29] On either side of the Virgin and Christ Child are grouped an impressive number of male and female saints including the Archangels Michael and Gabriel. As in the case of Duccio's *Maestà*, the kneeling saints in the immediate foreground of the painting represent Ansano, Savino,

---

[26] *Ibid.*, 68, citing a document in the Archives communales, Marseilles (BB 11), which records the deliberations of the city council on 22 May 1319. The relevant extract is published in M. H. Laurent, *Le culte de S. Louis d'Anjou à Marseille au XIVe siècle* (Temi e Testi, II, Rome, 1954), 48–50 (49).

[27] Giovanni Villani, *Cronica*, bk. 12, ch. 125, *ed. cit.* IV, 177. Matteo Villani, *Cronica*, bk. 1, ch. 20, *ed. cit.* I, 27, similarly describes how, in August 1348, the queen and her husband entered Naples under canopies.

[28] See Guenée in Guenée and Lehoux, *Les entrées royales françaises*, 19–22, drawing his evidence from fifteenth-century French sources. The fourteenth-century Florentine chronicler, Matteo Villani, standardly describes these objects as made of cloth-of-gold and silk ('ricchi palii d'oro e di seta'). See M. Villani, *Cronica*, bk. 1, ch. 20, bk. 5, ch. 23, *ed. cit.* I, 27, 416. Cloth of gold was also used for the canopies commissioned in 1327 by the Sienese Commune for the Duke and Duchess of Calabria (for which see note 15 above).

[29] [D]ILIGI/TE IUSTI/TIAM Q[U]I IUDICA/TIS TER/RAM. For colour illustrations of the Christ Child and his scroll, see Bagnoli, *La Maestà*, 27 (Pl. 28), 72 (Pl. 93), 73 (Pl. 94). For the discovery that this and another text in the painting were written on pieces of paper (not parchment) applied to the surface of the wall itself, see A. Bagnoli, 'I tempi della *Maestà*. Il restauro e le nuove evidenze', in *Simone Martini: atti del convegno (Siena, 1985)*, ed. L. Bellosi (Florence, 1988), 109–29 (109, 112, 116 n.5).

Crescenzio and Victor who – together with the Virgin herself – were the city's most revered patron saints.

The imagery of Simone Martini's treatment of the *Maestà* theme is further elaborated in the wide border of the painting which contains a series of roundels depicting the adult Christ, the four Evangelists, Old Testament prophets, the four Doctors of the Church and, at the centre of the lower border, a hybrid, allegorical figure of the Old and New Dispensation. These figurative paintings alternate with smaller roundels containing the civic emblems of the *balzana* and the lion of the *Popolo*, which, as already noted, also feature prominently on the painted canopy. In the lower border appear, additionally, the she-wolf suckling Romulus and Remus (another of Siena's emblems) and a painted replica of the front and back of one of the city's coins. This focus upon objects emphasizing Siena's civic identity and its principal political organisations continues again in the painted decoration of a second, much narrower, border that acts as part of the painted dado beneath the painting. In this area appear two highly accurate representations of the civic seal of Siena and the official seal of the *Capitano del Popolo*.[30]

Simone Martini's *Maestà* is, therefore, a painting replete with symbols and emblems denoting and celebrating Siena's political identity. Given the painting's prominence within what was then the city's principal council hall, this is hardly remarkable and can be found in other examples of contemporary painting belonging to such civic settings.[31] It is arguable, however, that Simone Martini also introduced into his *Maestà* imagery that belonged to contemporary rituals devised to signal notions of majesty both within the secular and the ecclesiastical spheres. Nowhere is this more obvious than in the expansive painted canopy, which occupies almost the entire width of the painting and a third of its height. Significantly absent from Duccio's *Maestà*, the canopy performs a number of important pictorial and compositional functions for the painting as a whole – thus contributing substantially to the painting's overall meaning and message.

In his depiction of this well-known ceremonial object, Simone Martini provides a convincing representation of an expansive canopy consisting of a large amount of crimson material, which, in itself, would denote magnificence and expense, due to the high cost of crimson dye.[32] The material, in turn, is rendered even more eye-catching and sumptuous by its chequered pattern, simulating woven or embroidered gold thread. From the way the

---

[30] For illustrations of all the figurative roundels, see E. Carli, *Simone Martini: La Maestà* (Milan, 1996), 149, 152–5. For the replica coins, *impresa* of the she-wolf, and the two seals, see Bagnoli, *La Maestà*, 41 (Pl. 43), 60–1 (Pl. 72), 67 (Pl. 84), 77 (Pls 97–9).

[31] Most strikingly in the late thirteenth-century painted decoration of the Sala del Consiglio (now known as the Sala di Dante) in the Palazzo Comunale of Siena's close neighbour, San Gimignano. For a detailed analysis of this room and its embellishment, see C. Jean Campbell, *The Game of Courting and the Art of the Commune of San Gimignano, 1290–1320* (Princeton, 1997), 44–106.

[32] Particularly if made from scale-insect dyestuffs imported from the East. For which, see D. Bomford *et al.*, *Art in the Making: Italian Painting before 1400* (London, 1989), 30–3.

material gently sags between the points of the eight supporting poles, it appears that the canopy is lined – thereby substantially adding to the impression of a costly, manufactured item. The edges of the canopy are even more ornately embellished with an elaborate sequence of heraldic devices, some of which are worked in expensive colours, such as ultramarine and crimson (Fig. 2). All these details are further embellished with gold and silver ornament. As a final ornamental flourish, the canopy is decorated by a series of flowing pennants attached to the top of each of the eight poles. The illusion given is that of a precious and intricately crafted object, closely mirroring what is known of the design and manufacture of canopies used for the ceremonial entries into the cities of fourteenth-century Italy and France.

The canopy also has an important role within the compositional and spatial organisation of the *Maestà*. Together with the ornate architecture of the throne, it creates an impressive framework for the principal cult figures of the Virgin and Christ Child (Fig. 1). By providing cover for the saints gathered around the throne, it also creates an exclusive space for this heavenly company and decisively sets them apart from the six kneeling figures in the foreground. Furthermore – as in the protocol for ceremonial entries – those who have been given the honour of carrying the poles supporting the canopy are all of extremely high status.[33] In short, the canopy functions as a means of creating a hierarchy between the various holy figures – effectively separating and distancing the Virgin and her saintly companions from the six kneeling figures in the foreground. They, in turn, in terms of their bodily comportment and gestures, appear as humble supplicants before the Virgin and her Son.

The subtle way that the canopy contributes to the meaning of the painting is further underlined by what can be reconstructed of the content and meaning of a number of painted texts that once appeared in the foreground of the *Maestà*. What survive now are two long texts: one executed in gold letters on a deep red ground and the other in gold letters on a black ground. The first is located along the edge of the pavement on which the angels and four patron saints kneel and therefore spans the entire width of the painting. The second appears on the edge of the dais on which the Virgin's throne is set and is framed by the figures of the two angels. Written in the vernacular and in the poetic verse of *terza rima*,[34] the two texts form an admonitory speech written on behalf of the Virgin and addressed to the kneeling figures of Saints Ansano, Savino, Crescenzio and Victor before her.

---

[33] Thus, the four front poles are carried by Saints Paul, John the Evangelist, John the Baptist, and Peter, whilst the four figures carrying the back poles have been identified, from left to right, as the apostles Bartholomew, James the Minor, James the Major and Simon. See Bagnoli, *La Maestà*, 157. For the protocol of who should be given the honour of carrying the ceremonial canopy in Angevin Provence, see Coulet, 'Les entrées solonnelles', 68.

[34] First explored by G. Mazzoni, 'Influssi danteschi nella "Maestà"' (Siena, 1315–16), *Archivio storico italiano*, 94 (1936), 144–62. For more recent studies on the relationship of these verses and Dante's *Divine Comedy*, see Bagnoli, *La Maestà*, 84–5.

It has generally been assumed that the two verses should be read in descending order, with the latter verse apparently relying on other texts that once appeared on scrolls held by the four patron saints – the outlines of which can only just be seen today.[35] It was previously argued, therefore, that the sequence of the dialogue begins with a reference to the flowers presented to the Virgin by the two angels and alludes to an enemy who 'despises' her and 'deceives' her 'land', then follows with a petition (now lost) from the four patron saints, and culminates in a reply where the Virgin acknowledges the saints' petitions but warns them against those who 'harm the weak'.[36] However, careful analysis of the verse structure has led me to believe that the two verses should be read in the opposite sequence. This would mean that the two verses make up a continuous reply by the Virgin in direct response to written petitions from the four patron saints, now completely lost.[37] Beginning with a heading entitled, 'The reply of the Virgin', the first part of her speech opens with the phrase 'my beloved ones' and continues with her acknowledgment of the saints' prayers on behalf of their devotees, her advice about the type of person they should not mediate for, and her preference for good counsel over the 'angelic flowers' of the 'heavenly field'. Her words end decisively with a final, unequivocal warning against 'some-one who, for his own estate, despises me and deceives my land'.[38] The two texts thus provide compelling evidence that the four patron saints were deliberately portrayed in the guise of supplicants, petitioning the Virgin for favours on behalf of the Sienese. She, in turn, appears as both Queen of Heaven and principal patron saint of Siena, graciously acknowledging their petitions and – on behalf of her Son – imparting her judgement about the merits of their case.

THE *MAESTÀ* AND CONTEMPORARY RITUAL

The presentation of a canopy at the moment of entry into the city was an emphatic acknowledgment of the high social status of the visitor – and in the specific case of the Angevin princes, their claim to royalty in southern Italy.

[35] Painted *a secco*, these scrolls and their texts have now all but disappeared. Bagnoli, *La Maestà*, 90, argues persuasively that these details were added by Simone Martini in the 1321 campaign of repainting the *Maestà*. See also note 37 below.

[36] For an example of the conventional way of reading the order of the two verses in the *Maestà*, see Martindale, *Simone Martini*, 207.

[37] Bagnoli, *La Maestà*, 83–5, argues on a number of technical and philological grounds that the upper text replaces an earlier text recording the saints' petition to the Virgin. At the time of the documented 1321 repainting of the *Maestà*, a second verse was introduced and the petition rewritten on scrolls placed in the hands of the four patron saints. Bagnoli's arguments thus support my view that the Virgin's 'reply' always began with the lower text, located in the immediate foreground of the painting.

[38] For the original Italian of the two verses, set out in the order suggested here, see *ibid.*, 87.

In the *Maestà*, the novel inclusion of the canopy decisively underlines the fact that the Virgin is represented here as the Queen of Heaven. A further characteristic of entries was the carefully programmed event of an exchange of speeches between the civic authorities and the royal visitor. This, in turn, might involve a petition where the royal guest was invited to impart his or her judgment over a particular case, such as the benevolent act of freeing prisoners.[39] Such elements of the ritual of ceremonial entries are again reflected in Simone Martini's treatment of the traditional subject of the *Maestà*. As noted, the four patron saints appear in the guise of supplicants engaged in an elaborate dialogue with the Virgin. In addition, the text that the Christ Child displays on his scroll further alludes to the notion of judgment and its application. Further comparisons can be drawn between the presence of heraldic insignia in both the painting and the descriptions of entries, signalling the identity and presence of various civic bodies at these ceremonial occasions. The hierarchical ordering of the various saints in the painting may also be construed as a reflection of the strict social hierarchy that would have characterized the subsequent procession though the city.[40]

The canopy was also, of course, a well-established feature of liturgical and ecclesiastical ceremony,[41] and Jean Campbell has raised the issue of whether, or not, Simone Martini's novel inclusion of the canopy within the *Maestà* reflects the emerging rituals surrounding the celebration of the feast of Corpus Christi.[42] In Siena, however, the earliest evidence for Corpus Christi processions becoming established as official civic events dates from the 1350s.[43] Moreover, although there was an altar in close proximity to Simone

---

[39] Guenée in Guenée and Lehoux, *Les entrées royales françaises*, 24, Coulet, 'Les entrées solonnelles', 64, 67–8.

[40] Women rarely featured in the ceremonial of entries, whereas in the *Maestà*, the Virgin is accompanied by a number female saints in close proximity to her; see Coulet, *ibid.*, 67, D. Norman, *Siena and the Virgin: Art and Politics in a Late Medieval City State* (New Haven and London, 1999), 55. It should also be noted that the principal visual impression of entries into the city would have been one of linear, sequential progression as the procession moved through the city to its destination. By contrast, the *Maestà* presents a highly formalized and static grouping of figures centred round the Virgin and Christ Child. In this respect, the image of the enthroned figures set beneath a ceremonial canopy is closer to that of contemporary coins and seals, such as the *pavillon d'or* issued in 1339 by the French king, Philip VI, which represents a single, highly-focussed image of the monarch, seated on a throne beneath a tent-like canopy (for which, see Guenée and Lehoux, *Les entrées royales françaises*, 15).

[41] As argued in Coulet, 'Les entrées solonnelles', 72–5, the canopy's survival as a ceremonial object, customarily used in late antiquity as a means of welcoming persons of high social status, owes a great deal to the practices adopted by early Christian popes and prelates, particularly in respect of the evolution of the liturgy for Palm Sunday.

[42] Campbell, 'The lady in the council chamber', 383–4, n.11, citing, in particular, A. B. Rave, *Fronleichnam in Siena: Die Maestà von Simone Martini in der Sala del Mappamondo* (Worms, 1986).

[43] See the essay by Machtelt Israëls in this collection. See also, F. Nevola, 'Cerimoniali per santi e feste a Siena a metà Quattrocento. Documenti dallo *Statuto di Siena*, 39', in *Siena e il suo territorio nel rinascimento*, ed. M. Ascheri (Siena, 2000), III, 171–84 (173–4, 180–1). Although a Corpus Christi procession was staged in Barcelona in either 1319 or 1320, the earliest evidence for the use of a canopy in the procession occurs in a manuscript illumination belonging to an Augustinian missal, dated 1362. See Guenée in Guenée and Lehoux, *Les entrées royales françaises*, 15–18, Fig. 1; Coulet, 'Les entrées solonnelles', 70, 80 n.60.

Martini's *Maestà* from the early fifteenth century onwards,[44] there is no evidence that the *Maestà* itself ever functioned as a mural altarpiece. It would not, therefore, have been used as a pictorial adjunct to the celebration of Mass, where the doctrine of the Corpus Christi is of special relevance.

Conversely, when first painted, the *Maestà* was specifically executed for the wall of the Sala del Consiglio, Siena's principal council hall. Here the city's principal legislative council met under the chairmanship of the *Podestà*, who would have sat on a ceremonial seat directly below the painting in question. Clearly, the prominent reference to the ideal of justice on the Christ Child's scroll was mainly directed towards the city's magistrates and councillors, whose function was to debate and vote upon laws governing Siena and its surrounding territories. In similar fashion, the words attributed to the Virgin as a direct response to a now lost petition, made on behalf of the Sienese by their four patron saints, also takes the form of a series of directives encouraging the assembled council to observe certain essential tenets of just and civilized behaviour.[45]

CONCLUSION

For the painting's first audience, familiar with the civic rituals for the reception of Angevin princes, the canopy in Simone Martini's *Maestà* would have acted as an immediate signifier of the majesty and the sanctity of the Virgin. In terms of design and distinctive heraldic ornament, it would also have mirrored the canopies standardly paid for by the Commune to honour illustrious visitors to the city – highly-crafted objects, in the production of which Simone Martini himself was involved. In addition, the well-established protocols for ritual entries – involving procedures for greeting and petitioning the honoured guest and for observing intricacies of social hierarchy – would have offered further associations between the painting and these events.

Modern scholars have argued that ritual also works in more subliminal ways for its participants and audience. Ritual performances are highly constructed events devised to 'produce a story people tell themselves about themselves'.[46] They are, therefore, deliberately devised both to influence and to control the perceptions of the people who repeatedly witness them. In late medieval society political rituals – such as entries into cities – often camouflaged

---

[44] This is the altar in the Cappella dei Signori, the earliest notice of which dates from 1405. See M. Cordaro in Brandi, *Palazzo Pubblico di Siena*, 83. The eighteenth-century antiquarian, Girolamo Gigli claims that the Cappella was dedicated first to Saint Luke and then to the Virgin, which might imply that there was an earlier chapel (and hence an altar) on this site. See G. Gigli, *Diario sanese* (1723), (Siena, 1854), II, 257. If this were the case, this would mean that there was always an altar set against the same wall as that of the *Maestà*, but well to the left of the painting.

[45] Norman, *Siena and the Virgin*, 53–7.

[46] E. Muir, *Ritual in Early Modern Europe* (Cambridge, 1997), 4, using a formula derived from Clifford Geertz's seminal study of the Balinese 'theatre' state, *Negara: The Theatre State in Nineteenth-Century Bali* (Princeton, 1980).

social tensions by giving an enhanced impression of the extent of political stability and harmony. It seems that the Angevin visits of 1310, 1314 and 1315 passed off without political threat or social tension, although all of the chronicle accounts of these three visits remark on the large number of armed retainers introduced into the city by these foreign guests.[47] In July of 1326, when Charles of Calabria visited the city and negotiated a term of office as Siena's *signore*, with the right to choose the city's *Podestà*, the political stakes were much higher. Nevertheless, the duke still received the customary reception and celebration in his honour. It may be, therefore, that the ritual events themselves were one of the ways in which the government successfully controlled and limited the Duke of Calabria's claims over Sienese political autonomy at that time.[48]

Similarly, the painted texts in the *Maestà* also reveal the fragility of Siena's power, referring, as they do, to specific, though unnamed individuals who threaten the city. Like contemporary ritual, however, the *Maestà* portrays an idealized model of what might be.[49] Five of the most prominent figures are Siena's principal patron saints – the Virgin and four petitioners who kneel before her – a familiar strategy in late medieval Italian art for appealing to an audience's sense of corporate, civic identity.[50] The only references to contemporary political office, institutions and allegiances appear in abstract form as heraldic devices and symbolic objects, such as the city seal, coin and canopy. Just as, in the early decades of the fourteenth century, civic processions and rituals were deliberately constructed to provide a compelling, if illusionary, demonstration of the stability and power of the Sienese government – a power bolstered by their allegiance to the royal house of Anjou – so the image of the *Maestà* must once have given Siena's councillors an empowering sense that their city state was, indeed, particularly blessed to be under the wise and prudent protection of the Virgin herself.

The Open University

---

[47] See notes 6, 8, and 11.

[48] For analysis of Charles of Calabria's 1326 visit and its political consequences for Siena, see W. M. Bowsky, *A Medieval Italian Commune: Siena under the Rule of the Nine 1287–1355* (Berkeley, 1981), 176–8; Caggese, *Roberto d'Angiò*, II, 88. For contemporary accounts of the celebrations staged for this visit, see 'Cronaca senese di autore anonimo' in *Cronache senesi*, 132–3, G. Villani, *Cronica*, bk. 9, ch. 356, *ed. cit.* II, 365–6. For its expense for the Commune, see Maginnis, *The Early Sienese Painter*, 68.

[49] Campbell, 'The lady in the council chamber', 374, has observed: 'The *Maestà* cannot . . . be described as a history painting. . . . The *Maestà* is, in fact, best described as a complex pictorial and poetic metaphor of sovereignty'.

[50] The relationship between the cults of patron saints and civic institutions in late medieval Italy has generated a substantial body of literature. See, for example: H. Peyer, *Stadt und Stadtpatron in Mittelalterlichen Italien* (Zurich, 1955); A. Vauchez, 'Patronage des saints et religion civique dans l'Italie communale à la fin du Moyen Age', in *Patronage and Public in the Trecento*, ed. V. Moleta (Florence, 1986); D. Webb, *Patrons and Defenders: The Saints in the Italian City States* (London and New York, 1996); G. Dickson, 'The 115 Cults of the Saints in Later Medieval and Renaissance Perugia: A Demographic Overview of a Civic Pantheon', *Renaissance Studies*, 12 (1998), 6–25.

3

Enter the emperor. Charles IV and Siena between politics, diplomacy, and ritual (1355 and 1368)*

GERRIT JASPER SCHENK

Siena, the guardian of the Via Francigena in the heart of Tuscany, was an important stopover for medieval Roman-German rulers on their traditional processions to the imperial coronation in Rome. The ceremonial entries organized in different ways reflected the relationship between city and ruler. Particular cultural traditions of receiving rulers,[1] the city's own social and political situation, urban topography and architecture with its ephemeral adornments – all this played a part in the way Siena stage-managed the *adventus*. Ritual, ceremony and politics combined to form a unique mix with its own performance dynamic. It is these that form the focus of the following study, which examines the ceremonial performance enacted by the city of Siena in order to receive Charles IV in 1355 and 1368.

The rulers from the empire north of the Alps went to Italy more and more rarely from the middle of the thirteenth century. Their claims to rule, collect taxes and assume political leadership were increasingly rejected by the largely autonomous local communities.[2] Yet the German king and Roman emperor constituted a considerable power factor, once he had actually progressed south of the Alps. If a community received him with full honours, he was then able to give the respective political leadership supreme imperial legitimation as his regents, representatives or imperial deputies (*regentes, locumtenentes, capitanei et vicarii*), for example.[3] It was also possible for them

* A variation on the title of the study by G. Kipling, *Enter the King. Theatre, Liturgy, and the Ritual in Medieval Civic Triumph* (New York, 1998), without seeking to adopt his position. I would like to thank the staff of the Archivio di Stato, Siena, for their help, Elaine Griffiths for the translation into English, and the editors for their useful comments.

[1] Cf. Kipling, *Enter*, 6–47; G. J. Schenk, *Zeremoniell und Politik. Herrschereinzüge im spätmittelalterlichen Reich* (Köln, Weimar and Wien, 2003), 34–38.

[2] Cf. E. Voltmer, 'Deutsche Herrscher in Italien. Kontinuität und Wandel vom 11. bis zum 14. Jahrhundert', in S. de Rachewiltz and J. Riedmann (eds.), *Kommunikation und Mobilität im Mittelalter. Begegnungen zwischen dem Süden und der Mitte Europas (11.-14. Jahrhundert)* (Sigmaringen, 1995), 15–26; M.-L. Favreau-Lilie, 'Vom Kriegsgeschrei zur Tanzmusik. Anmerkungen zu den Italienzügen des späteren Mittelalters', in B. Z. Kedar, J. Riley-Smith, and R. Hiestand (eds.), *Montjoie. Studies in Crusade History in Honour of Hans Eberhard Mayer* (Aldershot, 1997), 213–233; R. Pauler, *Die deutschen Könige und Italien im 14. Jahrhundert. Von Heinrich VII. bis Karl IV.* (Darmstadt, 1997); E. Widder, 'I Viaggi di Imperatori, Principi e Sovrani nel Tardo Medioevo', in S. Gensini (ed.), *Viaggiare nel Medioevo* (San Miniato, 2000), 163–194.

[3] On the concepts cf. M.-L. Heckmann, *Stellvertreter, Mit- und Ersatzherrscher. Regenten, Generalstatthalter, Kurfürsten und Reicsvikare in Regnum und Imperium vom 13. bis zum frühen 15. Jahrhundert* (2 vols., Warendorf, 2002), II, 660–666.

to join forces with the emperor to combat rivals in the internal Italian struggle for influence. Denying him admission, however, meant exposure to the threat of harmful imperial ban, unrest among the opposition inside your own walls or even siege and blockade.

King Charles IV, brought up at the French court and possessing great diplomatic experience, had long planned his procession to Rome for the imperial coronation.[4] When he entered Pisa in January 1355, the political situation was still unclear, and the southward journey on the Via Francigena was initially impeded: Florence, concerned for its independence, had long been trying, in coordination with the Tuscan cities of Siena, Arezzo, San Miniato, Pistoia, Perugia and Volterra, to mount an opposition against Charles IV.[5]

In Siena, the families of the oligarchic *Nove* (the Nine), who had emerged from a kind of 'grande bourgeoisie', had dominated the political life of the city since 1287. The rule of the *Nove* is considered the heyday of Siena, yet the stable facade concealed violent rivalry between different social groups.[6] Both the aristocratic magnates and the more 'petit bourgeois' *Popolo* were largely excluded from power. At times the *Nove* were threatened by the conspiracies and feuds between the magnate families of the Salimbeni and the Tolomei, and they reacted by setting up special troops recruited from their followers.[7] The bank failures of the 1340s and the fatal demographic, economic and political consequences of the first wave of plague from 1348 led to the demise of the *Nove*.[8]

When the envoys from the Tuscan cities presented their messages to the German king in Pisa on 30 January 1355, the Sienese, of all people, who could have blocked the Via Francigena, destroyed the diplomatic resistance so laboriously mounted by Florence. Until then the *Nove* had tended to

[4] Cf. E. Widder, *Itinerar und Politik. Studien zur Reiseherrschaft Karls IV. südlich der Alpen* (Köln, 1993), 125–192.

[5] Cf. with differing views Widder, *Itinerar*, 197–202; G. J. Schenk, *Der Einzug des Herrschers. 'Idealschema' und Fallstudie zum Adventuszeremoniell für römisch-deutsche Herrscher in spätmittelalterlichen italienischen Städten zwischen Zeremoniell, Diplomatie und Politik* (Marburg, 1996), 74–77, 81; R. Pauler, *Die Auseinandersetzungen zwischen Kaiser Karl IV. und den Päpsten. Italien als Schachbrett der Diplomatie* (Neuried, 1996), 98f., 103–106; Pauler, *Könige*, 181–204.

[6] Cf. W. M. Bowsky, *A medieval Italian commune: Siena under the Nine, 1287–1355* (Berkeley, Los Angeles, and London, 1981), 23–84; J. Hook, *Siena. Una città e la sua storia* (Siena, 1988), 27–44; E. Brizio, 'L'elezione degli uffici politici nella Siena del Trecento', *Bullettino Senese di Storia Patria* (hereafter 'BSSP'), 98 (1991), 16–62; O. Redon, 'Qualche considerazione sulle magistrature forestiere a Siena nel Duecento e nella prima metà del Trecento', in J.-Cl. Maire Vigueur (ed.), *I Podestà dell'Italia comunale Parte I: Reclutamento e circolazione degli ufficiali forestieri (fine XII sec.–metà XIV sec.)* (Rome, 2000), 666–670.

[7] Cf. W. M. Bowsky, 'The Medieval Commune and internal violence: police power and public safety in Siena 1287–1355', *American Historical Review*, 73 (1967), 1–17; A. Carniani, *I Salimbeni, quasi una Signoria. Tentativi di affermazione politica nella Siena del '300* (Siena, 1995), 191–197; R. Mucciarelli, *I Tolomei banchieri di Siena. La parabola di un casato nel XIII e XIV secolo* (Siena, 1995), 257–282.

[8] Cf. Bowsky, *Siena under the Nine*, 66–84, 304–314; Hook, *Siena*, 44; P. Cammarosano, 'Il comune di Siena dalla solidarietà imperiale al guelfismo: Celebrazione e propaganda', in: P. Cammarosano (ed.), *Le forme della propaganda politica nel Due e nel Trecento. Relazione tenute al convegno internazionale . . . Trieste, 2–5 marzo 1993* (Rome, 1994), 465f.

follow the 'foreign policy' positions of Florence.[9] Now, however, they surprisingly performed a *volte face*. In the words of the contemporary Florentine chronicler Matteo Villani '. . . they freely, and without any covenant, offered that city to his rule'.[10] However, when Charles IV called for a formal oath of allegiance from the Sienese, one of the envoys, the magnate Guccio Tolomei, refused to comply: he demanded that fresh deliberations be held in Siena before agreeing to this submission.[11] One can only speculate about the motives for this denial, which was doubtless disastrous for the reputation of the *Nove*. The Tolomei family entertained close connections with Florence and perhaps wanted to overturn the *Nove*'s new anti-Florentine policy, by demonstrating the internal disunity of the community to the outside world. With all his political experience, Charles IV seems to have understood this immediately. He quashed the resistance of Guccio Tolomei by according a general privilege for the magnates, so that the formal allegiance of the community[12] was finally sworn on 2 March in Pisa. In return, Charles swore to keep the *Nove* in power and to invest them as *vicarii* of the empire in Siena. That made three things clear: first, the *Nove* had to welcome Charles IV not just as the German king but also as the recognized *Signore* of the city. Second, it must have become clear to all concerned that the rule of the *Nove* was going through a particularly unstable period. Thirdly, the time to prepare for the entry had become comparatively short.[13]

We know relatively little about the actual preparations by the community. What can be said for example is that there were baldachins and flags with the imperial eagle and that the districts were prepared for the crowd of important guests in the pilgrim neighbourhoods near the two city gates

---

[9] Cf. M. Luzzati, 'Firenze e l'area toscana', in G. Galasso (ed.), *Storia d'Italia*, vol. 7/1 (Turin, 1987), 695; P. Torriti, *Tutta Siena, Contrada per Contrada. Nuova Guida illustrata storico-artistica della città e dintorni* (Florence, 1988), repr. 1992, 15f.; by contrast Pauler, *Auseinandersetzungen*, 98f., 103f. on a more pro-imperial stance of Siena.

[10] Matteo Villani, *Croniche di Giovanni, Matteo e Filippo Villani secondo le migliori stampe*, ed. A. Racheli (Trieste, 1857–59), II, 143f., book IV ch.54: '. . . magnificando con ornato sermone la serenità della maiestà imperiale, chiamandolo loro signore; e senza alcuno patto offersono quello comune liberamente alla sua signoria . . .' Cf. by contrast G. Canestrini, 'Di alcuni documenti riguardanti le relazioni politiche dei Papi d'Avignone coi comuni d'Italia avanti e dopo il tribunato di Cola di Rienzo e la calata di Carlo IV', *Archivio Storico Italiano*, Appendice 7 n.24 (1849), 405f. n.69. On Villani's Florentine perspective cf. L. Green, *Chronicle into History. An Essay on the Interpretation of History in Florentine Fourteenth-Century Chronicles* (Cambridge, 1972), 44–85.

[11] Cf. M. Villani, *Croniche*, book IV ch.53f., 61, ed. Racheli, II, 143f., 146; Donato di Neri, *Cronaca senese di Donato di Neri e di suo figlio Neri*, in *Cronache Senesi*, ed. A. Lisini and F. Iacometti (Bologna, 1947) (L. A. Muratori, *Rerum Italicarum Scriptores* 2nd ed., vol. 15/6), 576f.; Ranieri Sardo, *Cronica di Pisa*, ed. O. Banti (Rome, 1963), 111; O. Malavolti, *Historia De'fatti, e Guerre de'Sanesi, cosi esterne, come Civili. Seguite dall'Origine della lor Città, fino all'anno MDLV* (Venice, 1599), part II book 6, fol. 111r–112r; G. Tommasi, *Dell'historie di Siena Parte Prima* (Venice, 1625), 336. Guccio Tolomei: G. Pirchan, *Italien unter Kaiser Karl IV. in der Zeit seiner zweiten Romfahrt* (Prague, 1930), II, 146* No.98; Widder, *Itinerar*, 200–202, 386f., No.4. For more details see Schenk, *Einzug*, 85–92.

[12] The text of the oath of allegiance is not preserved.

[13] Cf. the generally longer preparatory period for other cities: Schenk, *Einzug*, 19–21.

along the Via Francigena.[14] The king, for his part, sent out a vanguard of 150 riders to Siena, under the command of a marshal, who swore an oath of obedience to the *Nove*, in accordance with the agreements made in Pisa. On 6 March, the king's representatives finally took symbolic possession of the city. An eyewitness, Donato di Neri, reports in his chronicle: '. . . they fixed the arms of the emperor to all the gates of Siena, and did likewise at the palace of the court of the *Signori Nove*, topping the windows with fine gold; it was lovely to behold.'[15] The seat of government of the *Nove* had since 1310 been the imposing Palazzo Pubblico on the Piazza del Campo[16], the public centre and the political heart of the city, on which all the streets converged. It was common to display the coats of arms of visiting princes at their temporary residence in Siena.[17] Since the Palazzo Pubblico was not intended to serve as quarters for Charles IV[18], this prominent flagging of what were for the community the central points of civic architecture – the gates and seat of government of the *Nove* – can be understood as a political and legal takeover of the city by Charles IV. A painting ascribed to Sano di Pietro, *San Bernardino preaching on the Campo*, reflects the state of the palace around 1444–1448 (Fig. 1), and can be taken as an indication of the appearance of the palace in the Middle Ages.[19] This shows the eagle of the empire with a single head, as was used during the kingship of Frederick III (1442–1452), affixed directly above the three gilded windows.[20] The positioning of the arms suggests imperial supremacy over the civic Balzana set into the windows tracery.[21]

---

[14] Cf. Donato, *Cronaca*, 577; Iohannes Porta de Annoniaco, *Liber de coronatione Karoli IV. Imperatoris*, ed. R. Salomon (Hannover and Leipzig, 1913), 72; Tommasi, *Dell'historie*, 338. Quarters: F. J. D. Nevola, '"Per Ornato Della Città": Siena's Strada Romana and Fifteenth-Century Urban Renewal', *The Art Bulletin*, 82 (2000), 29–31.

[15] Cf. Donato, *Cronaca*, 577: '. . . si féro l' arme de lo'nperadore a tutte le porti di Siena, e anco si fe' al palazo de la residenzia de' signori Nove, a capo le finestre a oro fino, bellissima'; on the author cf. P. Viti, 'Donato di Neri', *Dizionario Biografico degli Italiani*, 41 (Rome, 1992), 75–77. Before Sigismund's entry in 1432 the commune itself affixed the imperial coat of arms to it, cf. Favreau-Lilie, *Kriegsgeschrei*, 216.

[16] Cf. Torriti, *Tutta Siena*, 23–32; M. Cordaro, 'Le vicende costruttive', in C. Brandi (ed.), *Palazzo Pubblico di Siena. Vicende Costruttive e decorazione* (Milan, 1983), 29–143; L. Franchina (ed.), *Piazza del Campo. Evoluzione di una immagine. Documenti, Vicende, Ricostruzioni – Mostra didattica*, (Siena, 1987), 41; M. D'Angelico, *Die Datierungs- und Zuschreibungsproblematik des 'Giuncarico'-Freskos im Palazzo Pubblico von Siena und seine Einordnung in die sienesischen Territorialdarstellungen des Trecento* (Frankfurt a.M., 1997), 25–29.

[17] Cf. on the conditions in the empire north of the Alps Schenk, *Zeremoniell*, 255.

[18] Cf. below n.51.

[19] Cf. D. Balestracci and G. Piccinni, *Siena nel Trecento. Assetto urbano e strutture edilizie* (Florence, 1977), 103–105; G. Freuler, 'Sienese Quattrocento Painting in the Service of Spiritual Propaganda', in E. Borsook and F. Superbi Gioffredi (eds.), *Italian Altarpieces 1250–1550. Function and Design* (Oxford 1994), 81–116. The 'monogramma bernardiniano' between the upper, golden windows before the middle, third window dates to 1425, cf. G. Milanesi, *Documenti per la Storia dell'Arte Senese* (3 vols., Siena, 1854–1856, repr. 1969), II, 128f. No.89f.

[20] Cf. F. Gall, *Österreichische Wappenkunde. Handbuch der Wappenwissenschaft* (Wien and Köln, 1977), 41–43; O. Neubecker, *Wappenkunde* (München, 1980), 90f., 110–121.

[21] Cf. A. Cairola and E. Carli, *Il Palazzo pubblico di Siena* (Rome, 1963), 25f., 35f., 36; Cordaro, *Vicende*, 57. It is not clear whether the large city arms recognizable in 1444–1448 at Sano di Pietro (balzana and arms of the Popolo over the 1ˢᵗ storey) had already been placed there in 1355.

Fig. 1   Sano di Pietro, *Saint Bernardino preaching on the Campo*, 1448, tempera on panel, Museo dell'Opera del Duomo, Siena (photo reproduced with permission of Museo dell'Opera del Duomo, Siena)

On the evening of 23 March 1355, Charles IV and his wife Anna finally entered Siena.[22] The narrative sources link the report of the entry on 23 March with the description of the related uprising against the regime of the *Nove* on 24 and 25 March 1355. The exact sequence of the chaotic events

---

[22] Cf. sources for the following: Donato, *Cronaca*, 577; *Cronaca senese dei fatti riguardanti la città e il suo territorio di autore anonimo del secolo XIV*, in *Cronache Senesi*, ed. A. Lisini and F. Iacometti (Bologna, 1947) (L. A. Muratori, *Rerum Italicarum Scriptores* 2nd ed., vol. 15/6), 149; Ranieri Sardo, *Cronica*, 114–116 (with correct chronology); Johannes Porta de Annoniaco, *Liber*, 72f., 134; M. Villani, *Croniche*, book IV ch.80–82, ed. Racheli, II, 154f.; Tommasi, *Dell'Historie*, 338. On the reconstruction of events: Schenk, *Einzug*, 21–24 (*Occursus*), 95–103 (*Ingressus* and uprising on 24 and 25 March); Widder, *Itinerar*, 206–210; Pauler, *Könige*, 202f. By contrast,

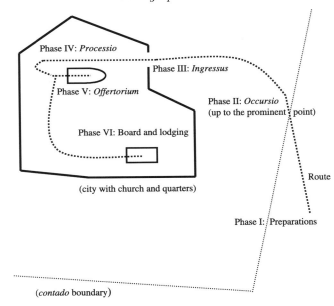

Fig. 2   Schematic diagram of an *Adventus* (map: G. J. Schenk)

appears to have been lost in the Sienese local chronicles, that have only been handed down in later copies. Ceremonial details of the entry might thus have been omitted by the authors since the uprising would have appeared more important in their eyes. The sources, for example, do not explicitly report on the usual *Occursio* – the traditional escort of honour from the border of the *contado* or another prominent point – which was provided by the Sienese contingent sent out to meet the party (Fig. 2). Nevertheless, a plausible reconstruction of events can be drawn from surviving sources.

The royal couple approached the city from the north, accompanied by 600 to 1000 knights and numerous foot soldiers. In the words of *Nove* supporter Giugurta Tommasi, writing long afterwards but well informed, the procession of high-ranking guests was received by the people of Siena outside the Porta Camollia with great pomp and circumstance.[23] The contemporary chronicler

uprising of 23–25 March in E. Werunsky, *Der erste Römerzug Kaiser Karl IV. (1354–1355)* (Innsbruck, 1878), 151–161; G. Luchaire (ed.), *Documenti per la storia dei rivolgimenti politici del comune di Siena dal 1354 al 1369* (Lyon and Paris, 1906), XXXI; P. Rossi, 'Carlo IV di Lussemburgo e la Repubblica di Siena (1355–1369). I. La prima discesa di Carlo IV in Italia e la caduta del governo dei Nove', *BSSP*, 38 (1930), 17; S. Moggi, 'Storia della repubblica Senese dal 1328 al 1355', *Miscellanea storica della Valdelsa*, 68 (1962), 55–73, 189; V. Rutenberg, 'La vie et la lutte des Ciompi de Sienne', *Annales. Economies, Société, Civilisation*, 20 (1965), 101f.; Carniani, *Salimbeni*, 215.

[23] Tommasi, *Dell'Historie*, 338: 'Fù fuor della porta a Camollia incontrato con pompa trionfale . . .'; on Tommasi cf. Schenk, *Einzug*, 84.

gives only a brief account, noting that the festively clad magnates and *Nove* rode out to meet the royal couple, flags flying, and accompanied by the Popolo.[24] The spectacle that met the eyes of the newcomers must indeed have been impressive.[25]

In the last third of the thirteenth century, the Antiportico di Camollia (or Porta Goltapalazzi) had been erected about 350 metres away from the older Porta di Camollia in order to block the Via Francigena and impede entry to the city. Since the first half of the fourteenth century an image of Mary, the patron saint of Siena, had adorned the exterior of the Porta Camollia perhaps – and certainly that of the Antiportico archway; the street had been paved since the end of the thirteenth century. The wording of the sources indicate that the Prato di Camollia served as a reception area, and this was later the case with the German kings Sigismund in 1432 and Frederick in 1452.[26] This area lay directly behind the Antiportico and a central gate[27], before the Porta Camollia itself came into sight, leading to a view of the towers and roofs of Siena. The open, spacious square had been laid out in 1309 at the expense of the community to offer an appropriate location for fairs etc. A Sienese panel (Fig. 3), showing the victory of Siena over the French in 1526 at the Porta Camollia, gives a relatively correct impression of the architectural design of the gates.[28] Yet Franceso Vanni, showing the situation in 1597, depicts the topographical situation without the central gate (Fig. 4).[29]

As soon as the royal couple appeared to the waiting crowd they were welcomed with loud music[30] and rode into the city under the baldachins. The published sources give little information about their style and manufacture,[31]

---

[24] Cronaca senese anonima, 149; Donato, *Cronaca*, 577; Raniero Sardo, *Cronica*, 116.

[25] Cf. on the following, with differing interpretations Balestracci and Piccinni, *Siena*, 19 n.5, 74f., 157; J. Gardner, 'An Introduction to the Iconography of the Medieval Italian City Gate', *Dumbarton Oaks Papers*, 41 (1987), 212–3; Torriti, *Tutta Siena*, 278; M. Israëls, 'New documents for Sassetta and Sano di Pietro at the Porta Romana, Siena', *The Burlington Magazine*, 140 (1998), 437 and n.7 and 12f.; Nevola, '*Per Ornato*', 36.

[26] Cf. Petrus Russius, *Senensis Historiae suorum temporum fragmentum*, ed. U. Benvoglienti (L. A. Muratori: *Rerum Italicarum Scriptores* 20) (Milan, 1731), col.40, Tommaso Fecini, *Cronaca Senese*, ed. A. Lisini and F. Iacometti (Bologna, 1947) (L. A. Muratori, *Rerum Italicarum Scriptores* 2nd ed., vol. 15/6), col.844 and Favreau-Lilie, *Kriegsgeschrei*, 216f. (Sigismund); H. Quirin, 'König Friedrich in Siena 1452', in H. Heimpel, W. Andreas and H. Grundmann (eds.), *Aus Reichstagen des 15. und 16. Jahrhunderts. Festgabe* (München, 1958), 60 (Frederick III).

[27] Cf. A. Lisini (ed.), *Il Costituto del Comune di Siena volgarizzato nel MCCCIX–MCCCX, edito sotto gli auspici del Ministero dell'Interno* (Siena, 1903), II, 134f., distinzione terza, No. CCXCI of 1309; E. Guidoni and P. Maccari (eds.), *Siena e i Centri Senesi sulla Via Francigena* (Rome, 2000), 73.

[28] Cf. A. Tomei (ed.), *Le Biccherne di Siena. Arte e Finanza all'alba dell'economia moderna* (Azzano San Paolo (Bergamo)/ Rome, 2002), 224f.: Attributed to Giovanni di Lorenzo, probably from a tax book cover.

[29] Cf. E. Pellegrini, *L'iconographia di Siena nelle opere a stampa. Vedute generali della città del XV al XIX secolo* (Siena, 1986), 105–109.

[30] Cf. Donato, *Cronaca*, 577. On the equipment and functions of civic musicians in Siena cf. Lisini, *Costituto*, I, 112f., distinzione prima No. CXII–CXIV, for processions see: F. A. D'Accone, *The Civic Muse. Music and Musicians in Siena during the Middle Ages and the Renaissance* (Chicago and London, 1997), 667–670.

[31] Donato, *Cronaca*, 577, '. . . uno palio fatto a oro fino, cioè uno baldachino sopra a lo'nperadore e un altro per la'nperadrice.'

Fig. 3   Giovanni di Lorenzo, *The victory of Porta Camollia*, 1526 tempera on panel, Museo delle Biccherne, Archivio di Stato, Siena (photo reproduced with permission of Archivio di Stato, Siena)

Fig. 4   Detail showing area between Porta Camollia and Antiportico, from Franceso Vanni, *Sena Vetus Civitas Virginis*, etching, 1597 (photo reproduced with permission of Biblioteca Comunale degli Intronati Siena)

Fig. 5   Niccolò di Giovanni Ventura, *Chronicle*, 1442, manuscript, *Procession with the Madonna Icon* (1260), Biblioteca Comunale degli Intronati Siena, A IV 5, fol. 5r (photo reproduced with permission of Biblioteca Comunale degli Intronati Siena)

yet a reconstruction can certainly draw on descriptions of entry baldachins from other cities[32] and of the Sienese procession baldachin. An example of the latter appears in a chronicle by Niccolò di Giovanni Ventura of 1442, illustrating the procession for the dedication of Siena to the Virgin Mary in 1260 (Fig. 5).[33] Presumably similar box-like canopies were used for the procession of 1355, borne with four rods and made of costly golden silk, probably adorned with the royal eagle and perhaps with the civic arms.[34] Such baldachins were familiar to Italian contemporaries; they were sacralizing and

---

[32] Cf. Schenk, *Einzug*, 59–63; Schenk, *Zeremoniell*, 448–455.

[33] Cf. B. Kempers, 'Icons, Altarpieces, and Civic Ritual in Siena Cathedral, 1100–1530', in B. A. Hanawalt and K. L. Reyerson (eds.), *City and Spectacle in Medieval Europe* (Minneapolis and London, 1994), 98f. and Fig. 4.5.

[34] Cf. a contemporary report on the baldachin for Sigismund in Siena in 1432 by Russius, *Senensis Historiae*, col.40, and Fecini, *Cronaca*, 844. In Siena in 1366/67 an order for the Corpus Christi procession of the Arte della Lana provided for a baldachin adorned with arms over the Corpus Christi, cf. M. Israëls, 'Sassetta's Arte della Lana altar-piece and the cult of Corpus Domini in Siena', *The Burlington Magazine*, 143 (2001), 542. Cf. furthermore Favreau-Lilie, *Kriegsgeschrei*, 216f. and Schenk, *Einzug*, 59–63.

honorific signs of dominance, used in ceremonies and processions such as those of the papal court and the Venetian doges.[35]

This entry under the baldachins marked the actual *Ingressus* over the threshold of the city. The contemporary chronicles reported a staged incident, where, with cries of joy the Sienese fell upon and tore up the silk fabrics processional banners.[36] Giugurta Tommasi describes more precisely that all flags and baldachins were ripped up, while the magnates seized the horse of the incoming king and rode joyfully through the city, followed by the mass of the people.[37] This spoliation, a sometimes even violent theft of baldachins and horses, is not unusual. In the empire to the north, and to the south of the Alps[38], people frequently laid claim to the baldachin and horse upon which the monarch rode into the cities on his coronation procession through the empire. This generally occurred during the entry through the city gate but also when he was about to go into the cathedral or his quarters.[39]

In fact, according to Anna Maria Drabek[40] such a practice can be traced to the example of the entry of the Roman king to his coronation in Aachen or Rome. Some ceremonial regulations actually specified that the clothes and the horse of the person entering the church for the coronation should be left behind for those who had helped the elected king or emperor to descend from his horse and don his robes.[41] One might speak of a kind of reward that the future rulers had to be seen to grant, in the spirit of the royal virtue of *largitio*. A model for this could be ritual elements from the specific

[35] Cf. n.xxxiii (processions); doges since 1275: Martin da Canal, *Les estoires de Venise. Cronaca veneziana in lingua francese dalle origini al 1275*, ed. A. Limentani (Firenze, 1972), 41, 246; A. Pertusi, 'Quedam regalia insignia. Ricerche sulle insegne del potere ducale a Venezia durante il Medioevo', *Studi veneziani*, 7 (1965), 87f. and Pl. 39; details: Schenk, *Zeremoniell*, 455–472.

[36] Cronaca senese anonima, 149: 'E quando furo per la terra fu sì grande la letizia e le grida che tutte le robe dello sciamitello si straciavano . . .'; Donato, *Cronaca*, 577: '. . . come fu scavalcato, tutte le bandiere e altri si stracioro.'

[37] Tommasi, *Dell'Historie*, 338: 'Non prima fu scavalcato l'Imperadore, che furono tutte le bandiere, ed i Baldacchini stracciati, e con dismodata allegrezza tolte le cavalcature, con le quali i nobili armati sequitato dal minuto populo allegri per tutta la Città trascorsero . . .'

[38] Cf. (with more literature): Schenk, *Zeremoniell*, 472–504 (north of the alps); south of the Alps cf. S. Bertelli, *The King's Body. Sacred Rituals of Power in Medieval and Early Modern Europe* (University Park, Pennsylvania, 2001), 97–113 and Schenk, *Einzug*, 66–72.

[39] See e.g.: Spoliation in the vicinity of the cathedral with Frederick III in Florence in 1452, cf. Commentarj di Neri di Gino Capponi di cose seguite in Italia dal 1419 al 1456. Alle quali Imprese si trovò il detto Neri in persona (L. A. Muratori: *Rerum Italicarum Scriptores* 20) (Milan, 1731), col.1211. In the king's quarters: Sigismund in Siena, 1432, cf. Fecini, *Cronaca*, 844; Frederick III in Siena, 1452, cf. P. Parducci, 'L'incontro di Federigo III Imperatore con Eleonora di Portogallo', *BSSP*, 13 (1906), 361 (Mariano di Matheo di Ceco); Quirin, *König*, 64 n.97, and Viterbo, cf. Aeneas Silvius de'Piccolomini, 'Historia Rerum Friderici III. Imperatoris', in A. F. Kollar (ed.), *Analecta Monumentorum omnis aevi Vindobonensia* (Vindobonae, 1762), II, col.273C f. and Niccola della Tuccia, 'Cronaca di Viterbo', in Ignazio Ciampi (ed.), *Cronache e Statuti della Città di Viterbo* (Firenze, 1872), 216f.

[40] Cf. A. M. Drabek, *Reisen und Reisezeremoniell der römisch-deutschen Herrscher im Spätmittelalter* (Wien, 1964), 38–43.

[41] On Aachen H. Herre and L. Quidde (eds.), *Deutsche Reichstagsakten unter Kaiser Friedrich III. Zweite Abteilung 1441–1442* (Stuttgart and Gotha, 1928), 172 No.100, 192 No.108, on Rome R. Elze (ed.), *Die Ordines für die Weihe und Krönung des Kaisers und der Kaiserin (Ordines coronationis imperialis)* (Hannover, 1960), *Ordo* no.14 §5 37, *Ordo* no.17 §2 and 7 62f.

ritual of investiture on the occasion of the ordination of bishops or, precisely in Renaissance Italy, a transfer of similar ritualized elements from the *adventus novi episcopi* onto his city.[42] Drabek explains the recourse to objects directly related to the ruler with a particularly sacral quality of the king as heir to the Germanic notions of *Königsheil*.[43] However, the baldachin used in the procession will have been understood by contemporaries as Christian, rather than Germanic, and – given the occasional coat of arms as decoration – even as a sign of imperial rule. The possession of articles that, like the baldachin, were clearly connected to the monarch, was a kind of 'symbolic capital' for the contemporaries; getting hold of such loot was therefore attractive and increased their social prestige.

However, this still does not explain the time and place of the plundering. That is why – appealing to recent research – I would like to propose a cultural anthropological interpretation of the phenomena, that is closely linked with concepts of space.[44] Accordingly, it is here a matter of a specifically late medieval *rite de marge* in the spirit of Arnold van Gennep and Victor Turner, combined with elements of initiation ritual and – shades of Max Gluckman – 'rituals of rebellion'.[45] The entry processions of rulers reveal the three-phase transition typical of *rites de passage* with significant change of status and space. The central, liminal phase (*rite de marge*) is characterized by special uncertainty, moderated by formal procedure. This familiar formality gives rise to Niklas Luhmann's 'Erwartungssicherheit' (certainty of expectation).[46] When rulers first enter cities that recognize them as their legitimate ruler, there is both a change of place and of status: the ruler turns from a distant imperial monarch to a city leader present in the flesh. By crossing the threshold into the city, and proceeding to its main church, the sacral manifestation of

---

[42] Cf. on the model of episcopal ordination E. Eichmann, *Die Kaiserkrönung im Abendland. Ein Beitrag zur Geistesgeschichte des Mittelalters mit besonderer Berücksichtigung des kirchlichen Rechts, der Liturgie und der Kirchenpolitik* (Würzburg, 1942), II, 257–279, on ritualized elements in Italian episcopal entries cf. Bertelli, *King's Body*, 97f.

[43] Cf. Drabek, *Reisen*, 43f.

[44] Cf. on the research approach with differences on details e.g. R. C. Trexler, *Public Life in Renaissance Florence* (New York inter alia, 1980), 297; C. Ginzburg, 'Saccheggi rituali. Premessa a una ricerca in corso', *Quaderni storici*, 65 (1987), 615–636; P. J. Arnade, 'Secular Charisma, Sacred Power: Rites of Rebellion in the Ghent Entry of 1467', *Handelingen der Maatschappij voor Geschiedenis en Oudheidkunde te Gent*, New Series 45 (1991), 69–94; A. Paravicini Bagliani, *Il Corpo del Papa* (Turin, 1994), 224–229; E. Muir, *Ritual in Early Modern Europe* (Cambridge, 1997), 153, 239–246; M. A. Bojcov, 'Ephemerität und Permanenz bei Herrschereinzügen im spätmittelalterlichen Deutschland', *Marburger Jahrbuch für Kunstwissenschaft*, 24 (1997), 89 with n.31; Bertelli, *King's body*, 97–113; Schenk, *Zeremoniell*, 496–504.

[45] Cf. A. v. Gennep, *Übergangsriten (Les rites de passage). Aus dem Französischen von Klaus Schomburg und Sylvia M. Schomburg-Scherff* (Frankfurt a.M., New York and Paris, 1986; French orig. 1909, Eng. trans. 1960), 21–23; V. W. Turner, *The ritual process: structure and anti-structure* (New York, 1995); M. Gluckman, *Order and Rebellion in tribal Africa. Collected Essays with an autobiographical introduction* (London, 1963), 110–136; on criticism of Gluckman's approach cf. S. Schröter, 'Rituals of Rebellion – Rebellion as Ritual: A Theory Reconsidered', J. Kreinath, C. Hartung and A. Deschner (eds.), *The Dynamics of Changing Rituals. The Transformation of Religious Rituals within Their Social and Cultural Context* (New York inter alia, 2004), 41–57.

[46] Cf. N. Luhmann, *Soziale Systeme. Grundriß einer allgemeinen Theorie* (Frankfurt a.M., 2nd ed. 1985), 411–422, 610–616.

the city as a 'cultic community'[47], or to their quarters, the ruler becomes head of the city, which becomes his city, an imperial city. The raising up of the baldachin may be perceived as almost offensive, and it is therefore taken from him in the act of spoliation, thus sharing the features of a rebellion ritual. For a short time the demonstrated domination is attenuated with a cathartic effect, but in the long term it is stabilized precisely through the dominance structure. The ceremonial apparatus therefore mitigates a delicate situation. The spoliations could consequently be understood in cultural anthropological terms as a ritualized element helping to render socially tolerable the ostentatious display of power by removing the symbols elevating the rulers above their subjects.

The *Ingressus* of Charles IV in 1355 apparently took place without the otherwise usual participation of the urban clergy.[48] This was possibly due to the fact that the obligatory visit to the cathedral had to be postponed to the next day, due to his late arrival, although it may have been a deliberate ceremonial decision on the part of the *Nove*, which might indeed have been interpreted as an affront to Charles IV.[49] Normally the city fathers presented the ruler on his entering their walls with signs of authority such as the keys of the city.[50] Generally he was happy to accept them with thanks, being its lawful Signore, and then hand them right back, in order to legitimize the city government in the public eye. But this important symbolic action was also apparently not performed by the *Nove* in 1355. Did they mistrust Charles IV, and is this also to be seen as a ceremonial affront?

After crossing the threshold of the gates, the festive procession proceeded to the ruler's quarters, the *castellare* of the magnate family, the Salimbeni (Fig. 6).[51] The route led along the main axis of the city, the gently curving *Strada Romana*. Even before the improvements of the fifteenth century it offered an imposing setting and may be considered an architectural showpiece of the city.[52] It was certainly no accident that Charles IV was accommodated in the home of the influential Salimbeni and not by a member of the governing *Nove*. The Salimbeni were soon to reveal themselves as partisans of the emperor and received in return a privilege over extensive possessions

---

[47] According to E. Voltmer, 'Leben im Schutz der Heiligen. Die mittelalterliche Stadt als Kult- und Kampfgemeinschaft', in: C. Meier (ed.), *Die Okzidentale Stadt nach Max Weber. Zum Problem der Zugehörigkeit in Antike und Mittelalter* (Munich, 1994), 213–242, following Max Weber.

[48] Cf. Schenk, *Einzug*, 30f., 40, 51–58; Favreau-Lilie, *Kriegsgeschrei*, 216f. (entry 1432); Quirin, *König*, 60f. (entry 1452).

[49] Only excommunicated rulers were refused the reception by the clergy, cf. Schenk, *Einzug*, 30f., 40.

[50] Cf. Schenk, *Einzug*, 32; Favreau-Lilie, *Kriegsgeschrei*, 217 (entry 1432); Quirin, *König*, 61 (entry 1452).

[51] Cf. Donato, *Cronaca*, 577; a more detailed account is given in Tommasi, *Dell'Historie*, 338.

[52] Cf. W. Braunfels, *Mittelalterliche Stadtbaukunst in der Toskana* (Berlin, 4th ed. 1979), 254 n.8 (Siena 1398); latterly Nevola, '*Per Ornato*'.

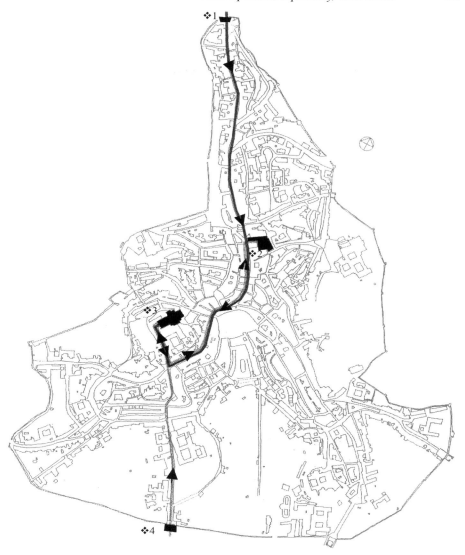

Fig. 6   Map showing the route of Charles IV's entry to Siena of 1355 and 1368. [Solid line marks 1355 processional route, grey line marks 1368 processional route] The numbers mark the major sites involved in the procession: (1) Porta Camollia (2) Palazzo Salimbeni (3) Duomo (4) Porta Tufi (map: F. Nevola)

in the Val d'Orcia.[53] The *castellare* itself was made up of several buildings; according to Donato di Neri Charles IV probably stayed in the central block, the *fondaco*, a grand, palatial structure.[54]

Next morning, the Sienese paid their respects to the king and presented him with the usual gifts on such occasions – grain, fish and wine.[55] Then, Charles IV proclaimed that all the citizens of Siena had to swear an oath of allegiance in the cathedral, which linked his visit to the cathedral, a routine part of advent ceremony (Fig. 2: *Offertorium*), to a more unusual oath-taking ceremony involving the entire citizenry.[56] His intention should be understood as a clear, public vote of no confidence towards the city government of the *Nove*. On the morning of 24 March, the king walked out with his entourage along the *Strada Romana* in the direction of the Piazza del Campo, continuing along the Via di Città and Via del Capitano to the cathedral (Fig. 6).[57] He took the opportunity of his visit to the cathedral to pardon thirty-nine Sienese prisoners, thereby demonstrating the *misericordia* and *clementia* of a Christian *rex pacificus*.[58] After he had attended the service in the cathedral, sworn *Syndici* (representatives of the city) then again swore the oath of allegiance to the king, recognising him – on behalf of all – as the signore of Siena. The great *piazza* in front of the cathedral, the religious heart of Siena, was certainly chosen deliberately as the place to swear the oath. The presence of the townspeople and proximity of Siena's patron, the Virgin Mary, invested the ceremony with civic and spiritual significance.[59]

It was probably immediately after this oath that the people of Siena rose up against the *Nove*.[60] Charles IV kept out of the fighting at first, yet city gates

[53] Cf. Widder, *Itinerar*, 208 n.432 on possible contacts to Henry VII, rejecting this Carniani, *Salimbeni*, 119–121; further Schenk, *Einzug*, 90f., 103f. Privilege: P. Rossi, 'Carlo IV di Lussemburgo e la Repubblica di Siena (1355–1369). II. La seconda discesa di Carlo IV in Italia e la caduta del governo dei Dodici', *BSSP*, 38 (1930), Appendix I, 232–234.

[54] On the Palazzo cf. F. Salimei, *I Salimbeni di Siena* (Rome, 1986) 10, 28–36; M. Merlini, 'L'evoluzione delle strutture architettoniche', in L. Bellosi (ed.), *La sede storica della Banca Monte dei Paschi di Siena. L'architettura e la collezione delle opere d'arte* (Siena, 2002), 12. Werunsky, *Erste Römerzug*, 150 n.2, 154 n.1 wrongly assumes Charles IV was accommodated in the Palazzo del Comune; a correct account is given by Rossi, *Prima discesa*, 15–17, Fig. 8.

[55] Cf. Ranieri Sardo, *Cronica*, 116; on the usual catering cf. Schenk, *Einzug*, 45–47.

[56] Cf. Ranieri Sardo, *Cronica*, 116; Schenk, *Einzug*, 39–42, 47f.

[57] Cf. Ranieri Sardo, *Cronica*, 116; Cronaca senese anonima, 149. On their route, see Nevola, '*Per Ornato*', 29 Fig. 3, and F.J.D. Nevola, *Urbanism in Siena (c. 1450–1512). Policy and Patrons: Interactions Between Public and Private* (Ph.D. thesis, Courtauld Institute of Art, University of London, 1998), 520 map 38: Standard ceremonial entry route; Balestracci and Piccinni, *Siena*, carta N.4.

[58] Archivio di Stato di Siena (hereafter ASS), *Consiglio generale* 472, fol. 41r–48r: undated 'offerta di carcerati'. Cf. Lisini, *Costituto*, I, 335f., distinzione prima no. DXXXIX and II, 360f., distinzione quinta n. CCCIV; on the argumentation cf. Schenk, *Einzug*, 48f., 106–110; in general Schenk, *Zeremoniell*, 356–359.

[59] Cf. Ranieri Sardo, *Cronica*, 116. On the square and its design with strong references to the city patron St Mary cf. R. Parenti, 'Una parte per il tutto. Le vicende costruttive della facciata dello Spedale e della piazza antistante' in E. Boldrini and R. Parenti (eds.), *Santa Maria della Scala. Archeologia e edilizia sulla piazza dello Spedale* (Florence, 1991), 20–94; M. Pierini, *Simone Martini. Con uno scritto di Alberto Olivetti. Appendice documentaria a cura di Paolo Brogini* (Milan, 2000), 190; Nevola '*Per Ornato*', 40 Fig. 17.

[60] Cf. on the course of the revolution Werunsky, *Erste Römerzug*, 151–165; Luchaire, *Documenti*, XXIX–XXXVIII; Rossi, *Prima discesa*, 17f.; Rutenberg, *Vie*, 101–103; Widder, *Itinerar*, 208–210. Reconstruction in the following according to Schenk, *Einzug*, 97–99, 110f.

and houses were burned down during the night; the *Nove* barricaded themselves in the Palazzo Pubblico and finally sent the king a kind of petition asking for help. In response, Charles IV appeared on the Piazza del Campo on 25 March, only to be urged to depose the regime, and rescinding his obligations towards them, he took swift possession of the Palazzo Pubblico and laid claim to the staff of office, the 'bachetta', the symbol of government.[61] There followed a day of plundering, excesses and killings; the archives were burned and the *Nove* fled. Charles IV imposed a ceasefire (26 March), made the citizens swear another oath and set up a provisional government of twelve magnates and eighteen *Popolari*, who came to be known as *Riformatori*. In support of the new regime, on setting out for Rome on 2 March, he appointed the Archbishop of Prague, Ernst of Pardubitz, as his deputy, leaving him behind in Siena well protected with troops.[62]

The return trip was much less spectacular. On 19 April, Charles IV entered Siena as the crowned emperor 'with great honour', according to Donato di Neri, probably through the grand Porta Romana, with its image of the town's patron, the Virgin Mary.[63] It appears that, during his entry, he hastily knighted an unusually high number of Sienese notables, before proceeding to his quarters, again the *castellare Salimbeni*.[64] His stay saw the establishment of a new government of *Dodici*, who took charge of civic affairs under the emperor's half-brother Nicolaus, Patriarch of Aquileia, who was the 'true Signore' and imperial vicar of Siena.[65] When Charles IV left the city on 5 May 1355, many citizens must have breathed a sigh of relief – but the real crisis was to come during the second visit of the emperor.

When Charles IV started his second procession to Rome in 1368, the political situation in and around Siena had changed considerably.[66] Hardly

---

[61] Donato, *Cronaca*, 577.

[62] Oath: Moggi, *Storia*, 194f. n.4. Cf. further Donato, *Cronaca*, 578f.; Cronaca senese anonima, 150; Luchaire, *Documenti*, 1 n.1; Matteo Villani, *Croniche*, book IV ch.89, ed. Racheli, II, 157; Malavolti, *Historia*, part II book 6, fol. 112r; F. Zimmermann (ed.), *Acta Karoli IV. Imperatoris inedita. Ein Beitrag zu den Urkunden Kaiser Karls IV.* (Innsbruck, 1891), 186 No.92: 'Arnestus . . . vicarius generalis et locumtenens in tota Tuscia et . . . regis procurator'; Widder, *Itinerar*, 209f.; Heckmann, *Stellvertreter*, II, 663.

[63] Donato, *Cronaca*, 579: 'Entrò in Siena con grande onore . . .'. Porta Romana: erected in 1327–50, probably provided before mid-century with a sinopia of the coronation of the virgin by Simone Martini, cf. Israëls, *New documents*, 437; Pierini, *Simone Martini*, 191.

[64] Cf. Donato, *Cronaca*, 579; Cronaca senese anonima, 150; Matteo Villani, *Croniche*, book V ch.14f., ed. Racheli, II, 163f. Cf. Widder, *Itinerar*, 231f.; L. Böninger, *Die Ritterwürde in Mittelitalien zwischen Mittelalter und Früher Neuzeit. Mit einem Quellenanhang: Päpstliche Ritterernennungen 1417–1464* (Berlin, 1995), 102 n.207; Pauler, *Auseinandersetzungen*, 120; on the group of knights Schenk, *Einzug*, 111–113.

[65] Cf. ASS, *Consiglio generale* 155, fol. 15v (appointment of the Dodici on 25 April 1355); Widder, *Itinerar*, 233f.

[66] For discussion 1355–1368 see Pirchan, *Italien*, I, 262–280; Rossi, *Seconda discesa*; D. Marrara, 'I Magnati e il governo del Comune di Siena dallo Statuto del 1274 alla fine del XIV secolo', in *Studi per Enrico Fiumi* (Pisa, 1979), 261–269; S. Moscadelli, 'Apparato burocratico e finanze del Comune di Siena sotto i Dodici (1355–1368)', *BSSP*, 89 (1982), 29–118; V. Wainwright, 'Conflict and popular government in fourteenth century Siena, il Monte dei Dodici, 1355–1368', in *I ceti dirigenti nella Toscana tardo comunale. Comitato di studi sulla storia dei ceti dirigenti in Toscana. Atti del III Convegno: Firenze, 5–7 dicembre 1980* (Firenze, 1983), 57–80; V. Wainwright, 'The Testing of a Popular Sienese Regime. The "Riformatori" and the Insurrections of 1371', *I Tatti Studies. Essays in the Renaissance*, 2 (1987), 118–120; Widder, *Itinerar*, 315–317; Carniani, *Salimbeni*, 218–229; Schenk, *Einzug*, 115–119.

six weeks before the entry of Charles IV into the city, the unstable regime of the *Dodici* was brought down by an uprising of a number of magnates allied with the Tolomei and members of the Salimbeni family. They set up a government consisting of noble *consoli* and asked the emperor to legitimize their rule.[67] Yet both the deposed *Dodici* and some members of the Salimbeni family asked the emperor for assistance.[68] Once again Charles IV was able to tip the balance by throwing his political weight behind one party.

The ceremony of his entry was therefore almost completely marked by political circumstances.[69] The emperor's not peaceful-looking 'vanguard,' this time consisted of 800 knights, led by the *condottiere* Malatesta Ungaro from Rimini.[70] The regime of the noble *consoli* obviously did not know how to react to this threat but finally decided not to open the gates to a vanguard of this sort. Soon after 11 September, the troops of Malatesta Ungaro occupied a position to the north of the closed Porta Camollia. On 23 September, an uprising broke out in the city against the *consoli*.[71] The gates were opened to Malatesta Ungaro, the combat against the *consoli* was fierce but soon victorious. The Condottiere, now imperial governor, occupied the Palazzo Pubblico: a new city government made up of *Popolari*, *Dodici* and *Nove* was set up, called the *Riformatori*, who were particularly supported by members of the Salimbeni family.[72] They hastily began the preparations for the imperial visit.

A committee was entrusted with the preparations for a 'fortunate entry' without 'tumult and unrest'.[73] The citizens were told to make a vow of allegiance to the emperor, the people, the constitution and the Salimbeni dynasty, while some *Riformatori* were supposed to prepare the request to the emperor for recognition of their new regime. Malatesta Ungaro moved into the Castellare of the magnate Malavolti, and the guest quarters in the city were prepared.[74] The community sent a splendid delegation to meet and

---

[67] Cf. Donato, *Cronaca*, 619; ambassadors according to ASS, *Concistoro 2403*, fol. 112r: 'Misser Vanni Malavolti, Francescho di Misser Petro Forteghuerra, Mino Dagnolo Talomei . . . Symone di Fecino andaro ambasciadori alomperadore ad XI d' settembre . . .'.

[68] Cf. Donato, *Cronaca*, 619: 'E' Salimbeni subito per denaro trattaro con certi de' Dodici e . . . segretamente mandaro a lo'mperadore . . .'; Rossi, *Seconda discesa*, 208; Carniani, *Salimbeni*, 239f.

[69] Cf. on the reconstruction of the events in the following Pirchan, *Italien*, I, 280–289; Widder, *Itinerar*, 317–321; Schenk, *Einzug*, 119–132.

[70] Malatesta Ungaro was loyal to the Pope; on the papal intervention for Siena and on the pro-papal policy of Charles IV cf. Widder, *Itinerar*, 318; Pauler, *Auseinandersetzungen*, 203f.; Schenk, *Einzug*, 116f.

[71] Cf. Donato, *Cronaca*, 619.

[72] Cf. Luchaire, *Documenti*, LXVI–LXXIV, nos.51–60; Pirchan, *Italien*, II, 151* f. No.102; Brizio, *L'elezione*, 37–49; Carniani, *Salimbeni*, 240f.

[73] Cf. Pirchan, *Italien*, I, 287; Luchaire, *Documenti*, 158–161 No. 61f.: 'Item quod capitula sint ista que habeant dicere . . . domino Imperatori . . . : . . . vj° quod sint ipsi previdentes . . . coram prefato domino Imperatore et verbis et opere defendant status presentem contra omnem personam . . . quod nullus sit tumultus et rumor in eius introitu felici prefato.' Details: Schenk, *Einzug*, 121–123.

[74] Katharina, the emperor's daughter, lodged in the Albergo del Gallo, cf. Donato, *Cronaca*, 620, that was partly in owned by the Salimbeni, cf. M. Tuliani, *Osti, Avventori e Malandrini. Alberghi, locande e taverne a Siena e nel suo contado tra Trecento e Quattrocento* (Siena, 1994), 84f., 210f.

escort the emperor back, while a reception committee was sent to the *contado* border, to Massa Marittima. Perhaps it was only then that the emperor decided to make his surprisingly short visit to Siena at the request of the Sienese reception committee; it was not included in his original itinerary to Rome via Grosseto, Magliano and Viterbo.[75]

On 12 October, Charles IV and Anna approached the city from the southwest, in order to be received by the Sienese outside the Porta ai Tufi.[76] Everyone appeared for the *Ingressus* with 'garlands on their heads, olive branches in their hands and in a happy mood', although again the city clergy were absent.[77] The *Dodici* came on foot, while the Salimbeni were on horseback, surrounded by many *Popolari*. The new city council solemnly wanted to present the emperor with the keys of the city and the 'segni de' cassari', signs of authority over the *contado* of Siena. Yet the emperor refused to accept the symbols of domination, with the words 'Look after them well'.[78] Then, under baldachins of gold and silk brocade, they proceeded over the threshold into the city – this time apparently without the Emperor being plundered. During the cheering and festive music the imperial couple rode directly to their quarters, the well-guarded *castellare Salimbeni*. The route is not described in the sources but they were likely to have taken the grand route along the present Via Pier Andrea Mattioli, Via San Pietro, Via di Città and Banchi di Sopra (see Fig. 6).

Nearly every medieval imperial *adventus* suggests the ancient motif of Jesus' entry into Jerusalem (Ps 118: 26; Mark 11: 1–10), which was also quite apparent to the people of Siena, due to the annual re-enactment in the Palm Sunday processions.[79] The ruler entering the city turned, at least liturgically,

---

[75] Escort: ASS, *Concistoro* 2403, fol. 115v. Reception committee: ibidem; ASS, *Concistoro* 1776, No.43: Letter from 'Jachomo di Tofano . . . datum i[n] Massa di X dottobre' to Malatesta, apparently with information on the emperor's original itinerary ('. . . che misser lo nperadore per la più dritta via che potra chapitara a Grossetto, e poi ne va al santo padre dritto a Magliano o per la più presso che potra. Et per questa cagione ser Giovanni e Lando sono cavalchati a Grosseto per dare ordine . . .'); cf. A. Giorgi, 'Il Carteggio del Concistoro della repubblica di Siena (Spogli delle lettere: 1251–1374)', *BSSP*, 97 (1990), 343 No.342.43. Cf. Pirchan, *Italien*, I, 286–293 and Widder, *Itinerar*, 319–323 with map 540.

[76] Cf. Donato, *Cronaca*, 621, unlike the later chroniclers Giugurta Tommasi, *Storie di Siena. Autogr. Parte II* (Biblioteca Comunale di Siena (hereafter BCS), Ms. A.X.74), fol. 28r ('Porta a Sanmarco') and Malavolti, *Historia*, part II book 7, fol. 130v, followed by Rossi, *Seconda discesa*, 212 with n.1.

[77] Donato, *Cronaca*, 621: '. . . ciascuno con grillande in capo, con ulivi in mano e con allegreza e festa grandissima.' Cf. Schenk, *Einzug*, 124–132.

[78] Cf. Donato, *Cronaca*, 621: '. . . e lui disse: "serbatele voi", e scavalcò in casa Salimbeni.' Contrary to the views of Pirchan, *Italien*, I, 287f., this inhabitual gesture must be interpreted as a vote of no confidence in the city government.

[79] Cf. on the systematic distinction between two models, that of the *Adventus* of Jesus into Jerusalem as a bringer of peace ('historical type') and the Second Coming of Christ as messianic judge ('eschatological type') first E. H. Kantorowicz, 'The "King's Advent" and the enigmatic panels in the door of Santa Sabina', *The Art Bulletin*, 26 (1944), 207–231, latterly Kipling, *King's Advent*, 6–47; criticism of this systematic distinction: Schenk, *Einzug*, 51–58. On the Palm Sunday procession in Siena cf. M. Marchetti (ed.), *Ordo offitiorum ecclesiae senensis. Oderigo e la liturgia della Cattedrale di Siena (Inizi secolo XIII). Edizione del testo del codice G.V.9 della Biblioteca Comunale di Siena* (Siena, 1998), 138 ch.LXXXVIII: 'De ordine processionis in Die Ramis Palmarum.' A further model could be civic traditions like Corpus Christi processions, cf. in general Schenk, *Zeremoniell*, 461–468, in Italy P. Helas, *Lebende Bilder in der italienischen Festkultur des 15. Jahrhunderts* (Berlin, 1999), 38–45, on the traditional Corpus Christi processions in Siena cf. note xxxiv.

into a kind of imitation of Christ, a welcome to Christ the King, the long-awaited *rex pacificus*. Precisely in comparison with Charles IV's entry in 1355 it is striking that the *Riformatori* in 1368 resorted to this traditional pattern of the entry into Jerusalem with their use of olive branches as props for the *Ingressus*. The symbolic message perhaps even contained a specific Sienese allusion: the need for peace was, of course, not just an urgent problem of the city. Social peace, security and harmony were felt to be the responsibility of a good government even under the *Nove*; indeed they were found to be so central that Ambrogio Lorenzetti decorated the walls of the official hall of the *Nove* in the Palazzo Pubblico in 1338/39 with a complex allegory of the 'good' and the 'bad' government. A central figure of the fresco called by contemporaries *la Pace e la Ghuerra* was the white-clad personification of *Pax*, wearing a laurel-wreath and bearing an olive branch.[80]

The educated ruler certainly knew Lorenzetti's fresco from his stay in 1355. It may be assumed with good reason that in 1368 the emperor knew exactly what the city wanted to tell him in symbolic form; the need for visible legitimation of the new government and his help in the reconciliation with the escaped magnates.

As in 1355, the emperor went to the cathedral the next day, attended Holy Mass, and in a political gesture, made three Sienese knights, and pardoned prisoners.[81] On his return from the cathedral the *Riformatori* paid a visit to the emperor, presenting him with comparatively generous gifts and offering him again the symbols of lordship over the city and *contado*. This time the emperor accepted the symbols of power but, to the disappointment of the *Riformatori*, did not give them back. Instead, he handed them over to Malatesta Ungaro of Rimini, who was supposed to stay in Siena as his governor (*referendarius et locum tenens*).[82] His cool disregard for the visible desire of the city that he bring them peace and harmony as the highest earthly judge was therefore deliberate politics.

On the next day (14 October) the emperor took the road to Rome without having settled the internal rivalries and fundamental political problems of the city.[83] The disregard of the communal needs for peace and political stability was, however, to explode during his stay in Siena after his return from Rome, and led to his eviction and ultimately to the failure of his political line towards Siena.[84]

[80] Quote: Cronaca senese anonima, 78; on the fresco cf. J. M. Greenstein, 'The Vision of Peace: Meaning and Representation in Ambrogio Lorenzetti's Sala della Pace Cityscapes', *Art History*, 11 (1988), 492–510; R. Starn, *Ambrogio Lorenzetti. The Palazzo Pubblico, Siena* (New York, 1994), 60f.

[81] Cf. Donato, *Cronaca*, 621: Three knights (Reame de' Salimbeni, Bartali de' Salimbeni, Niccolò de' Salimbeni) contrary to the position of Pirchan, *Italien*, I, 288 (two knights); cf. regarding Salimbeni, *Salimbeni*, 132, albero IV and index; Carniani, *Salimbeni*, 285.

[82] Cf. Donato, *Cronaca*, 621; Tommasi, *Storie Autogr.*, fol. 28r (delegation of Riformatori) and Widder, *Itinerar*, 320f. Quote: Luchaire, *Documenti*, 173–175 No. 69; overlooked by Heckmann, *Stellvertreter* (see index).

[83] Tommasi, *Storie Autogr.*, fol. 28v: 'Dopo la partenza dell'Imperatore molte cose in un tempo premevano la città.' Cf. Widder, *Itinerar*, 320f., 330–332; Carniani, *Salimbeni*, 245f.

[84] Cf. Pirchan, 339–362; Rossi, *Seconda discesa*, 213–232; Widder, *Itinerar*, 331–336; Carniani, *Salimbeni*, 246f.; Schenk, *Einzug*, 133–137; Pauler, *Auseinandersetzungen*, 202–207.

The entries of Charles IV in Siena in 1355 and 1368 prove to be both typical and exceptional. The city and the monarch resorted to the local usage of traditional entry ceremonies, while adapting them to the particular circumstances. Three factors deserve special attention: First, the performative dynamic of the respective ceremonies is noteworthy. Each time the ceremony reflects not just the social situation of the parties involved, but set in motion a series of events that go beyond the intentions of those concerned. In 1355 the *Nove* ultimately fell due to the visible distrust of the king, while in 1368 the plans of Charles IV failed due to his disregard for the civic desire for peace and reconciliation between rivals on the internal political scene. Second, the entry of the monarch seems not just a traditional ceremony or archaic ritual, but rather a means of political communication. The emperor is no longer the politically defining factor, however, but just a catalyst. He only plays a role in the struggle for power in the city by 'tipping the balance'. Third, ceremony, ritual and politics prove to be inseparably interwoven with topography and architectural staging in a city. With the ritually devised crossing of the threshold into the cultic community of the city, the procession passes under the image of its patron saint, while the processional route shows the city from its best angle and touches on important points of its religious and political topography. Indeed a city's architecture and topography are not only the stage for politics, ceremonies and rituals but they are also decisive in performing them. By the same token, this means that urban construction has to be understood as the expression in stone of the living organism of a community. However, monuments will remain mute if there is no reconstruction of the human activities pertaining to them.

University of Stuttgart

4

Altars on the street: the wool guild, the Carmelites and the feast of Corpus Domini in Siena (1356–1456)*

MACHTELT ISRAËLS

The book cover of Siena's financial *Biccherna* office for the second semester of 1367 shows an unusual image: the Trinity seated above an altar (Fig. 1).[1] This eucharistic image reflects a recent event in Sienese public life,[2] for that very year, the powerful Sienese guild of woolworkers, the *Arte della Lana*, had instituted its patronage over the feast of Corpus Domini.[3] The treasurer of the *Biccherna* magistrates that commissioned the panel, Bartoloccio Dini, is presented as a woolworker. Saint Nicholas, one of the saints flanking the Trinity, refers to the church of San Niccolò al Carmine, the centre for the feast of Corpus Domini in Siena at this time.[4] A third party is the city of Siena whose involvement in the observance of the cult manifests itself through its civic colours of black, white and red which line the altarcloth.[5]

The iconographical significance of the *Biccherna* panel can be gleaned through Carmelite arguments of only three years earlier.[6] In 1364, the friars petitioned the city government to help finance the commissioning of a monstrance, by stressing the redemptive powers of the Eucharist, as being identical to 'the body of Christ that had been crucified and saved mankind from hell'.[7] On the *Biccherna* panel, the redemptive notion is made even

* I would like to express my gratitude to Julian Gardner, Christa Gardner von Teuffel, Henk van Os, Frances Andrews, Victor Schmidt, Ludwin Paardekooper, Philippa Jackson and Fabrizio Nevola, for their comments and suggestions. This paper is the historical continuation of my article 'Sassetta's Arte della Lana Altar-piece and the Cult of Corpus Domini in Siena', *The Burlington Magazine*, CXLIII (2001), 532–43.

[1] L. Borgia, E. Carli, M. A. Ceppari et al. (eds.), *Le Biccherne. Tavole dipinte delle magistrature senesi (Secoli XIII–XVIII)* (Rome, 1984), 114; M. Boskovits, *Frühe Italienische Malerei* (Berlin, 1987) (mus. cat. Berlin, Gemäldegalerie), 182–3. The relative register has not been preserved.

[2] As was common for these bookcovers, see A. Tomei (ed.), *Le Biccherne di Siena. Arte e finanza all'alba dell'economia moderna* (Azzano San Paolo (Bergamo)/Roma, 2002).

[3] Israëls, 'Lana', 535, 542 doc. I; and see note 8.

[4] The other saints have not been identified with certainty; see note 1.

[5] The Commune had donated candles to be carried in the Corpus Domini procession, paid for by the *Biccherna* from 1356; Archivio di Stato di Siena (hereafter 'ASS'), Consiglio Generale, 157, fol. 7v; Israëls, 'Lana', 534.

[6] S. Borghesi and L. Banchi, *Nuovi documenti per la storia dell'arte senese* (Siena, 1898), 29; Israëls, 'Lana', 534.

[7] ''l corpo di Yhesu Cristo, el quale fu passionato nel legno della croce, ricuperò l'umana generazione dall'onferno.'; ibidem.

Fig. 1   Niccolò di Buonaccorso (?), Biccherna bookcover: *The Trinity between Saints*, 1367, tempera and gold on panel, 42,3 × 30,6 cm Berlin, Staatliche Museen zu Berlin – Preußischer Kulturbesitz, Kunstgewerbemuseum, inv. nr. K 9223

more explicit through the sacrificial Lamb at the feet of the Crucified Christ. In their subsidy request for the monstrance, the Carmelites went on to state that, through the Holy Sacrament, Christ makes himself palpably visible to mankind in his trinitarian glory: 'tutto vivo et vero alli occhi delli umani'.[8]

[8]   In the Eucharist 'el celestiale filliuolo del Padre Eterno si dà, e si mostra a noi colla Trinità'. On St Catherine of Siena's Trinitarian conception of the Eucharist: B. Rossi, 'L'Eucaristia nella spiritualità di Santa Caterina da Siena', in: C. Alessi and L. Martini (eds.), *Panis Vivus. Arredi e testimonianze figurative del culto eucaristico dal VI al XIX secolo* (Siena, 1994) (exh. cat. Siena, Palazzo Pubblico, 1994), 251–2; and see J. Oliver, 'Image et dévotion: le rôle de l'art dans l'institution de la Fête-Dieu', in A. Haquin (ed.), *Fête-Dieu (1246–1996). Actes du Colloque de Liège, 12–14 septembre 1996* (Louvain-la-Neuve, 1999), I, esp. 153–5, 163–4. Compare the suggestion that Masaccio's *Trinity* extolled Corpus Domini; E. Borsook, 'Cults and Imagery at Sant'Ambrogio in Florence', *Mitteilungen des kunsthistorischen Instituts in Florenz*, 25 (1981), 158.

Set in these terms, the *Biccherna* image evokes the vision of the devotee contemplating the Holy Sacrament on an altar and shows how powerfully it fulfilled a deep desire to physically behold the Divine.

The mendicant, guild and civic significance of the Corpus Domini ritual celebrations from 1356 (when they make their first documented appearance) until 1456 (when the feast was formally appropriated by the Commune in Siena) are examined in this paper. What objectives did the Carmelites, the guild and the city government pursue by participating in this ritual? What message did they convey through ceremonial practice and visual form? In particular, special attention will be given to the procession and the erection of outdoor altars and comparison with other centres will show what is peculiar to the ritual significance and impact of the Sienese Corpus Domini celebrations.[9]

This feast is celebrated on the Thursday following the octave of Pentecost. It was first celebrated in Liège in 1246 and the cult, albeit instituted by Pope Urban IV and provided with its own liturgy by Thomas Aquinas in 1264,[10] only really spread throughout Europe after its confirmation by Pope Clement V in 1314.[11] On average, people took communion only once a year, at Easter, as it demanded serious spiritual and corporal preparation. The veneration of the Eucharist was therefore, above all, a visual affair, the ardently desired contemplation of the Real Presence of Christ in the transubstantiated host.[12]

The feast initially spread slowly, gaining impetus only with Pope John XXII's renewed efforts to promote its observance in 1317, when the first public processions can also be consistently documented in Europe.[13] On the Italian peninsula, Venice moved exceptionally quickly and by 1258 had already incorporated the new feast in its statutes, while the first public procession seems to have taken place in Vicenza (1311), followed by other centres,

[9] On the lack of a general rite for the procession; P. Browe, *Die Verehrung der Eucharistie im Mittelalter* (Rome, 1967), 108.

[10] R. Busa (ed.), *S. Thomae Aquinatis Opera Omnia* (Stuttgart, 1980), VI, 580–1; P.-M. Gy, 'L'office du Corpus Christi et la théologie des accidents eucharistiques', *Revue des Sciences Philosophiques et Théologiques*, 66 (1982), 81–6; Idem, 'Office liégois et office romain de la Fête-Dieu', in Haquin, *Fête-Dieu*, I, 117–26.

[11] M. Rubin, *Corpus Christi. The Eucharist in Late Medieval Culture* (Cambridge/New York etc., 1991) (its restriction to England criticized by N. Orme, in *English Historical Review*, 107 (1992), 386–8); Browe, *Die Verehrung*; C. Caspers and M. Schneiders, 'Bibliographie de la Fête-Dieu 1946–1997', in: Haquin, *Fête-Dieu*, I, 193–225.

[12] P. Browe, *Die häufige Kommunion im Mittelalter* (Münster, 1938), esp. 133–63; A. Eijenholm Nichols, 'The Bread of Heaven: Foretaste or Foresight?', in: C. Davidson (ed.), *The Iconography of Heaven* (Kalamazoo, Michigan, 1994), 40–68; C. M. A. Caspers, '*Meum summum desiderium est te habere*: l'eucharistie comme sacrement de la rencontre avec Dieu pour tous les croyants (ca.1200–ca.1500)', in Haquin, *Fête-Dieu*, I, 127–51. Bernardino preached on the subject in his 1425 Sienese sermons: C. Cannarozzi (ed.), *San Bernardino da Siena. Le prediche volgari* (Florence, 1934), II, 248–66, 312–26, III, 324–44, 385–99.

[13] Early Northern European processions did not yet pass through the city's streets but were restricted to the domains of single churches: A. Löther, *Prozessionen in spätmittelalterlichen Städten. Politische Partizipation, obrigkeitliche Inszenierung, städtische Einheit* (Cologne, Weimar, Vienna, 1999), esp. 50–99; O. Nußbaum, *Die Aufbewahrung der Eucharistie* (Bonn, 1979), 150–9; Browe, *Die Verehrung*, 91–8; Rubin, *Corpus Christi* 176–85. Good insight into the factors that slowed down the dissemination of new feasts is provided by R. W. Pfaff, *New Liturgical Feasts in Later Medieval England* (Oxford, 1970), esp. 4–5.

such as Milan (1335) and Orvieto (1337).[14] In Siena, observance of the feast may have been encouraged by the Dominican Bishop Ruggero da Casole (1307–17), who probably nurtured his Order's fervour for the solemnity. He had Duccio's *Maestà* installed on the eve of Corpus Domini with a famous procession, albeit not yet a theophoric one.[15]

However, a public celebration of Corpus Domini in Siena is first mentioned in the year 1356, when the city government decided to offer candles that were to be carried in the procession by the Carmelites. The Commune intended to incite feelings of solidarity in its citizens: the Holy Sacrament would 'through its charity set the minds of the Sienese aglow, kindle indivisable unity'.[16] This aim reveals a remarkable early understanding of the feast's potential by the Sienese government. At the same time, this deliberation makes the Carmelite

[14] E. Muir, *Civic Ritual in Renaissance Venice* (Princeton, 1981), 223; M. Casini, *I gesti del principe. La festa politica a Firenze e Venezia in età rinascimentale* (Venice, 1996), 158; G. Vio, 'La devozione all'Eucarestia nella Venezia dei dogi e la processione del "Corpus Domini" monopolio del governo della Repubblica', in: A. Niero (ed.), *San Marco: aspetti storici e agiografici* (Venice, 1996), 170; H. Niedermeier, 'Über die Sakramentsprozessionen im Mittelalter. Ein Beitrag zur Geschichte der kirchlichen Umgänge', *Sacris Erudiri*, XXII (1974–75), 422–8, 432–4, 426 for Vicenza, with a reference to S. Rumohr, *Riccordi Eucaristici a Vicenza* (1924); Nußbaum, *Die Aufbewahrung*, 157 note 436; A. Tamborini, *Il Corpus Domini a Milano* (Rome, 1935), 54–5; G. Freni, 'The Reliquary of the Holy Corporal in the Cathedral of Orvieto: Patronage and Politics', in: J. Cannon and B. Williamson (eds.), *Art, Politics, and Civic Religion in Central Italy. 1261–1352. Essays by Postgraduate Students at the Courtauld Institute of Art* (Aldershot and Brookfield, 2000), 123–4, 152–3 doc. III.

[15] As erroneously postulated by P. Seiler, 'Duccio's *Maestà*: The Function of the Scenes from the Life of Christ on the Reverse of the Altarpiece: A New Hypothesis', in: V. M. Schmidt (ed.), *Italian Panel Painting of the Duecento and Trecento* (Washington, 2002), 251–77 and A. B. Rave, *Fronleichnam in Siena. Die Maestà von Simone Martini in der Sala del Mappamondo* (Worms, 1986), 26–7. Though the choice of date might be significant, this was an incidental procession with the altarpiece as its fulcrum. Evidence for associating the back of the *Maestà* with the preservation of the host remains conjectural, especially since Seiler misinterprets the 1435 inventory, which describes a curtain with the painted representation of a tabernacle before the high altarpiece, not a curtain *and* a physical tabernacle ('una tenda vermoglia per coprire la tavola del detto altare con grangio di seta dipinta nel mezzo due angioli che tengono uno tabernacolo dipento el corpo di Cristo'); ASS, Opera Metropolitana, 30, fol. 17r). See also J. Tripps, *Das handelnde Bildwerk in der Gotik* (Berlin, 2000), 219–20. For the procession see e.g. J. I. Satkowski, *Duccio di Buoninsegna. The Documents and Early Sources* (University of Georgia, 2000), 97–108, 112–4.

[16] Four *doppieri* of six *libbra* each were accorded 'Ut in devotissima processione dicta die fienda per dictos fratres per civitatem Senensis, dicti doppieri portentur accensi ad reverentiam sanctissimi et sacratissimi Corporis Domini, ut dignetur sue caritatis ardere mentes Senensium, accendere ad individuam unitatem.' See note 5. The phrase calls to mind Ambrogio Lorenzetti's vivid representation of *Concordia* in the *Good Government*. On the cult of the Eucharist as expressing unity, but also differentiation and tensions in society and politics: E. Muir, *Ritual in Early Modern Europe* (Cambridge, 1997), 158–65; Rubin, *Corpus Christi*, 243–71, criticizing the alleged social connotations of the Host as body put forward by M. James, 'Ritual, Drama and Social Body in the Late Medieval English Town', *Past and Present*, 98 (1983), 3–29, as does C. Zika, 'Hosts, Processions and Pilgrimages: Controlling the Sacred in Fifteenth-Century Germany', *Past and Present*, 118 (1988), 43–4. Ritual language is credited with the power to forge the political reality of a city by R. C. Trexler, *Public Life in Renaissance Florence* (New York, London etc., 1980) and S.R.F. Price, *Rituals and Power. The Roman imperial cult in Asia Minor* (Cambridge, London etc., 1984). On political manipulation of Corpus Domini e.g. C. Bernardi, 'Il teatro politico del Corpus Domini (1300–1500)', in: F. Paino (ed.), *Dramma Medioevale Europeo, 1996. Atti della I Conferenza Internazionale su 'Aspetti del Dramma Medioevale Europeo, Camerino, 28–30 giugno 1996* (Camerino, 1996), II, 83–108. A more pragmatic, case-specific approach in: Löther, *Prozessionen*; idem, 'Rituale im Bild. Prozessionsdarstellungen bei Albrecht Dürer, Gentile Bellini und in der Konzilschronik Ulrich Richentals', in: A. Löther, U. Meier et al. (eds.), *Mundus in imagine. Bildersprache und Lebenswelten im Mittelalter. Festgabe für Klaus Schreiner* (Munich, 1996), 99–123; A. J. Fletcher, 'Playing and Staying Together: Projecting the Corporate Image in Sixteenth-Century Dublin', in: A. F. Johnston and W. Hüsken (eds.), *Civic Ritual and Drama* (Amsterdam/Atlanta, 1997), 15–37.

predominance over the feast unambiguously clear. The precise date upon which the Sienese Carmelites first celebrated Corpus Domini with special pomp is not known, although a confraternity dedicated to the cult had found shelter underneath the Sienese church of San Niccolò al Carmine by 1325.[17] Around a decade later, the office of Corpus Domini appeared in their graduals, with a miniature of the *Communion of the Apostles*.[18]

In order to explore the Carmelite incentive for embracing this feast, it is necessary to consider the circumstances of their arrival in Siena. The Carmelites settled in the city around 1256, adapting for their own use the church of San Niccolò.[19] Only after the 1247 mitigation of their rule, necessitated by their migration from eremitical life in the Holy Land, had Carmelites started to settle in cities of the West.[20] The Carmelites had to make up for both the absence of a charismatic founder and for their late arrival in cities compared to their rivals, the Dominicans and the Franciscans, whose settlements in Siena dated to 1221 and *circa* 1231 respectively, and who shortly after the turn of the century far outnumbered them.[21] During the early Trecento, the Carmelite choice of the Virgin Mary came under fierce attack from the Dominicans, who had long regarded her as their exclusive patron.[22] This may have stimulated the Sienese Carmelites to seek another focus for their devotion, as the Order's traditional dedication to the Virgin Mary was hardly a distinguishing feature in the *Civitas Virginis*. In order to enhance their profile and prestige in the city, the Carmelites grasped the possibilities offered by the novel feast of Corpus Domini, a move not apparently typical of other settlements of the Order.[23] By this adoption, they linked themselves to a cult that was gaining tremendous popularity, judging, for example, by the feverish devotion to the Eucharist fostered by St Catherine of Siena (1347–1380).[24]

[17] M. Butzek and H. Teubner, in: P. A. Riedl and M. Seidel (eds.), *Die Kirchen von Siena* (Munich, 1985–), I.1, 16, 52, 505, doc. 68.

[18] C. De Benedictis, G. Freuler and A. Labriola, *La miniatura senese. 1270–1420* (Milan, 2002), 120, 315–6, Fig. 258.

[19] V. Lusini, *La chiesa di S. Niccolò del Carmine in Siena* (Siena, 1907), 6–7; R. Francovich and M. Valenti, *C'era una volta. La ceramica medievale nel convento del Carmine* (Florence, 2002) (exh. cat. Siena, Santa Maria della Scala, 2002), 14–22.

[20] A. Jotischky, *The Carmelites and Antiquity. Mendicants and their Pasts in the Middle Ages* (Oxford, 2002), 13–25. J. Smet, *I Carmelitani. Storia dell'Ordine del Carmelo* (Rome, 1989), I, 146–9.

[21] Riedl and Seidel, *Kirchen*, II.1.2, 452, 491, 890 doc. 99; A. Liberati, 'Chiese, monastery, oratori e spedali senesi. Chiesa e convento di San Francesco', *Bulletino Senese di Storia Patria* (hereafter *BSSP*), LXV (1958), 142. The Franciscan and Dominican houses were three times as populated as the Carmelite one in 1307; D. Waley, *Siena and the Sienese in the Thirteenth Century* (Cambridge, 1991), 135–6.

[22] As Julian Gardner suggested to me. See Jotischky, *Carmelites*, 109–10, 181–2.

[23] The Carmelite Order observed the feast from 1306; Browe, *Die Verehrung*, 79. The Dominicans took the lead in the Florentine Corpus Domini; Borsook, 'Cults', 150. A further justification could have been found in the figure of their mythical founder Elijah, whose miraculous feeding (I Kings: 6–8) served as a prefiguration to the Eucharist in the Corpus Domini office; Busa, *S. Thomae*, 580.

[24] Rossi, 'L'Eucaristia', 251–7; A. Vauchez, 'Dévotion eucharistique et union mystique chez les saintes de la fin du Moyen Age', in: D. Maffei and P. Nardi (eds.), *Atti del Simposio Internazionale Cateriniano-Bernardiniano (Siena, 17–20 aprile 1980)* (Siena, 1982), 298–300.

In turn, the Carmelites attracted the special attention of the second party involved in Corpus Domini, the *Arte della Lana*. Another masterstroke in the Carmelite battle for authenticity and antiquity was their claim that they descended from Elijah.[25] In an analogy to the prophet and his fountain in the desert at Mount Carmel, the Carmelites claimed to possess a divine ability to govern water supplies. This found contemporary visual expression in the high altarpiece of the Sienese Carmelite church, painted by Pietro Lorenzetti in 1329, with *Hermits at the Fountain of Elijah* as one of its predella panels.[26] As if to corroborate this, the friars dug a well in their orchard in the early Trecento and claimed to have found the mythical river of the Diana.[27] In 1367, when the *Arte della Lana* decided to adopt the Carmelite feast of Corpus Domini, this association with water must have been a strong attraction for the guild, ever dependent on plentiful supplies. The Carmelites therefore seem to have served the *Arte della Lana* as spiritual intercessors for a continuous provision of water. Such was the guild's involvement with the Carmelites that in 1431 they acquired patronage rights over the main chapel of the Carmine.[28]

In Siena the powerful *Mercanzia* exerted control over all guilds, an exception being made for the *Arte della Lana*, due to civic interests in the wool-trade. During the government of the *Dodici* (1355–1368) the guild-system was restructured, establishing electoral power for the guilds and resulting for the *Arte della Lana* in a high number of dependent crafts.[29] This consolidation of its importance may have triggered the guild to espouse the conspicuous religious festivity of Corpus Domini in 1367, which could ritually evince their newly bolstered standing in the city.

The feast of Corpus Domini also appealed to the wool guild, because it could be turned into a showcase for their craft. From its inception, the

---

[25] This historical claim is the subject of Jotischky, *Carmelites*.

[26] Jotischky, *Carmelites*, 56–7, 132; J. Cannon, 'Pietro Lorenzetti and the History of the Carmelite Order', *Journal of the Warburg and Courtauld Institutes*, 50 (1987), 18–28; H. van Os, *Sienese Altarpieces. 1215–1460. Form, Content, Function* (Groningen, 1988 and 1990), I, 91–9.

[27] A Sienese obsession ridiculed by Dante; *Purgatorio* XIII, 152–4. The myth was probably a graceful later invention antedating the episode to the twelfth century, in the Carmelites' never-ceasing desire for venerable antiquity; G. Gigli, *Diario Senese* (Siena, 1723) (2nd edition Siena, 1854), II, 28 and G. Faluschi, *Chiese Senesi, circa* 1821, Biblioteca Comunale di Siena (hereafter BCS), E.V.17, quire 61, fols. 4ʳ–5ʳ, give the date as 1157, referring to the *Cronaca* of Agnolo di Tura, where, however, the story cannot be found. F. Bargagli Petrucci, *Le fonti di Siena e i loro acquedotti* (Siena/ Florence/Rome, 1903), I, 9–10 note 2, refers to *Croniche di Giovanni Bisdomini* (copied by Tommaso Mocenni in 1718), ASS, Manoscritti, D 36, 39–40 (s.a. 1176)), but earlier copies do not contain the Diana story. The earliest mention is probably S. Tizio (1458–1528), *Historiae Senenses*, I, BCS, B.III.6, 554–556 (s.a. 1177). The well had certainly been constructed by 6 August 1330 or 1335, as inscribed on a stone found inside and as suggested by the financial help towards its construction accorded by the Consiglio Generale in 1328; M. Pierini (ed.), *A ritrovar la Diana* (Siena, 2001), 113–9.

[28] Israëls, 'Lana', 534, 543 doc. VII.

[29] ASS, *Arti*, 63, fol. 35v (29 December 1355); V. Wainwright, 'Conflict and Popular Government in Fourteenth-Century Siena: il Monte dei Dodici, 1355–1368', in: *I Ceti dirigenti nella Toscana tardo comunale (Atti del III Convegno di studi sulla storia dei ceti dirigenti in Toscana, Firenze, 5–7 dicembre 1980)* (Florence, 1983), 67–9. For the situation of the Arte della Lana in Siena see M. Ascheri, *Siena nel Rinascimento. Istituzioni e sistema politico* (Siena, 1985), 109–37; idem, 'Per la storia del tessuto a Siena: qualche aspetto', in: M. Ciatti (ed.), *'Drappi, Velluti, Taffettà et altre cose'* (Siena, 1994) (exh. cat. Siena, Sant'Agostino, 1994), 239–44.

hallmark of the Corpus Domini processions, which fell in the warm season between 23rd May and 24th June, was that the woolworkers' cloth spanned the streets. The 1367 guild statutes ordained that 'la piaza di Sancto Pellegrino si cuopra di panni di lanaiuoli', so that the entire square of the *Arte della Lana* headquarters (the present-day completely remodelled Piazza dell'Indipendenza) was covered with a canopy of cloth.[30] Such a clever marketing technique similarly induced the guild of the *Pizzicaiuoli* (grocers) to adopt the feast of the Purification of the Virgin or Candlemas, traditionally characterized by the blessing of candles, goods that were sold by the *Pizzicaiuoli*.[31] Elsewhere guilds would manifest themselves during festivals by exhibiting their products, as occurred in the *mostra* preceding the feast of the Baptist in Florence, while in Dublin as early as 1498 they provided for pageants in the Corpus Domini procession, some with biblical representations that had a bearing on their craft.[32]

The city's aim for solidarity, the Carmelites' search for distinction and venerability and the guild's preoccupation with water and with the display of its wares, all contributed to the growth of the cult of Corpus Domini. According to the 1367 guild statutes, festivities started on the vigil with vespers on the square of the *Arte della Lana*. The following day, a solemn mass was held in San Niccolò al Carmine, ushering in a procession with the consecrated Host. It wound its way 'per tucta la città', no specifications as to its precise route being given. The consuls, the treasurer, the notary and thirty senior guild members carried lit two-branched candelabra in attendance of the Holy Sacrament, while three candelabra were left to adorn the Carmelite high altar.[33] Other woolworkers were invited to join the procession, provided they could afford their own candles. Musicians played trumpets, shawms and kettledrums.[34] Piazza San Pellegrino must have been a stunning setting for the culmination of the procession. The square was spanned with woollen cloths, embellished with rushes brought from the wool guild's estates in the *contado*, and an outdoor altar was erected there. The choice of this location underlined the importance and identity of the feast's patron, just as the civic significance of the Assumption was underlined by celebrating it on the Campo.[35]

---

[30] Israëls, 'Lana', 535, 542 doc. I.

[31] Muir, *Ritual*, 61–2. C. B. Strehlke, in K. Christiansen, L. B. Kanter and C. B. Strehlke, *Painting in Renaissance Siena* (New York, 1988) (exh. cat. New York, The Metropolitan Museum of Art, 1988), 218.

[32] The latter phenomenon known in England too; Fletcher, 'Playing', 22–23. For Florence e.g. P. Pastori, 'Le feste patronali fra mito delle origini, sviluppo storico e adattamenti ludico-spettacolari', in: P. Pastori (ed.), *La festa di San Giovanni nella storia di Firenze. Rito, istituzione e spettacolo* (Florence, 1997), 14, 17.

[33] If my assumption is correct that 'altare d'esso Corpo di Cristo' refers to the high altar.

[34] On the meaning of musicians in the procession: D. Altenburg, 'Die Musik in der Fronleichnamsprozession des 14. und 15. Jahrhunderts', *Musica Disciplina*, XXXVIII (1984), 21.

[35] F. Glénisson – Delannée, 'Fête et société: l'Assomption à Sienne et son évolution au cours du XVIe siècle', in: F. Decroisette and M. Plaisance (eds.), *Les fêtes urbaines en Italie à l'époque de la Renaissance. Vérone, Florence, Sienne, Naples* (Paris, 1993), 78–82; B. Treffers, 'La pala di Benvenuto di Giovanni per la festa e la tela dogmatica della Compagnia del Corpus Domini', in: B. Bonucci, *Festa e mercato nella Montalcino industriosa del Quattro-Cinquecento* (San Quirico d'Orcia, 2003), 132–3, suggests the square held civic connotations, but the *Biccherna* office had long since moved and the nearby intersection of the city's *terzi* had no ritual significance.

The wool guild repeatedly required that 'li signori de la festa', those in charge of organising the feast, should spend no more than 25 florins, suggesting the event was overly lavish.[36] Vespers at the altar in Piazza San Pellegrino completed the guild celebrations.

The procession must have wound through all three *Terzi* of the city, as appears from Tizio's record of specially ornamented areas for the festivity of 1371.[37] When this chronicle is considered with the woolworker's statute remark that they processed 'per tucta la città' and with Gigli's later account, it can be seen that the Holy Sacrament and its cortège called at the following locations and the likely route can be surmised (Fig. 2): from San Niccolò al Carmine (*1) as the starting point, via the church of San Marco and the cloth-shaded Casato to the Campo (*2), passing in front of the Palazzo Pubblico, to San Martino (*3)[38], Via del Porrione and the Vicolo dei Magalotti (the setting for torch-lit dances and meals), further to the Mercanzia, Piazza Tolomei (*4), the Dogana (*5) and then a long détour via San Vincenzo to Porta Camollia (*6). The cortège would then have turned and found its way to San Domenico (*7), from where it passed through the woolworkers' district, along the Fondaco di Sant'Antonio, to Piazza San Pellegrino (*8).[39] The way back to San Niccolò al Carmine (*1) via the Casato would again have touched at the Campo (*2), where in fact, in 1371, the stretch from Palazzo Accarigi at the Costarella dei Barbieri to the Palazzo Pubblico was ornamented. Evidence from other centres suggests that the processional route was carefully designed to unite both various districts and important churches.[40] In Siena the long *parcours* called at its three *Terzi* and encompassed locations of civic importance such as the Campo and Porta Camollia, but also those of particular interest to the Carmelites and to the *Arte della Lana*. The guild's three districts were comprehended, just as were the churches where it venerated

---

[36] In 1368 and 1423; Israëls, 'Lana', 535, 542 docs. III–V.

[37] Tizio, *Historiae*, III, BCS, B.III.8, 440–1 (s.a. 1371).

[38] A particular importance of the cult in San Martino might be attested by its inventory of 7 April 1419 mentioning '.I. tabernacolo da portare el corpo di Cristo. [. . .] .I. velo da portare el corpo di Cristo di drappo a oro.'; ASS, Notarile ante-cosimiano, 270, loose papers. The confraternity of Sant'Antonio housed beneath the church lists expenditures for Corpus Domini in 1388 for clearing the square and for adorning it with greenery, lamps and presumably an altar ('soldi uno per bulete per l'altare') while they probably exposed a figure of Saint Anthony and a crucifix ('Per achonciatura il chrocifisso e rifreschatura santo Antonio al maestro Lando dipentore a dì 24 di maggio soldi vintidue'); *Compagnia di S. Antonio Abate di Siena. Libro dell'entrata e dell'uscita. 1388–1416*, BCS, A.I.5, fols. 28'–29'.

[39] Gigli, *Diario*, I, 583. G. A. and P. Pecci (eds. E. Innocenti and G. Mazzoni), *Giornale Sanese (1715–1794)* (Monteriggioni, 2000), 11, stating in 1717 that it was a 'gita assai lunga'. Parts of the route can be identified by seventeenth-century invitations to the woolworkers to carry the poles of the baldachin for certain stretches; ASS, *Arti*, 75, II nrs. 196 (1661), 172 (*s.a.*).

[40] Zika, 'Hosts', 38–9; Freni, 'The Reliquary', esp. 124, 131, 152–3 doc. nr. III; M. Poisa, 'La processione del Corpus Domini a Brescia nei secoli XV–XVI', *Civiltà bresciana*, 8 (1999), 83–7. In Siena, the procession of St Catherine visited locations of importance to the saint's life and to the participating Dominicans, confraternities and *contrade*; V. Grassi, 'Antiche cerimonie per la festa di S. Caterina', *Studi Cateriniani*, XVII (1939), 3–5.

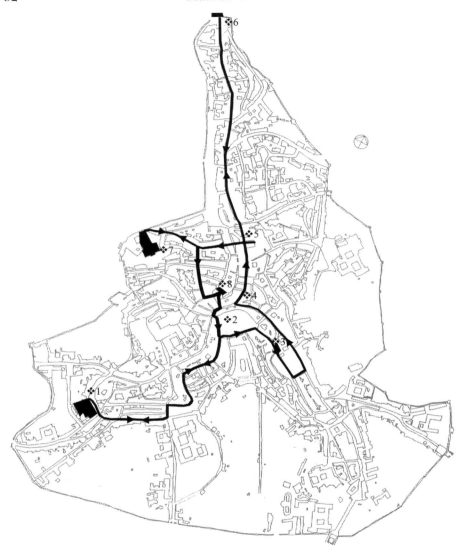

Fig. 2   Hypothetical route of the Sienese Corpus Domini procession between 1367 and 1448. The numbers mark the major sites involved in the procession: (1) San Niccolò al Carmine (2) Piazza del Campo (3) San Martino (4) Loggia del Mercanzia (5) Dogana (6) Porta Camollia (7) San Domenico (8) San Pellegrino (map: F. Nevola)

Fig. 3 Giovanni di Lorenzo (attr.), *Coat of arms of the Arte della Lana*, panel of a baldachin, 1544, gold and paint on silk, *ca.* 60 × 28 cm, San Niccolò al Carmine, Siena (Siena, Fotografia Lensini)

its older patron saints, St Anthony Abbot at the church of the same name and the blessed Ambrogio Sansedoni at San Domenico.[41]

During the procession, the Holy Sacrament itself was displayed in its monstrance and carried on a 'barella di legname',[42] under a baldachin. The *Arte della Lana* priors took turns in carrying this canopy.[43] When they assumed the patronage of the feast, they ordered the guild's coat of arms to be painted on it. A surviving baldachin of 1544, probably by Giovanni di Lorenzo, shows the guild's coats of arms, as well as an image of the Virgin Mary, of the Crucified Christ and a tabernacle with the Holy Sacrament on its silk panels (Fig. 3).[44] During

[41] The woolworkers were concentrated in three 'conventi': 'L'Arte Lunga' (San Pellegrino to the Sapienza), 'Diacceto' (San Pellegrino to the Baptistery) and 'Casato' (ASS, Arti, 64, fol. 15v; D. Balestracci and G. Piccinni, *Siena nel trecento. Assetto urbano e strutture edilizie*, (Florence, [1977]), 127. Israëls, 'Lana', 533). H. Teubner in Riedl and Seidel, *Kirchen*, II.1.2, 503–5, for the cult of 'santo Ambrogio'.

[42] F. Nevola, 'Cerimoniali per santi e feste a Siena a metà Quattrocento. Documenti dallo Statuto di Siena 39', in: M. Ascheri, *Siena e il suo territorio nel Rinascimento/Renaissance Siena and its Territory* (Siena, 2001), 179.

[43] Documented for the seventeenth century, see note 39.

[44] M. Ciatti, 'Appunti per una storia dei tessuti a Siena e il patrimonio delle contrade', in: *Paramenti e arredi sacri nelle contrade di Siena* (Florence, 1986) (exh. cat. Siena, Museo Civico, 1986), 38–9 (figs. 32–5), 43, 68; G. Palei, in: Ciatti, *Drappi*, 133–4 nr. 44. A previous baldachin had been ordered in 1425; Israëls, 'Lana', 536.

the Carmelite predominance over the feast, they continued to use the monstrance ordered by the friars in 1365[45] and *Arte della Lana* heraldry graced both the monstrance, the candelabra and the musical instruments of the procession.[46]

Siena's Corpus Domini was famous way beyond the city's borders for its *dimostrazioni*, ceremonial practices and, in particular for the shading of streets with cloths, called *cieli*, of tapestries, religious paintings, greenery, flowers and numerous altars that adorned houses along the route.[47] Of these the most striking must have been the spanning of squares and streets by cloths of wool, a phenomenon that spread from Piazza San Pellegrino to other parts of the city.[48] Such awnings are documented at other feasts that fell in the warm season, such as that of the Baptist in Florence, where Piazza San Giovanni would be covered with blue cloth decorated with heraldic devices, as would the square in front of Pistoia Cathedral during this city's festival of San Jacopo.[49] But the spanning of cloths over wooden structures seems to have particularly distinguished Corpus Domini in Italy. Aeneas Silvius Piccolomini (Pius II) beautifully described the enchanting effect of the sun filtering through these canopies in the lavish Corpus Domini celebrations in Viterbo in 1462. He likened the 'parietes laneos' shading the open-air altar to a celestial setting, the 'summi Regis habitaculum'.[50] Filippo Lippi seems to have used this heavenly analogy when setting his Maringhi *Coronation* against a *cielo* made of long blue cloths sewn together.[51] In Venice from 1454, the guild of woolworkers had to lend white cloths to span a temporary passage around Piazza San Marco, and in early fifteenth-century Brescia, the entire route through the city was spanned by woolworker's cloth. The wool guilds in these cities, unlike in Siena, assumed no further role of importance in their government-centred feast.[52] Corpus Domini celebrations in Montalcino around 1500 were similarly celebrated outside 'sotto vari tendoni stesi ad uso di chiesa'.[53] The vision of woollen cloths spanning Siena's squares and streets thus seems

---

[45] Unfortunately melted down in 1765; Faluschi, *Chiese*, fol. 79v.

[46] Israëls, 'Lana', 535, 542 doc. I.

[47] Gigli, *Diario*, I, 583.

[48] 'tanta fuit hominum curiositas, ac religionis reverentia, ut lanarii Sancti Peregrini plateam pannis laneis totam adumbrant superne extensis'; Tizio, *Historiae*, III, BCS, B.III.8, 440 (s.a. 1371).

[49] G. Vasari (ed. G. Milanesi), *Le Vite* (Florence, 1906), III, 199–200 (Life of Il Cecca); Trexler, *Public Life*, 247; H. L. Chretien, *The Festival of San Giovanni. Imagery and Political Power in Renaissance Florence* (New York, 1994), 108; Pastori, 'Le feste', 15, 17.

[50] E. S. Piccolomini (ed. L. Totaro), *I commentarii* (Milan, 1984), VIII.8, 1596–7.

[51] He could have witnessed the Sienese tradition as sub-prior of the Sienese Carmine (1428–29) (Israëls, 'Lana', 535), but would have been familiar with Florentine awnings too. For eucharistic connotations of the Maringhi *Coronation*; Borsook, 'Cults', 164–72.

[52] Vio, 'La devozione', 171, 174; Muir, *Civic Ritual*, 224; Poisa, 'La processione', esp. 77, 81–2.

[53] T. Canali, *Notizie istoriche della città di Montalcino*, eighteenth-century ms., Biblioteca Comunale di Montalcino (for the quote). I thank Ludwin Paardekooper for this reference and for showing me the manuscript of this part of his forthcoming dissertation: *Altaarstukken in het Sienese territorium: opdrachtgevers en functie, 1450–1500*, Rijksuniversiteit Groningen. Celebration of the feast in Montalcino can be traced to 1452. For the particularly detailed 1518 *Liber ordinum* (based upon an older one predating 1462 according to Paardekooper): Bonucci, *Festa*, esp. 19–20, 26–8, 74–4 nrs. 18–20 & 22–3, 77 nr. 34.

Plate 1

Plate 2

Plate 3

Plate 4

to have served the purpose of temporarily transforming the open air city into a heavenly church worthy of housing the Holy Sacrament in procession.

What can be said of the ritual purpose of the outdoor altar, an important feature of Corpus Domini processions?[54] The tradition of erecting altars before the houses along a processional route goes back to antiquity.[55] According to the special legislation for the Christian *altare portatile*, one of its functions was to serve those occasions on which a church was not large enough to house the influx of its congregation.[56] This certainly applied to the Corpus Domini masses on Piazza San Pellegrino. In Siena, outdoor altars were also erected for once-only religious events, fashionable sermons and processions. In 1425 Bernardino borrowed an altarpiece from the guild of stonemasons as well as a wooden altar from the *Opera del Duomo*, to accompany his sermons on the Campo (Fig. 4).[57] The feast in honour of his canonisation in May 1450 was distinguished by arches of greenery around the Campo shading the altars.[58]

However, the *Arte della Lana* altar had a precise practical, as well as symbolic, significance for the cult of Corpus Domini, beyond the general tradition of outdoor altars. Firstly, a practical significance, because an altar was the only possible place were the Holy Sacrament in its shining monstrance could fittingly be placed during an outdoor mass such as at Piazza San Pellegrino. During Pope Pius II's celebration of Corpus Domini in Viterbo, all the city's relics and precious liturgical objects were placed on a multitude of outdoor altars lining the processional route at which priests said mass.[59] A similar custom seems to have been observed in Siena, as Gigli records that altars were erected throughout the city, brought onto the streets from the churches. He likens those altars to tables ready to accommodate the 'Sagratissimo Pane degli Angeli'.[60] Secondly, the wool guild's altar had a symbolic significance because the altar was a metaphor for Christ himself, the protagonist of the feast.[61]

In 1423, the Sienese guild expressed its shame at annually having to borrow an altarpiece to adorn the temporary altar on their square and thus commissioned

[54] See e.g. F. G. Véry, *The Spanish Corpus Christi Procession: A Literary and Folkloristic Study* (Valencia, 1962), 11–20; A. Alejos Moran, *La Eucaristía en el arte valenciano* (Valencia, 1977), I, 297–8; Bonucci, *Festa*, 20, 28, 77 nr. 35, 84 nr. 66; Poisa, 'La processione', 81, 86, 89, 104; Nußbaum, *Aufbewahrung*, 158; Tamborini, *Corpus Domini*, 82–4; M. Calore, 'Spettacoli sacri negli stati estensi. I. Le rappresentazioni sacre a Modena come manifestazione collettiva', *Quadrivium*, XIX (1978), 33, 57, 58.

[55] Price, *Rituals*, 112.

[56] J. Braun, *Der Christliche Altar in seiner geschichtlichen Entwicklung* (Munich, 1924), I, 43.

[57] Israëls, 'Lana', 539. See note 62.

[58] S. Tizio (ed. P. Pertici), *Historiae Senenses* (ante 1528), III (tomo IV) (Rome, 1998), 271 (27 May 1450); A. Provedi, *Relazione di Pubbliche Feste* (Siena, 1791), 25–6 (25 May 1450); D. Arasse, 'Fervebat pietate populus. Art, dévotion et société autour de la glorification de S. Bernardine de Sienne', *Mélanges de l'Ecole Française de Rome. Moyen Age Temps Modernes*, 89 (1977), 192–3, 227, (citing a contemporary record by Agostino Dati); R. L. Mode, 'San Bernardino in Glory', *The Art Bulletin*, LVI (1973), 59. When the Sienese rejoiced about the coronation both of Pius II (1458) and of Pius III (1503), an altar was erected on the Campo; C. Mazzi, *La Congrega dei Rozzi nel secolo XVI* (Firenze, 1882), I, 35, 45; see also essay by Fabrizio Nevola in this collection.

[59] Piccolomini, *Commentarii*, 1594–613.

[60] Gigli, *Diario*, I, 583. See note 38.

[61] Braun, *Der Christliche Altar*, I, 750–3.

Fig. 4 Sano di Pietro, *Bernardino preaching on the Campo*, 1448, tempera on panel, 162 × 101.5 cm, Museo dell'Opera del Duomo, Siena (photo: Soprintendenza B.A.S. of Siena, with permission of the Ministero per i Beni Culturali e Ambientali)

an altarpiece especially for the Sienese feast. In order to remedy the situation, they levied taxes to pay for an elaborate triptych by the painter Sassetta. This huge structure was kept in a cupboard inside the palazzo of the *Arte della Lana*, waiting to be carried out on the sturdy backs of the woolworkers once a year. Sassetta's sophisticated altarpiece first made its appearance in 1425 (Fig. 5).[62]

[62] The reconstruction is based on eighteenth-century descriptions, prior to its sad dismantling; Israëls, 'Lana', with further literature. In Montalcino too, prior to the commissioning of the Benvenuto di Giovanni, the Commune borrowed an altarpiece from the Compagnia dei Santi Jacomo e Cristofano to stand on top of its outdoor altar during Corpus Domini; Paardekooper, *Altaarstukken.*

Fig. 5 Author's hypothetical scaled reconstruction of Sassetta's Arte della Lana altarpiece, 1423–1425

The central panel showed the Eucharist in a monstrance adored by angels, hovering over a landscape.[63] Its composition refers to the Host as the *Panis Angelorum* and pertains to a passage in the gospel of Saint John, associated with the Eucharist: 'Ego sum panis vivus qui de caelo descendi'.[64] Sassetta's predella illustrated the origins and miraculous power of the Holy Sacrament, with *The Institution of the Eucharist* as well as with a eucharistic miracle and the burning of a heretic doubting transubstantiation. In these panels, Sassetta

[63] The tentative reconstruction is based on a miniature by painters of the generation preceding Sassetta, to which Christa Gardner von Teuffel kindly drew my attention; G. Freuler, 'La miniatura senese degli anni 1370–1420', in: Labriola, De Benedictis, Freuler, *Miniatura*, 197–204, 342, tav. CXXXII–III; E. Cioni, entry in Alessi and Martini, *Panis Vivus*, 102–3 nr. 28.

[64] John: 6:51; part of the Corpus Domini office; Busa, *S. Thomae*, 581. Rubin, *Corpus Christi*, 142–7.

transposed the subject to a Sienese context by including Carmelite friars as well as members of the wool guild with their banner, a sign of the Order's and the guild's backing of the dogma underlying Corpus Domini. This militant position had been adopted at the Council of Siena of 1423, which had condemned the heretics Jan Hus and John Wyclif.[65] The Carmelite Order was involved in this sacramental debate, for example through the important English Carmelite theologian Thomas Netter.[66] The central Coronation pinnacle of Sassetta's altarpiece was accompanied by pinnacles of the Annunciation that referred to the Incarnation, as repeated in the prayer 'Ave verum corpus natum de Maria Vergine' popularly used to address the Holy Sacrament.[67] Saint Thomas Aquinas added eucharistic weight to the altarpiece, while the figure of Saint Anthony paid tribute to an earlier patron saint of the wool guild. In between, two half-length figures of the prophets Elijah and Elisha genuflected towards the Carmelites. Pilasters showed the doctors of the church and Siena's patron saints, the latter again embedding the work in a Sienese context. Sassetta's Corpus Domini altarpiece thus interwove the interests of the three main parties: the wool guild, the Carmelites and the Commune.

This altarpiece, designed for an annual outdoor feast, was not as unique as might at first seem. Quite an array of altar antependia were designed to be exposed once or twice a year, during the major feasts of churches, as emerges from records for silver *palliotti* in Florence, Pisa and Lucca.[68] In Arezzo, according to Vasari, Parri Spinelli's *Madonna della Misericordia* high altarpiece of 1435–7 was taken from the church of Santi Lorentino e Pergentino to an outdoor altar in front of it every year on the eve of the feast of the titular saints.[69] Nor was the *Arte della Lana* alone in Siena in its initiative of an altarpiece displayed in the open air. The phenomenon of open-air chapels with altarpieces was widespread. In Siena, the Cappella di Piazza boasted an altarpiece

[65] Association of the altarpiece-project and the Council: P. Scapecchi, *La Pala dell'arte della lana del Sassetta* (Siena, 1979); idem, 'Chiarimenti intorno alla Pala dell'Arte della Lana', in: Alessi and Martini, *Panis Vivus*, 239–49. In this context, the cathedral inventory of 1423 is of interest, mentioning a new choir book (not yet present in 1420) with 'officii nuovi solfati', amongst them that of 'el corpo di Cristo'; ASS, Opera Metropolitana, 29, fol. 3v.

[66] Thomas Netter or Walden (*circa* 1375–1430) attended the Council of Constance, which condemned the heretics Wyclif and Hus. His treatise was eagerly awaited by Pope Martin V in 1427; E. Monsignanus and I. Ximenez (eds.), *Bullarium Carmelitanum* (Rome, 1715–68), I, 177–8 (8 August 1427). On the Carmelites and their battle against heresy especially in England, see Jotischky, *Carmelites*, 183–9; Smet, *Carmelitani*, 76–81. The Carmelites were represented at the Council of Siena by Tuscan provincial Matteo d'Antonio of Florence and by Antonio di Matteo of Pisa; W. Brandmüller, *Il Concilio di Pavia-Siena 1423–1424. Verso la crisi del conciliarismo* (Siena, 2004) (translation of *Das Konzil von Pavia-Siena 1423–1424* (Paderborn, 2002)), 143.

[67] Browe, *Die Verehrung*, 53; H. Caspary, *Das Sakramentstabernakel in Italien bis zum Konzil von Trient. Gestalt, Ikonographie und Symbolik, kultische Funktion* (Munich, 1961), 101.

[68] For a Pisan palliotto ordered in 1358; Israëls, 'Lana', 539 (note 51); for Lucca's thirteenth-century 'tabula argentea': M. Giusti, 'L'antica liturgia lucchese', in: *Lucca, il Volto Santo e la civiltà medioevale (Atti del convegno internazionale di studi, Lucca, Palazzo Pubblico, 21–23 ottobre 1982)* (Lucca, 1984), 42; for the silver dossal of the Florence Baptistery: H. Hager, *Die Anfänge des italienischen Altarbildes. Untersuchungen zur Entstehungsgeschichte des toskanischen Hochaltarretabels* (Munich, 1962), 188 note 63.

[69] Vasari, *Vite*, II, 283–4; M. J. Zucker, *Parri Spinelli. Aretine Painter of the Fifteenth Century* (PhD Columbia University, 1973), 111–2.

from its construction.[70] Cortona's chapel on Piazza Sant'Andrea, with an altarpiece commissioned in 1411, is another case in point.[71] In 1425, Gentile da Fabriano painted his now lost *Madonna dei Notai* for the Sienese notaries' guild. The polyptych adorned the wall above the benches against the facade of the Palazzo dei Notai on the Campo.[72] In 1744, Gentile's polyptych served as a ritual departing and returning point for the procession of the notaries' patronal feast.[73] This might well be an echo of an older guild ritual and the function of Gentile's polyptych resembled that of its exact contemporary, Sassetta's *Arte della Lana* altarpiece. Antependia, but also altarpieces, were occasionally brought into the open air, such as the stonemasons' polyptych borrowed by Bernardino, the unidentified altarpiece borrowed by the *Arte della Lana* prior to 1423, or the Florence Baptistry *palliotto*, put on an altar on Piazza San Giovanni, together with relics, to celebrate the expulsion of the Medici in 1530.[74]

Straightforward parallels for altarpieces designed to appear outside once a year have so far only rarely been documented. Close in function to the Sassetta was Benvenuto di Giovanni's altarpiece, *Salvator Flanked by Sts Michael and Giles* of the early 1490s, commissioned for Corpus Domini at Montalcino, where the city magistrates had this 'tavola . . . deputata a tale celebratione' installed at their outdoor altar on their central square.[75] Comparable, once-yearly use may have been made of a now-lost retable in Valencia by Juan Rexach of 1461, commissioned by the local guild of butchers and intended for the exposure of the Eucharist during the octave of Corpus Domini.[76]

---

[70] Sodoma's fresco was preceded by an altarpiece with the figure of Christ by Cristoforo di Bindoccio and Meo di Pietro (paid 1392) and by a work by Guidoccio Cozzarelli; G. Borghini, 'La decorazione', in: C. Brandi (ed.), *Palazzo Pubblico di Siena. Vicende costruttive e decorazione* (Milan, 1983), 347 note 335; E. D. Southard, *The Frescoes in Siena's Palazzo Pubblico 1289–1539: Studies in Imagery and Relations to other Communal Palaces in Tuscany* (New York and London, 1979), 129–32.

[71] Now Piazza Signorelli. G. Mancini, *Cortona nel Medio Evo* (Florence, 1897), 282. In commemoration of the victory that brought Cortona under the supremacy of Florence on the nameday of St Anthony Abbot, the 1411 statutes for Cortona ordain that on both this saint's day and on that of St John the Baptist, 'solennitates fiant et fieri debeant ad altarem dictorum sanctorum quod ad eorum laudem et reverentiam a principio factum est in platea domini capitanei iuxta ecclesiam Sancti Andree de Cortona'; Archivio di Stato di Firenze (ASF), *Statuti delle Comunità Autonome e Soggette*, 280, fol. 35v. The chapel is mentioned in a notarial act drawn up 'iuxta et ante capellam Sancte Marie de platea,' on 1 October 1420: ASF, *Notarile antecosimiano*, 18905, unfol., ad annum. In this respect also roadside-chapels merit attention: R. Stopani, *I Tabernacoli Stradali* (Poggibonsi, 1998); idem, *Una Cappella Stradale affrescata del Quattrocento. L'oratorio dei Pianigiani a Casanuova di Ama nel Chianti* (Poggibonsi, 1994).

[72] K. Christiansen, *Gentile da Fabriano* (Ithaca/New York, 1982), 50–5, 137; A. De Marchi, *Gentile da Fabriano. Un viaggio nella pittura italiana alla fine del gotico* (Milan, 1992), 193–4.

[73] ASS, *Arti*, 1, fols. 7ᵛ. I intend to discuss the function of the *Madonna dei Notai* elsewhere.

[74] Hager, *Anfänge*, 188 note 63.

[75] Montalcino, Museo Civico e Diocesano d'Arte Sacra. Bonucci, *Festa*, 11–2, 28, 71 nr. 11, 77 nr. 37 (for the quote); Treffers, 'Pala', 131–8. Paardekooper, *Altaarstukken*, convincingly argues that, around the middle of the Quattrocento, Corpus Domini replaced the city's older feast of the Salvator, thereby explaining the iconography of Benvenuto di Giovanni's bloodshedding Christ. He also shows that Benvenuto's arrangement of his figures, the patron saints of Montalcino's *terzi*, reflects ritual prescriptions for representatives of the *terzi* during the festivities.

[76] Alejos Moran, *Eucaristía*, I, 250, II, 47, nr. LXXV. Altarpieces incorporating a tabernacle were common in Spain, South-Germany and to some extent Italy; *ibidem*, I, 244–54, II, 45–9; Tripps, *Das handelnde Bildwerk*, 216–22, Nußbaum, *Die Aufbewahrung*, 429–30, 434, 438–40.

Sassetta's altarpiece, a permanent and venerable ornament for the patron feast of the woolworkers, probably has to be seen as a precursor or perhaps a contemporary of other ornamentation and ephemera provided for such occasions. Tapestries and paintings were displayed on houses along the processional route according to the 1545 city statutes.[77] This probably reflects an older custom, apparent in the Sienese celebrations of the canonisation of Bernardino in 1450, when images of the novel saint, some of them on altars, adorned the streets, showing a noteworthy fluency between art-historical functional types.[78] Theatrical elements probably graced Sienese Corpus Domini, even though only sixteenth- and seventeenth-century records survive. In 1545, pageants with tableaux vivants ornamented the processional cortège[79], while confraternity members stood on top of the brotherhood altars erected along the route, dressed up as their patron saints making an offering to the Signoria upon the latter's passing by.[80] Since an early date, pageants had featured in the feast of the Assumption in Siena and they are consistently known in Italy by the first half of the fifteenth century, appearing, for example, in the procession at the vigil of San Giovanni Battista in Florence.[81] In turn, the tableaux vivants are reminiscent of similar theatrical elements present in the Sienese festivities surrounding the canonisations of Bernardino (1450) and Catherine (1461), their ascension into paradise rendered on the Campo, or of the enactments of the Assumption of the Virgin staged in honour of the coronation (1458) and festive entry (1460) of Pope Pius II.[82] Furthermore, since the momentous victory of Montaperti on the name day of St George in 1260 until well into the fifteenth century, the *Giuochi Giorgiani* had featured the performance of the warrior saint's battle with the dragon.[83] In Florence, according to Gregorio Dati writing in the first years of the Quattrocento,

[77] M. Ascheri (ed.), *L'ultimo statuto della Repubblica di Siena (1545)* (Siena, 1993), 376; payments for the decoration of the guild's square for Corpus Domini in 1661, include entries for 'un contadino per portare quadri [. . .]' and 'chiodi per attaccare quadri'; ASS, Arti, 75, II, nr. 148. In Montalcino at Corpus Domini all street tabernacles were embellished; Bonucci, *Festa*, 81 nr. 58.

[78] Arasse, '*Fervebat*', 193, 227. Two banners ('*labari*') in Siena Cathedral, showing the figure of Bernardino, were lent by the Concistoro for the use of memorial services in June 1444; M. Bertagna, *L'Osservanza di Siena. Studi storici* (Siena, 1964), II, 8–9. Processional banners were sometimes 'stored' on an altar, serving as altarpieces; M. Bury, 'Documentary evidence for the materials and handling of banners, principally in Umbria, in the fifteenth and early sixteenth centuries', in: C. Villers (ed.), *The Fabric of Images. European Paintings on Textile Supports in the Fourteenth and Fifteenth Centuries* (London, 2000), 19–30, esp. 21, 26–7; J. R. Banker, *The Culture of San Sepolcro during the Youth of Piero della Francesca* (Ann Arbor, 2003), 168–9. See note 38.

[79] Ascheri, *Ultimo statuto*, 376.

[80] Gigli, *Diario*, I, 583–4 with a reference to Giulio Mancini that I was unable to trace.

[81] They originated in Spain. Glénisson-Delannée, 'Fête', 71, 99. For Florence: Trexler, *Public Life*, 252–5; Chretien, *Festival*, 35; Pastori, 'Le feste', 19–20. A good general introduction is Ph. Helas, *Lebende Bilder in der italienischen Festkultur des 15. Jahrhunderts* (Berlin, 1999), esp. 38–45 with further literature.

[82] Mazzi, *Congrega*, 26–39, 52; Arasse, '*Fervebat*', 189–263, esp. 193–6, 209–13, 227–8; Mode, 'San Bernardino', 59–60.

[83] Mazzi, *Congrega*, I, 6–7, 22. For a 1257 enactment of the Passion; *ibidem*, 4–5.

confraternity members dressed up as angels produced theatrical representations relating to their patron saints.[84]

Finally, a consideration of the altarpiece's later history gives us another clue as to its significance. In 1460, the woolworkers started to construct a chapel on Piazza San Pellegrino to house Sassetta's altarpiece, 'come conveniva alla detta tavola', where it would also form the backdrop for daily masses, encouraging woolworkers to gather in their district.[85] Such collective relevance also applied to the Cappella di Piazza, where mass was said on market days, to be heard by all merchants and their customers alike, a trumpet sound marking the elevation of the Host.[86] In his 1575 apostolic visitation, Bishop Bossi fiercely condemned the public character of both chapels.[87] He was evidently unsuccessful though, as in 1750 Giovan Antonio Pecci, local historian and woolworker, defended the 'publica scoverta cappella', because according to him the Corpus Domini celebrations were 'un lustro così onorifico', the chapel 'un gius dell'arte nostra molto antico', and above all the altarpiece solicited immense popular devotion.[88] The outdoor altar and its altarpiece expressed the civic, mendicant and guild interests in the feast of Corpus Domini, and were religious manifestations of the guild's invitation to solidarity.

Towards the middle of the fifteenth century, due to its powerful organizers and its effective ornamentation, the feast of Corpus Domini had acquired such momentum as to attract renewed interest from religious as well as civic authorities. In 1433 Pope Eugenius IV, as well as reinforcing the indulgences granted to those attending the offices by Pope Urban IV and Pope Martin V (1429), attached another indulgence specifically to those participating in the procession, much enhancing its importance.[89] On 21 May 1447, Pope Nicholas V ordained that in Siena the cathedral should be the centre of the Corpus Domini celebrations, depriving the Carmelites of their privileged rôle.[90] The friars then organized a secondary procession of their own on the Sunday following Corpus Domini.[91]

---

[84] Chretien, *Festival*, 34–5. Compare the profuse evidence in N. Newbigin, *Feste d'Oltrarno. Plays in Churches in Fifteenth-Century Florence* (Florence, 1996).

[85] Israëls, 'Lana', 536–8.

[86] F. A. D'Accone, *The Civic Muse. Music and Musicians in Siena during the Middle Ages and the Renaissance* (Chicago and London, 1997), 465–6; Gigli, *Diario*, II, 210–1.

[87] Israëls, 'Lana', 537–538, 543 doc. IX; F. Bossi, *Visita Apostolica*, Archivio Arcivescovile di Siena, Sante Visite 21, fol. 147v (27 July 1575 – ad Cappella di Piazza). For similar ordinances regarding the Montalcino square chapel; Bonucci, *Festa*, 102–4, 120–2.

[88] G. A. Pecci, *Miscellanee*, BCS, A.III.7, fols. 37ʳ–38ʳ, Israëls, 'Lana', 538, 543 doc. X.

[89] Rubin, *Corpus Christi*, 211; Browe, *Die Verehrung*, 97.

[90] Israëls, 'Lana', 536 note 30. With a date of 1448: A. Liberati, 'Chiese, monasteri, oratori e spedali senesi. Ricordi e notizie. Chiesa di San Niccolò al Carmine', *BSSP*, XLVII (1940), 161; A. M. Carapelli, *Notizie delle chiese e cose riguardevoli di Siena*, 1718, BCS, B.VII.10, fols. 32ᵛ, 69ᵛ; Tizio/Pertici, *Historiae*, 251; *Cronaca del Fecini*, BCS, A.VI.9, fol. 396r.

[91] It is unclear when the Sunday 'Carmelite' procession was first organized. In the seventeenth century it departed from the Carmine, moved to San Marco, Santa Marta, via delle Cerchia, Sant'Agostino (by then home to the confraternity of Corpus Domini) and back via Postierla to the Carmelite house; ASS, Arti, 75, II, nr. 173 (1659), nr. 183 (1660), nr. 196 (*s.a.*). Gigli, *Diario*, I, 586, II, 169. For the Arte's *perpetua* in the form of candles for the Sunday procession; ASS, Conventi, 2550 (Carmine), fol. LXIIIIr.

The cathedral works took their task seriously and by 1448 had already ordered, 'per la festa del Corpo di Cristo di nuovo principiata in Duomo', greenery to adorn both the interior and the exterior of the cathedral as well as a gilded wooden tabernacle by the goldsmith Francesco di Antonio.[92] The following year, the *Opera del Duomo* paid the painters Fruosino di Nofrio and Antonio di Giusa for banners showing the coats of arms of the *Arte della Lana*, that now took part in both the Carmelite and the cathedral-sponsored processions.[93] In 1450, Francesco di Antonio made a definitive silver tabernacle for the cathedral.[94]

The city government took only a few more years to realize the potential offered by participation in the procession, which would link their civic authority with the supernatural power of the Eucharist.[95] In 1456, a long rubric was added to the city statutes, officially establishing the *Signoria*'s participation in the celebration.[96] The *Arte della Lana* now processed from its headquarters to the Palazzo Pubblico to fetch the high representatives of the Commune and the other guilds on their way to the cathedral. After mass, the Holy Sacrament was carried in procession, as shown in a miniature by Girolamo da Cremona (Fig. 6). The sequence of the participants was subject to strict rules. For the first time all the guilds were to participate, as a mirror of the social, professional stratification of the city.[97] The feast of Corpus Domini thereby differed from Siena's prime feast of the Assumption, which reflected the political and administrative organisation of the city and its subject towns (the latter absent in Corpus Domini provisions).[98] Confraternities led the procession, followed by the religious orders, the woolworkers accompanied by trumpeters and the other guilds in ascending order of importance. The cortège culminated with high guild officials, especially from the *Arte della Lana*, closest to the Holy Sacrament beneath its baldachin and immediately followed by representatives of the city government, arranged in decreasing order of importance. Following the 'padiglione', possibly shaded Piazza San Pellegrino, the cortège was reshuffled to include the high clergy, now parading guilds, confraternities, the religious, musicians, the canons, the Holy Sacrament, a cardinal and bishops, city-magistrates with released

---

[92] Archivio dell'Opera della Metropolitana di Siena, 710 (502 numeration Moscadelli), fols. 106ʳ–107ʳ. Testimony to earlier Corpus Domini celebrations in the cathedral (1390s): D'Accone, *Civic Muse*, 160, and compare note 65.

[93] Along with other adornments for the festivity; AOMS, 710 (Mosc. 502), fols. 120ʳ⁻ᵛ.

[94] G. Milanesi, *Documenti per la storia dell'arte senese* (Siena, 1854–56), II, 259–60, doc. 184; payments in AOMS, 710 (Mosc. 502), fol. 130r; AOMS, 24 (Mosc. 28), fol. 19r (s.a. 1449).

[95] After the beautiful phrase in Muir, *Ritual*, 68.

[96] Nevola, 'Cerimoniali', esp. 173–5, 180–1 doc. 2. The Florentine magistracy participated since 1425; Casini, *Gesti*, 113–4; Borsook, 'Cults', 156. See note 16.

[97] A phenomenon widely commented upon, e.g. Rubin, *Corpus Christi*, 243–71; Nevola, 'Cerimoniali', 172, 176.

[98] Glénisson – Delannée, 'Fête', 65–129. For participation of the *contado* in civic ritual: G. Chittolini, 'Civic Religion and the Countryside in Late Medieval Italy', in: T. Dean and C. Wickham (eds.), *City and Countryside in Late Medieval and Renaissance Italy* (London, 1990), 69–80.

Fig. 6   Girolamo da Cremona e Liberale da Verona, *Procession of Corpus Domini*, in Graduale. A Resurrectione Domini usque ad festum Corporis Christi, 1472–1473, Siena, Cathedral, Libreria Piccolomini, cod. 23.8, fol. 132ʳ (Siena, Fotografia Lensini)

prisoners and, last but not least, the *Arte della Lana*.[99] The hierarchy thus seems to have moved inward towards the procession's fulcrum, the Eucharist, with a secular accent in the first sequence and a religious one in the second. Through its inclusion of all the guilds, the procession proclaimed a comprehensive

[99] Both procession-orders are centred around the Eucharist, so it is unlikely they pertain to the situation *ante* and *post* mass in the cathedral as suggested in Nevola, 'Cerimoniali', 175. 'padiglione' can not refer to the baldachin above the monstrance, mentioned subsequently. In Pistoia, the awning spanning the cathedral square during the festivity of San Jacopo was known as 'paviglione' at the end of the thirteenth century; Chretien, *Festival*, 108. Alternatively this later addition in the statute might be a later alteration, replacing the primitive sequence.

image of the city, calling to mind the 'indivisible unity' already aspired to by the government in 1356, which at the same time did not prevent the wool guild from standing out in the arrangement. Wax candles were still paid for by the *Biccherna* and in the end equally divided between the cathedral and the Carmine.[100]

The celebration of Corpus Domini had grown into a ritual capable of expressing civic values, whereas it had first served to enhance the profile of a guild and a mendicant order. Through altars, altarpieces, theatrical representations, music, light-filtering cloths over the streets, abundant greenery and hierarchically ordered processions, the city was temporarily transformed into a celestial sphere contemplating the Real Presence of Christ.

Amsterdam

---

[100] Ascheri, *Ultimo Statuto*, 375–6. For the order of the procession in 1726–29, see G. A. Pecci, *Miscellanee*, BCS, A.III.9, fols. 149r–v. See also Gigli, *Diario*, I, 576–82.

5

*Ritual geography: housing the papal court of Pius II Piccolomini in Siena (1459–60)**

FABRIZIO NEVOLA

A well-known *Biccherna*, a Sienese tax book cover, painted by Lorenzo di Pietro, 'il Vecchietta' in 1458, illustrates *The Coronation of Pius II* (Fig. 1).[1] The pope is shown being crowned in the presence of the College of Cardinals, with a view of Siena appearing immediately below as a cityscape, separated from the *Coronation* by only a narrow gilt band. In this 'Sienese' representation of the papal coronation, the international event was translated into an occasion of local significance through the mediatory power of the urban portrait. Thus, while no visual references connect the coronation ceremony to Rome, the prominence of the city-view reinforced the Sienese origins of the Piccolomini pope, and claimed his appointment as a specifically local achievement.

Vecchietta's small panel glossed over the troubled political relations that existed between the pope and the Sienese government, offering instead an idealized vision of their peaceful coexistence.[2] The painted image thus followed in a Sienese tradition that might be traced as far back as Lorenzetti's 'Sala della Pace' fresco cycle, of altering real places, events and political circumstances, and presenting 'corrected' visions of contemporary scenes for

* Primary research for this paper, in Rome and Siena archives, has been generously funded by the AHRB. My warm thanks also go to the staff and library of Villa I Tatti, the Harvard University Centre for Renaissance Studies in Florence, the privileged setting in which I wrote up the final text. I am also very grateful to Georgia Clarke for her careful and incisive comments.

Translations, unless otherwise stated, are my own.

Dating is modern style (note that Sienese style began the year on 25 March).

[1] Museo delle Biccherne, Archivio di Stato, Siena. See, *Le Biccherne. Tavole dipinte delle magistrature senesi (secoli XIII–XVIII)*, U. Morandi et al. eds. (Rome 1984), 166; L. Cavazzini, 'Incoronazione di Pio II, 1460', in L. Bellosi ed., *Francesco di Giorgio e il Rinascimento a Siena* (Siena-Milan 1993), 114; most recently, *Le Biccherne di Siena. Arte e Finanza all'alba dell'economia moderna*, ed. A. Tomei (Azzano San Paolo [Bergamo]/Rome, 2002), 196.

[2] The complex political relations are discussed in I. Polverini Fosi, '"La Comune Dolcissima Patria": Pio II e Siena', in D. Rugiadini ed., *I ceti dirigenti nella Toscana del 'Quattrocento*, (Atti del V et VI convegno: Firenze, 10–11 dicembre 1982; 2–3 dicembre 1983) (Florence 1987), 516–8; also now, P. Pertici, 'Il viaggio del papa attraverso il territorio senese: le tappe di una vita', in *Il sogno di Pio II e il viaggio da Roma a Mantova. Atti del Convegno Internazionale. Mantova: 13–15 aprile 2000* (Centro Studi L. B. Alberti, *Ingenium* n.5), ed. A. Calzona, F. P. Fiore, A. Tenenti and C. Vasoli (Florence 2003), 143–62. Pius summarized the conflict of interests in a reported speech to the *Concistoro*, see A. S. Piccolomini, *I Commentarii*, ed. A. van Heck (Vatican City 1984) I, 139–42(bk. II, chapter 21).

Fig. 1   Lorenzo di Pietro, 'il Vecchietta', *The coronation of Pope Pius II* (Museo delle Biccherne, Archivio di Stato, Siena)

posterity.[3] While the slippery nature of paintings in this respect has some-times been noted, and cautioned against, the similar functions of ephemeral displays and temporary architecture, prepared for ceremonial occasions such as triumphal entries to cities, is commonly described as having such

[3] This theme cannot be explored further in this essay, but is considered in Chapter 1 my forthcoming *Architecture and Government in Renaissance Siena. Fashioning Urban Experience (1400–1555)*. A similar analysis of Lorenzetti's frescoes, that opposes its interpretation as a 'mirror of society', is found in M. Baxandall, 'Art, Society and the Bouguer Principle', *Representations*, 12, 1985, 32–43; such themes have recently been addressed by Luke Syson in a paper, 'Representing the Domestic Interior in the Fifteenth Century: Record or Convention, Myth and Model', presented at the conference '*A Casa*: people, spaces and objects in the Renaissance interior', held at the Victoria and Albert Museum, London (May 2004).

intentions.[4] Thus, where civic theatre and ritual is assumed to distort reality through artistic licence, such premeditated alteration of 'real' events, is more rarely brought to the analysis of art works.

In fact, in the case of Vecchietta's *Biccherna*, artist and local officials had converged towards the similar objective of rendering the remote event of Pius II's coronation in Rome more 'Sienese'. Such an aim was admirably and somewhat remarkably achieved by what might be described as a live relay re-enactment of the papal coronation taking place in Rome, staged on Siena's Piazza del Campo, where an elderly priest stood in for the pope, in a ceremony which took place on the very same day of the Rome event, 3 September 1458.[5] This theatrical spectacle, which blurred the boundaries between fact and fiction, quite literally borrowed the visual form and technical machinery of the Assumption *sacre rappresentazioni*, as the Virgin Mary descended from her heavenly throne to crown the proto-pope.[6] Again it is significant, as in Vecchietta's panel, that it was the Virgin Mary – Siena's advocate and divine Queen – who performed the coronation, thus demonstrating her agency as protector of the city in Aeneas Silvius Piccolomini's ascent to the pontifical throne.

Rather than explore further the complex and symbolically charged rituals of re-enactment, honouring and reception of the pope in Siena, however, this article considers the impact of the pope and his court on the everyday and ritual life of Siena, in two visits of 1459 and 1460. Nonetheless, both the Sienese 'coronation' ceremony and the two sojourns are united by the common theme of the overlap between the local and curial significance of events, and their staging in the public space of the city.

HOUSING THE PAPAL COURT: A CITY WITHIN THE CITY

The papal visits to Siena of 1459 and 1460 followed a fairly standard model for the entry, reception and accommodation of important

---

[4] That ephemeral displays allowed temporary license to alter and 'reinvent' the familiar is a fundamental theme for their scholarly perception, which in part derives from studies of more extreme topsy-turvy occasions, such as the carnivals, most provocatively formulated by M. Bakhtin, *Rabelais and His World* (trans. H. Iswolsky; Bloomington 1984).

[5] Extensive documentation, survives for this event, which is examined in further detail in my 'Metaurbanistica e cerimoniale: Pio II ed la corte papale in Siena', in *Pio II e le Arti al debutto del Rinascimento*, Acts of the conference, ed. C. Crescentini and A. Antoniutti (Rome 2006) 377–87. The key account is the eyewitness record of one of the organisers, Francesco Luti, see F. Luti, *Notizie di Papa Pio II e sue lettere a varii potentati*, Biblioteca Comunale di Siena (hereafter BCS), Ms. B. V. 40, fol. 3–5. See also Tommaso Fecini, 'Cronaca Senese (1431–1479)', in A. Lisini and F. Iacometti eds., *Cronache Senesi*, *RIS*, 15. 6 (Bologna 1931); 868; A. Allegretti, 'Ephemerides Senenses ab anno MCCCCL usque ad MCCCCXCVI italico sermone scriptae', in *Rerum Italicarum Scriptores*, ed. L. Muratori, vol. 23 (Milan 1733), 770; Archivio di Stato di Siena (hereafter ASS), *Consiglio Generale*, 228, fol. 48v (20 August); S. Tizio, *Historiae Senenses*, BCS, B. III. 9, fol. 507.

[6] It is highly probable that the apparatus used three weeks before, for the Assumption *sacra rappresentzione* was re-used for Pius' coronation. On Assumption *sacra rappresentazione* see, D. Arasse, '*Fervebat Pietate Populus*: Art, dévotion et société autour de la glorification de Saint Bernardin de Sienne', *Mélanges de l'Ecole Française de Rome*, 89, 1977, 189–263; also useful are W. Heywood, *Our Lady of August and the Palio of Siena* (Siena 1899) and C. Mazzi, *La congrega dei Rozzi di Siena nel secolo XVI* (Florence 1882), I, 33–6.

visitors.[7] Indeed, the official decisions regarding the planning of the visit specifically mentioned that the organization should adhere to 'those means and ways that were employed for the visit of Pope Eugenius IV,' appealing thus to well established precedents.[8] Once the visit had been approved, numerous measures were adopted to ensure that it would reflect favourably on the Commune.[9] A committee was established 'pro honorantia et ornato adventu;' it was the task of these officials to supervise the decoration of the city, the organisation of banquets and ceremonies and the provision of food and lodging for visitors.[10] Funding for entries and stays, which could often be quite long and expensive, were either drawn directly from public funds, or were collected by a forced loan, usually levied at a rate of 0.4–0.8% of taxable income.[11] The visits of Pius II appear to have been paid for directly from the public purse, and in spite of attempts to limit the budget allocated to the visits, top-up payments were made throughout both stays.[12] Nonetheless, in spite of the costs involved, visits favoured the Sienese economy by providing large numbers of visitors, increased consumption of luxury products and extraordinary income from house letting, which was often tax exempt.[13]

Pius visited Siena for the first time in February 1459 for two months, while en route for Mantua.[14] Possibly in view of the difficulty of finding sufficient properties to house the numerous visitors, nine officials were elected 'sopra le stanze da deputarsi' as well as the usual committee elected 'sopra la honoranza del Sommo Pontefice nel advenimento suo'.[15] The housing officials selected numerous city properties to lodge the cardinals and their retinues, and stables for their horses.[16] Documentary evidence for this stay is less complete

[7] I have discussed the question of entries to Siena (with bibliography) in '"Lieto e trionphante per la città": Experiencing a mid-fifteenth-century imperial triumph along Siena's Strada Romana', *Renaissance Studies*, 17:4 [2003], 581–606; a detailed analysis of entries is offered in Gerrit Schenk's essay in this collection.

[8] ASS, *Consiglio Generale* 228, fol. 84r (13 February 1458/9). On the seven-month visit of Eugenius IV in 1443, see Maria Assunta Ceppari, 'I Papi a Siena', *Istituto Storico Diocesano di Siena: Annuario 1998–1999* [Siena 1999], 345–54; the visit is also discussed by P. Pertici, '"I sacri splendori": Eugenio IV e Siena in un affresco di Domenico di Bartolo', in *Bullettino Senese di Storia Patria*, CVI, 1999 [2001], 484–94.

[9] ASS, *Consiglio Generale* 228, fol. 82v (31 January 1458/9). The model is discussed for Florence by R. Trexler, *Public Life in Renaissance Florence* (New York-London 1980), 303–6; for Venice, P. Fortini Brown, 'Measured Friendship, Calculated Pomp: The Cermonial Welcomes of the Venetian Republic', in *Triumphal Celebrations and the Rituals of Statecraft, (Papers in Art History from the Pennsylvania State University, VI, Part 1)* (Pennsylvania 1990), 136–40.

[10] E.g. for Pius ASS, *Consiglio Generale*, 228, fol. 82v (31 January 1459) and ASS, *Consiglio Generale*, 230, fol. 84 (29 January 1464); for Duchess of Ferrara ASS, *Consiglio Generale*, 235, fol. 64v (25 May 1473).

[11] Figures derived from deliberations for the visits of the Duchess of Ferrara, ASS, *Consiglio Generale*, 235, fol. 64v (25 May 1473); for Ippolita Sforza, ASS, *Concistoro*, 2482, fol. 2 (2 and 13 June, 8 and 22 July 1465).

[12] ASS, *Concistoro*, 560–563 for numerous entries, January–September 1460.

[13] ASS, *Concistoro*, 2154, fol. 22 and 105 (9 December 1460 and 11 February 1462); see also below.

[14] A. Allegretti, 'Ephemerides Senenses', 770 (24 February 1459); ASS, *Concistoro*, 2477 (24 Feb–23 April). Initial plans for lodgings, which do not appear to have been adopted, are listed in ASS, *Concistoro* 554, fol. 37v–38 (14 February).

[15] ASS, *Concistoro*, 2477, fol. 0v (31 January 1459).

[16] ASS, *Concistoro*, 2477 lists restorations and rent costs; see discussion below.

than for that of the following year, but it is evident that the Commune chose to lodge as many of the visitors as possible in monasteries, which were presumably taken rent-free, rather than in private palaces, which were quite expensive to rent (Tables 1 and 3).[17] All the properties were adapted in preparation for their illustrious visitors, and payments document re-plastering of rooms and the construction of additional walls, as well as unspecified works of painting.

As Table 1 shows, a number of monasteries benefited from restoration work, although it is not known which cardinals they housed, while six cardinals were lodged in private properties, and numerous stables were hired for the large number of horses which came with the court. Of six private properties rented to cardinals, the two most expensive were the palace of Giovanni Bichi, let to the papal chancellor Rodrigo Borgia, and the palace of Battista Bellanti, provided for Cardinal Pietro Barbo; it is noticeable that Battista Bellanti was on the housing committee, while Giovanni Bichi was represented on it by his brother Lorenzo.[18] Evidently, though the government was keen to keep the costs of the visit low, private interests ensured that rent income favoured committee-members!

While it is possible to draw some conclusions regarding the housing choices made for the cardinals and the pope on their first visit to Siena, it is more rewarding to compare the evidence from 1459 with the more comprehensive documentation of 1460. In 1459 the pope, cardinals and members of the *curia* came to Siena for the first time, for a brief stay; in 1460 they proved to be more exacting guests, knowledgeable about the city's housing-stock and layout, while also the length of the visit meant that the papal presence was far more deeply felt. Reports sent back to Siena between September and October 1459 from the Sienese ambassadors in Mantua, Niccolò Severini and Lodovico Petroni, prepared the ground for Pius' plans for a longer visit to Siena in January 1460.[19] In addition to the understandable discussion of political issues, these letters show considerable concern for the housing arrangements to be made for the papal court, and contain what amount to reservations for specific palaces and buildings, placed through the ambassadors on behalf of the cardinals and the pope. Correspondence issuing from the papal chancery pursued similar objectives.[20]

---

[17] Rents paid for the month are in ASS, *Concistoro*, 1995, fol. 100v; restorations and other costs in ASS, *Concistoro*, 1995, fol. 1–99. It has proved difficult to collect tangible evidence suggesting that links between host monastic institutions and cardinals (e.g. protectors or members of an order) influenced residence choices.

[18] ASS, *Concistoro*, 1995, fol. 1 and 100; committee was Battista di Giovanni Bellanti, Lorenzo di Ghino di Bartolomeo Bichi, Bernardino di Leonardo Arduini (*Nove*); Tommaso di Giovanni Giovanneschi, Lorenzo di Antonio Venturini, Francesco di Pietro (*Popolo*); Giorgio Luti, Giovanni di Stefano di Magio, Spinello di Giovanni Spinelli (*Riformatori*).

[19] ASS, *Concistoro*, 1995, fol. 56, 66, 78, 88 (September–October 1459).

[20] Brief letter from G. Lolli, confirming death of Cardinal of Portugal and the fact that his rooms in Santa Maria dei Servi might be offered to Cardinal Zamorense, ASS, *Diplomatico Riformagioni*, 31 August 1459; reference to this and other correspondence in ASS, Ms. B 15: 'Ristretto del contenuto ne' contratti e ne' brevi et bolle pontificie [. . .]', fol. 374–5.

Table 1   Properties restored for Pius II's visit of 1459, and their occupants (*Concistoro* 2477)[1]

Restored Property (used by the Papal court)	Occupant (rent cost if known-in lire)
Private Lodgings	
Albergo del Gallo	Pope's *familia* and horses (96)
Giovanni di Guccio Bichi house	Chancellor and his *familia* (433)
Battista Bellanti house	Cardinal Barbo (250)
Lodovico Marescotti house	Cardinal Calandrini (128)
Tommaso Allegretti house	Cardinal Colonna (162)
Pietro di Cristofano Vitelli house	Cardinal Torquemada (70)
Antonio di Goro house	Cardinal Orsini and *familia* (40)
Filippo di Cristofano house	*Familia* of Cardinal
in Pian Mantellini	Lodovico Mila (15)
Antonia donna fu di Savino house	Ambrogio Spannocchi
on Piazza dello Spedale	
Monasteries	
Vescovado	Pope Pius II
Santa Maria dei Servi	Cardinal Juan de Mella
San Agostino	Cardinal Scarampo
San Niccolo al Carmine	Cardinal Lodovico Mila
San Domenico	Cardinal de Coëtivy?
La Magione	?
Stables	
Ambrogio Sozzi for stable behind house	Cardinal Bessarion (8)
Petrone di Francesco stable in S Leonardo	Cardinal Capranica (?) (8)
Giovanni Cristofani stable	Cardinal Orsini (20)
Mariano di Giacoppo Petrucci stable	Cardinal Colonna (8)
Stables in Palazzo Salimbeni	
Stables at Pian dei Servi in front of S M Maddalena	
Stables in S Francesco	
Stables prepared under Santa Maria Scala	
Stables behind S Marco	
Stables under house of Fabrizio Sozzini	
Stables near Umiliati	
Stables at Sperandie	
Stables of Santa Marta at San Agostino	

[1] Identification of Cardinals from Eubel (1914).

These requests were made specifically in light of the court's previous experience of Siena, and reveal a good deal about the housing preferences of the pope and his cardinals, especially when they are considered in relation to the arrangements made the year before. With the exception of the pope, who was traditionally lodged in the Bishop's Palace next to the cathedral, only

Cardinal Borgia stayed in the same private palace when the court returned to Siena in 1460, but others returned to monasteries.[21] Implicit in the correspondence is the fact that if suitable arrangements were not made, in the words of Cardinal Pietro Barbo to the ambassadors, 'non se fermarà in Siena ala tornata ma per rectas vias andarà ad Roma'.[22]

On 25 September 1459, the Sienese ambassadors very perceptively commented to the Commune that:

> Alexandro Mirabilli has told us that Your Excellencies would do well to prepare as many lodgings for the cardinals as you can, without assigning these to anyone without the approval of the pope. Now, Your Excellencies are very wise, and will provide what they consider appropriate for the public good and purse. Your Excellencies should be advised, however, that Mantua now is honoured by the presence of many prelates and lords, of ambassadors and of numerous courtiers; and it is a beautiful Mantua, and in addition to this, large, dignified and beautiful lodgings have been provided. And there is no shortage of anything. We write this so that Your Excellencies understand the matter in full, so that you may provide as necessary, because as Your Excellencies know, the courtiers hold great sway with the pope, particularly if they are treated badly.[23]

The ambassadors had observed the efforts being made in Mantua to make the city an honourable setting for the Congress, noting that the magnificence with which visitors to the city were to be treated, benefited diplomatic contacts and political discussions, and suggesting that similar measures should be taken in Siena.[24] Numerous property restorations mentioned below, as well as more wide-ranging urban improvements and zoning provisions, were intended to do just this.[25]

---

[21] Cardinal Barbo, ASS, *Concistoro*, 1995, fol. 66v (2 October 1459); Cardinal Borgia, ASS, *Concistoro*, 1995, fol. 56 (25 September 1459). Some monasteries were re-used, see below. The Bishop's Palace is used throughout to denote the residence of the bishop, although the elevation of Siena to archbishopric means that the building was, from 1460, the Archbishop's Palace.

[22] ASS, *Concistoro*, 1995, fol. 66v (2 October 1459).

[23] ASS, *Concistoro*, 1995, fol. 56 (quoted in I. Polverini Fosi, '"La Comune Dolcissima Patria,"' 515), 'ci ha dicto che V. S. farieno bene a provedere a più stanze per li cardinali che sia possibile senza consegnarle ad alcuno se non quanto piaccia al Summo Pontefice. Hora le V. S. sono sapientissime che provederanno quanto lo parrà conveniente per lo honore e debito publico. Advisando le vostre excellentie che Mantova hoggi è molto ornata di prelati e signori, di Ambasciatori e di molta corte, et è una bella Mantova ed. oltra a questo c'è molte stanze belle e grandi e degne. Ecci habundantissimo di ogni cosa. Questo scriviamo acciò che V. S. intendino ad pleno et possino provvedere perchè come sa la S. V. ei cortigiani possono assai nel papa non essendo bene tractati'.

[24] On Mantua, see H. Burns, 'The Gonzaga and Renaissance Architecture', in *Splendours of the Gonzaga*, ed. D. Chambers and J. Martineau (London 1981), 28–9. See also, most recently R. Signorini, 'Alloggi di sedici cardinali presenti allla Dieta', in *Il sogno di Pio II*, 315–389, with identification of residences in Mantua and bibliography on cardinals present; and D. S. Chambers, 'Spese del soggiorno di Papa Pio II a Mantova', in the same volume, 391–402, for discussion of the lavish treatment reserved for the papal court.

[25] ASS, *Concistoro*, 2481 covers the 1464, without reference to building preparations.

Reflecting the government's desire to secure the papal visit to Siena, the ambassadors' reports contained each request made to them, as 'every cardinal is anxious to secure his lodgings'.[26] These included 'repeat bookings' by Cardinal Bessarion for rooms in San Francesco, Cardinal Juan de Mella, for rooms in Santa Maria dei Servi, Cardinal Juan Torquemada for Giovanni Pecci's palace and the vice-chancellor, Cardinal Rodrigo Borgia for Palazzo Bichi-Tegliacci.[27] Cardinal Rodrigo had evidently been very struck by Palazzo Bichi, expressing to the ambassadors his 'great desire to lodge in the palace where he had stayed previously, and that His Holiness had already written to this effect to Luigi Tegliacci, on account of his having recently acquired the palace'.[28] The palace was one of the best-appointed private buildings of the late 1450s in Siena, and its design included a gothic façade and a magnificent internal arrangement distributed around a classicising courtyard and loggia.[29] Centrally located, near the cathedral precinct, the palace also had wonderful views of the countryside as well as a chapel for which Pope Nicholas V had granted the right to a private altar in 1452.[30]

Just as Cardinal Rodrigo had liked the Bichi palace, so the pope interceded for Cardinal Lodovico Scarampo, so that 'you will see fit to provide him with a palace and not a monastery, which is as close as possible to the Bishop's Palace, and should be able to accommodate one hundred horses and have a kitchen garden'.[31] Likewise, Cardinal Pietro Barbo stated that 'on account of the fact that I have a large entourage, I ask your Excellencies that if you are unable to get a big enough palace, you should find two or three neighbouring ones,' stating bluntly that he did not want to be lodged in the house of Battista Bellanti in the district of San Donato, where he had stayed the year before.[32] Such comments clearly indicate that some cardinals preferred the comforts of modern palaces to the rigours of monastic cells, and needed ample space to accommodate their large retinues. Cardinal

---

[26] ASS, *Concistoro*, 1995, fol. 66v (2 October 1459), 'ognuno [cardinal] fastima di provvedere per la stanza'. In addition to these letters, a series of communications directly from the pope are reported in ASS, Ms. B 15: 'Ristretto del contenuto ne' contratti e ne' brevi et bolle pontificie [. . .]', fol. 374: 31 Aug, 1459 and September 1459, fol. 375: 10 February 1459[60].

[27] ASS, *Concistoro*, 1995, fol. 56, 66, 78, 88 (September–October 1459); cardinals identified from C. Eubel, *Hierarchia catholica medii aevi sive Summum Pontificorum, 1431–1503* (Münster 1914), II, 8–14.

[28] ASS, *Concistoro*, 1995, fol. 66v (2 October 1459), 'desiderare molto la stanza dove ste e che di questo la Santita di Nostro Signore ne haveva scripto uno breve al Luigi Tegliacci per cagione dela vendita di essa casa'.

[29] The palace is discussed most recently by P. Pertici, 'Per la datazione del *Libro d'ore* di Feliziana Bichi', in *Siena ed il suo territorio nel rinascimento*, III, ed. M. Ascheri (Siena 2001), 165–8; also useful are G. Cecchini, 'Il Castello delle Quattro torri e i suoi proprietari', *Bullettino Senese di Storia Patria*, 55, 1948, 3–32 and 'Minime di storia dell'arte senese: Un'altro palazzo gotico del Rinascimento', *Bullettino Senese di Storia Patria*, 68, 1961, 241–50.

[30] ASS, *Diplomatico Bichi Borghesi*, Ms. B 25, vol. I, fol. 36 (16 January 1452).

[31] ASS, *Concistoro*, 1995, fol. 56 (25 September 1459) 'vi degniate farli provvedere una stanza et non convento di religiosi più vicino al palazzo [bishop's] che sia possibile, la quale stanza sia almeno capace per cento cavalli et con orto [. . .]'.

[32] ASS, *Concistoro*, 1995, fol. 66v (2 October 1459), 'havendo grande famiglia che la Signoria Vostra non possendosi provedere d'una stanza conveniente, senne trovi due o tre contigue [. . .] non vuole per niente quella dove stè di Misser Baptista'; Battista Bellanti, ASS, *Lira*, 147, fol. 125 (1453).

Fig. 2 Anonymous. Pope Pius II seated between two cardinals. Cover of the account book (ASS, *Concistoro* 2479) kept of the expenses for lodgings of the pope and his cardinals in Siena, 1460 (Archivio di Stato, Siena)

Barbo was, in fact, lodged in the house of Tommaso Luti, in the central district of Pantaneto, which had been restored at considerable expense by the Commune before the court's arrival, and was also given the neighbouring houses of Tommaso's cousin Francesco, and of Leonardo di Andrea Tolomei.[33] For his part, Pius II required more space than had been made available on his first stay in the Bishop's Palace, and thus also demanded the palace of Tommaso Pecci across the street, for which he asked 'that a bridge be made to cross from one side of the street to the other'.[34] While the palace was granted to the pope, there is no evidence that the bridge he requested was ever built.

There can be no doubt that on their second stay, which was to last around seven and a half months, the papal court was treated with greater magnificence and a far larger economic outlay was made for lodgings (Fig. 2). Monasteries continued to be used, possibly because, as the ambassadors informed the

[33] ASS, *Concistoro*, 2479, fol. 6–7, 56, 71 for restorations costing 3200 *lire* (1459–60); ASS, *Lira* 144, fol. 38, 59, 136.

[34] ASS, *Concistoro*, 1995, fol. 56 (25 September 1459), 'si faccia uno ponte per passare dall'uno canto all'altro'.

papal court in Mantua, 'large palaces are hard to come by in Siena on account of the hilly terrain', although it is also very clear from Table 3 that the Commune was prepared to rent more than one neighbouring property in order to satisfy the cardinals' and their households' needs.[35] Restoration and rent costs were consequently enormously high for the 1460 visit, amounting to 7,200 lire for rent alone, as against 1,243 in 1459.[36] These greater expenses can be explained both by the court's longer stay, and the fact that the city had much longer notice of the court's arrival, which meant that more preparations could be made to create a suitable court setting in Siena.

In partial response to the cardinals' requests, and following the instructions of the committee charged with preparing housing for the papal stay, numerous palaces, monasteries and churches became the focus of frenetic building activity during the winter of 1459 (Table 2).[37] The extraordinary effort was meticulously assessed and recorded by the government surveyor, Pietro dell'Abaco, and the work involved countless builders, as well as well-known masters such as Urbano di Pietro, Luca di Bartolo da Bagnocavallo and Antonio Federighi, all paid from government funds.[38]

It is possible to identify most of the properties that were provided for the cardinals and their retinues. A clear logic governed the assignation of lodgings, with the pope placed at the religious centre, in the Bishop's Palace adjacent to the cathedral, and the cardinals distributed along four principal arteries that led out from Piazza Duomo towards the major monastic houses on the periphery (Fig. 3). Such choices reflect the intention to provide a court-like setting for the transaction of papal and curial life, which was overlaid upon the civic fabric of fifteenth-century Siena. The palace was thus established as an alternative *locus* of authority to the civic Palazzo Pubblico, with the palaces of the Sienese elite serving as courtiers' residences, distributed about the city much in the same way as the cardinals were spread about papal Rome (and Avignon before).[39]

---

[35] ASS, *Concistoro*, 1995, fol. 56 (25 September 1459), 'stanze [palaces] essere molto difficili trovare in Siena perchè è terra montuosa'. A number of monasteries had guest houses that may have been used for the cardinals, as for example was the case for the sizeable apartements at S. Agostino, for which see restoration costs and construction of a new kitchen block in preparation for the visit of Emperor Sigismund (1432), ASS, *Concistoro* 2475; also *Die Kirchen von Siena*, P. A. Riedl and M. Siedel eds., I, Munich 1985, 27–30.

[36] ASS, *Concistoro*, 2477, fol. 100 (1459); ASS, *Concistoro*, 2480, fol. 80–1 (1460). It is notable that rent costs seem to have been kept lower for the second stay. There are no totals for restoration costs. ASS, *Concistoro*, 2478–9 for preparations and expenses during stay.

[37] ASS, *Concistoro*, 2479.

[38] ASS, *Concistoro*, 2479; on Pietro dell'Abaco see N. Adams, 'The Life and Times of Pietro dell'Abaco, a Renaissance Estimator from Siena (active 1457–86)', *Zeitschrift für Kunstgeschichte*, 48, 1985, 384–95; Luca di Bartolo and Antonio Federighi are discussed in my 'Revival or Renewal: Defining Civic Identity in Fifteenth-century Siena', in *Shaping urban identity in the middle ages*, eds. P. Stabel and M. Boone (Leuven/Apeldoorn 2000), 111–34.

[39] On the distribution of cardinals' residences in Avignon, see B. Guillemain, *La cour pontificale d'Avignon, 1309–1376. Étude d'une société* (Paris 1966), 181–276 and 497–532; more summary is Y. Renouard, *The Avignon Papacy, 1305–1403* (London1970; original French ed. 1954), 80–96. The ceremonial implications of the distribution of cardinals' residences around the city to do not seem to have been pursued, for Avignon or Rome during the fourteenth–fifteenth centuries.

Table 2 Properties restored for Pius II's visit of 1460 (*Concistoro* 2479) and their occupants (*Concistoro* 2478 and 2480)[2]

Restored Property	Occupant
Private Houses	
Giovanni di Niccolo Mannini	?
Palazzo Salimbeni	?
Fabbiano di Gasparre	?
Tommaso Luti	Cardinal Barbo
Salvadore di Gasparre	?
Casa di Santa Marta	Cardinal Sassoferrato
Giovanni Bichi/Tegliacci	Cardinal Borgia
Andrea di Cristofano	Cardinal Calandrini
Giovanni Pecci	Cardinal Torquemada
Filippo di Caterino	Cardinal Nicholas of Cusa
Iacomo di Buccio	Cardinal Eroli
Bartolomeo di Antonio Petrucci	Giovanni Saracini, 'spenditore del papa'
Antonio di Toro Treasurer	Ambrogio Spannocchi, Papal Treasurer
Antonia di Savino tintore	Papal Secretary
Caterina di Nanna	G. Lolli, Secretary
Giovanni di Cola fornaio	Papal bakery
Niccolò di Andreoccio Petrucci	Papal 'scudieri'
Giovanni di Bartolomeo Petrucci	Papal 'scudieri'
Bartolo di Iacopo Petrucci	Datary
Giulia donna di Bartolomeo Gallerani	Antonio Ribigli, 'maestro delle cerimonie'
'All'osteria'	Ambassadors to the pope
'All'osteria'	'Simonetto'
'All'osteria'	Braccio da Perugia
Monasteries/Churches	
San Marco	?
San Francesco	Cardinals Scarampo/Orsini/Bessarion
Santa Maria dei Servi	Cardinal Juan de Mella
Abbadia San Donato	Cardinal Colonna
Convento dei Mantellini,	Cardinal Lodovico Mila
San Niccolò al Carmine	
San Domenico	Cardinal de Coëtivy
Church of San Martino	?
Casa di San Martino	Cardinal Scarampo (?)
San Agostino	Cardinal d'Estouteville
Stables	
Rede di Pietro di Agostino	Stable for C. Calandrini
Pietro di Giovanni	Stable for C. Calandrini
Lorenzo di Senso	Stable for C. Calandrini
Ghilberto di Bindo	Storeroom for Pope
Meo della Massa	Stable under Salimbeni for C. Mila
Chele manischalco	Stable at San Marco for C. Borgia
Meo del Bianco	Stable for C. Bessarion
Ciarpelone di Tura	Stable in S. Martino for C. Calandrini
Iacomo di Renaldo Pecci	Stable Fontebranda for C. Calandrini
Antonio di Narni	Stable for Mons. Tiano
Francesco di Lorenzo	Stable in San Salvatore for Mons. Tiano

[2] Identification of Cardinals from Eubel (1914).

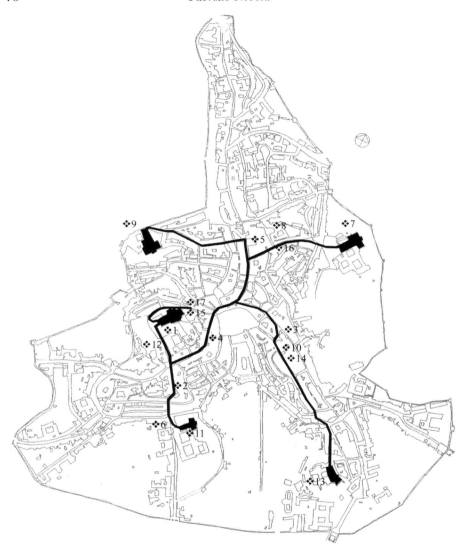

Fig. 3 Map showing the location of the lodgings of Pope Pius II and the Papal Court in Siena, 1460. (1) Pius II: Palazzo Arcivescovile, (2) Cardinal Borgia: Palazzo Bichi, (3) Cardinal Bessarion: Palazzo Luti, (4) Cardinal Bessarion: Palazzo Marescotti, (5) Cardinal Juan de Mila: Palazzo Salimbeni [?], (6) Cardinal Sassoferrato: Casa di Santa Marta, (7) Cardinal Scarampo or Orsini: San Francesco, (8) Cardinal Colonna: Abbadia San Donato, (9) Cardinal de Coëtivy: San Domenico, (10) Cardinal Scarampo: Casa di San Martino, (11) Cardinal d'Estoutville: San Agostino, (12) Cardinal Torqemada: Casa di Giovanni Pecci, (13) Cardinal Zamorense: Santa Maria dei Servi, (14) Cardinal Barbo: Casa di Tommaso Luti, (15) Datario: Casa di Bartolo di Iacopo Petrucci, (16) Antonio Robioli: Casa di Bartolomeo Gallerani, (17) Giovanni Saracini: Casa di Bartolemeo di Antonio Petrucci (information drawn from *Concistoro* 2478 and 2480. Map: author)

Around the papal accommodation in the Bishop's Palace were grouped a number of officials in the service of the pope; this was only partially put into practice in 1459, when the pope's *depositario* Ambrogio Spannocchi, who did not yet have a palace in Siena, was lodged on the Piazza Duomo.[40] The concept was applied more thoroughly in 1460, when ten properties were hired, in addition to the Bishop's Palace, to house the pope and his close advisors; while it is not possible to locate all these buildings, four of seven tentatively identified were in the vicinity of the cathedral.[41] Three houses belonging to the Petrucci clan were taken to house the papal equerries, the Datary, as well as the papal procurator Giovanni Saracini; a short distance from the papal court a bakery was hired to supply the daily needs of the palace.[42] The pope was thus able to create his court in the immediate vicinity of the cathedral, the religious centre of the city, on a site which was well connected to the cardinals' lodgings and the civic centre, but which also had its own public space in the square facing the Bishop's Palace and the cathedral.

It is clear that in 1460 most cardinals' lodgings lined the routes that led from the cathedral precinct to the religious complexes of Santa Maria dei Servi, San Francesco, San Domenico and Sant' Agostino (see Fig. 3). Thus for example, Cardinal d'Estouteville was lodged at Sant' Agostino, and along the route to that monastery (Via del Capitano and Via di San Pietro) were the palaces assigned to Cardinal Torquemada (Palazzo Pecci), Cardinal Borgia (Palazzo Bichi-Tegliacci) and Cardinal Sassoferrato (Casa di Santa Marta). A similarly coherent selection process can be seen in the case of the route leading to Santa Maria dei Servi where Cardinal Juan de Mella was lodged (Piazza Piccolomini and along Via del Porrione); along that route were the residences of Cardinal Bessarion (Palazzo Luti), Cardinal Scarampo (Casa di San Martino) and Cardinal Barbo (also in a Luti palace).

It is, of course, to some extent perhaps obvious that the palaces of Siena's leading citizens should be on the main streets of the city centre, but this does not wholly explain the choice of palaces for the cardinals, or their distribution. It is, for instance, noticeable that none of the palaces around the central Piazza del Campo, or along the *Strada Romana* (the main street through Siena) were selected, but rather that it was subsidiary streets that led from the civic and religious centre out to the monastic complexes distributed on the four compass points of the city that were chosen. It seems probable that this choice was in part governed by ceremonial and aesthetic considerations.

[40] On Spannocchi, see my 'Ambrogio Spannocchi's "bella casa": Creating Site and Setting in Quattrocento Sienese Architecture', in *Renaissance Siena: Art in Context*, ed. L. A. Jenkens, (Kirksville 2005), 141–156; ASS, *Concistoro*, 2477, fol. 72v.

[41] Pius, his secretaries, treasurer, Datary, stable-hands and baker (Table 3); located in ASS, *Lira*, 137, fol. 76, 105, 360 and house of Tommaso Pecci. On Giovanni Saracini's role as paymaster for papal projects in Siena, is documented in Archivio di Stato di Roma [henceforth ASR], *Camerale 1: Tesoreria Segreta (Entrata e uscita)* 1288 and 1289.

[42] ASS, *Lira* 140, fol. 216.

Table 3 Properties let to the Papal court in 1460 (1 Feb–10 Sept; *Concistoro* 2480)[3]

fol.	Owner	Visitor/Use	Period of Stay	Cost
fol. 2	Matteo di Antonio di Buonsignori	?	7 months 10 days	2542 lire
fol. 3	Luigi di Giovanni Tegliacci	House C. Borgia	7 months 10 days	850 lire
fol. 4	Bonaventura di Agostino Borghesi	House C. Borgia	1 month	117 lire
fol. 5	Biagio di Antonio di Pietro Turchi	House C. Bessarion	1 month	88 lire
	Bartolomeo Luti	House C. Bessarion	1 month	88 lire
fol. 6	Pietro Turegli	House C. Bessarion	1 month	64 lire
	Francesco Luti	House C. Barbo	7 months, 27 days	379 lire
fol. 7	Tommaso di Maurizio Luti	House C. Barbo	(as above)	379 lire
	Leonardo di Andrea di Bartolomeo	House C. Barbo	(as above)	284 lire
fol. 8	Andrea di Cristofano	House C. Calandrini	7 months 10 days	528 lire
	Francesco Arringhieri	House C. Calandrini	(as above)	350 lire
fol. 9	Chele manischalco	Stable at San Marco for C. Borgia		28 lire
	Tome di Docio	House C. Bessarion	1 month 28 days	112 lire
fol. 10	Lorenzo Marescotti	House C. Bessarion	1 month 28 days	88 lire
	Lodovico Marescotti	House C. Bessarion	1 month 28 days	82 lire
fol. 11	Domenico di Francscone	House C. Bessarion	1 month 26 days	23 lire
	Antonio di Toro	House	7 months 10 days	146 lire
fol. 12	Tommaso di Nanni Pecci	House for Pius II	7 months 10 days	1085 lire
fol. 13	Giovanni di Pietro Pecci	House for C. Torquemada	6 months	340 lire
	Antonia di Savino tintore	House for Papal Secretary	7 months 10 days	176 lire
fol. 14	Caterina di Nanna	House for G. Lolli, Secretary	7 months 15 days	205 lire
	Giovanni di Cola fornaio	Bakery for Pope	7 months 10 days	190 lire
fol. 15	Rede Bartolomeo Gallerani	House for Captain	7 months 10 days	58 lire
	Cicerone d'India- 'Albergo del Gallo'	House for C. Bessarion	1 month 26 days	52 lire
fol. 16	Filippo di Caterino	House for C. Nicholas of Cusa	7 months 10 days	102 lire
	Iacomo di Buccio	House for C. Eroli	7 months 10 days	205 lire
fol. 20	Lodovico e Antonio dei Tondi	House for C Colonna	7 months 10 days	205 lire
	Improvement work to above			20 lire
	Antonio di Toro	House for Papal Treasurer	7 months 10 days	146 lire
fol. 21	Paolo di Astolfo	Casetta	7 months 10 days	58 lire
	Meo del Bianco	Stable for C. Bessarion	7 months 10 days	117 lire

Table 3 *Continued*

fol.	Owner	Visitor/Use	Period of Stay	Cost
fol. 22	Ciarpelone di Tura	Stable in S. Martino for C. Calandrini	7 months 10 days	15 lire
	Battista di Vanni	As above	5 months	60 lire
fol. 23	Bartolomeo di Antonio Petrucci	House for Giovanni Saracini, 'spenditore del papa'	7 months 10 days	140 lire
fol. 24	Niccolò di Andreoccio Petrucci	House for Papal 'scudieri'	7 months 10 days	146 lire
	Giovanni di Bartolomeo Petrucci	House for Papal 'scudieri'	7 months 10 days	58 lire
	Rede di Pietro di Agostino	Stable for C. Calandrini	5 months	15 lire
	Pietro di Giovanni	Stable for C. Calandrini	5 months	17 lire
fol. 25	Lorenzo di Senso	Stable for C. Calandrini	5 months	15 lire
	Ghilberto di Bindo	Storeroom for Pope	7 months 10 days	29 lire
	Meo della Massa	Stable under Salimbeni for C. Mila	7 months 10 days	29 lire
fol. 26	Giovanni di Niccolò	House for C. Eroli	6 months	120 lire
	Battista di Antonio di Tuccio	House for C. Eroli	6 months	48 lire
	Madonna Antonia	House for C. Eroli	6 months	48 lire
fol. 27	Alberto di Damaso-	House for C. Colonna	7 months 10 days	58 lire
	Bartolo di Andrea	'Casa tenne il papa per la sua famiglia quando fe il nipote cardinale'	5 months 20 days from 20 March	226 lire
fol. 28	Iacomo di Renaldo Pecci	Stable Fontebranda for C. Calandrini	7 months 10 days	55 lire
	Antonio di Narni	Stable for Mons. Tiano	6 months 28 days	6 lire
	Francesco di Lorenzo	Stable in San Salavtore for Mons. Tiano	6 months 28 days	6 lire
fol. 32	Petrone Petroni	House for Capitano di Giustizia, 'perche il chavamo da Santa Marta e mettemoci monsignor di Sasso Ferrato'	6 months 26 days	137 lire
fol. 34	Bartolo di Iacopo Petrucci	House for Datario	7 months 10 days	170 lire
	Giulia donna di Bartolomeo Gallerani	House for Antonio Ribigli, 'maestro delle cerimonie'	4 months	41 lire

³ Identification of Cardinals from Eubel (1914).

RITUAL GEOGRAPHY: THE CEREMONIAL USE OF URBAN SPACE

The papal visits of Pius II to Siena were an important catalyst for the process of urban renewal and beautification that was the responsibility of the recently founded office of the *Maestri sopra all'ornato.*[43] At the same time as the nine officials 'sopra le stanze' were busy procuring rooms to house the pope and cardinals, a number of legislative measures were applied in order to improve the appearance of the *Strada Romana.*

Among the most strenuously enforced measures were zoning provisions against noisy and dirty professions that practiced their trade along the *Strada Romana* and in general, in the centre of the city. In the lead-up to the second papal visit, a decree of 25 October 1459, stated that

> [. . .] it would be a good and honourable thing, particularly on account of the imminent visit of the Papal court [. . .] that it were decided and ruled that blacksmiths should on no account have their workshops along the Strada Romana from San Donato a Montanini as far as the Cathedral and the Piazza Piccolomini.[44]

By removing the noisy and dirty blacksmiths' workshops from the main city streets, a clear relationship was established between zoning restrictions and urban improvements, with the specific intention of creating a suitable setting to receive the papal court of Pius II.[45] In March 1460, these rulings were followed by further legislation that forced butchers to relocate to the south-western valley of Fontebranda, specifically because 'our city is much criticized by courtiers and other foreigners who are in the city [. . .] because they [the butchers] are in the main streets'.[46] In turn, these negative zoning restrictions were complemented by policies that encouraged the concentration of luxury *botteghe,* selling gold, cloth and finished leather goods, as well as banks, along the central street, the *Strada Romana.*[47] All of these hoped to benefit from the visitors' custom.

---

[43] On the work of the *Ornato,* see P. Pertici, *La città magnificata: interventi edilizi a Siena nel Quattrocento* (Siena 1995); on coincidence with papal sojourns, see my '"Ornato della città": Siena's Strada Romana as Focus of Fifteenth-century Urban Renewal', *Art Bulletin,* 82 [2000], 26–50.

[44] *Concistoro* 2125, fol. 10 (quoted from P. Pertici, *La città magnificata,* 71); 'sarebbe bene e honorevole cosa, et maxime havendoci ad venire la corte romana [. . .] si deliberasse e statuisse e ordinasse che per la strada maestra da la chiesa di San Donato presso a Montanini infino al Duomo e infino alla Piazza Piccolomini inclusive non possino stare a buttiga fabbri di veruna ragione per alcuno modo'.

[45] On Renaissance zoning see J. Ackerman and M. Rosenfeld, 'Social Stratification in Renaissance Urban Planning', in *Urban Life in the Renaissance,* ed. S. Zimerman and R. Weissman (Newark 1989), 21–49; also L. B. Alberti, *On the Art of Building in Ten Books,* ed. and trans. J. Rykwert, N. Leach and R. Tavernor (Cambridge, Mass. 1991), 191–2 (VII.1).

[46] ASS, *Statuto di Siena* 25, fol. 330 (21 March 1460), 'civitas nostra sit multus damnata a cortigianis et allis forensibus existentibus in civitate Senensis' because 'per stratas magistras stent'.

[47] See my '"Più honorati et suntuosi ala Republica": *Botteghe* and Luxury Retail along Siena's Strada Romana', in *Buyers, sellers and salesmanship in medieval and early modern Europe,* ed. B. Blondé, P. Stabel and E. Welch (Brepols 2006) [forthcoming].

Furthermore, the period surrounding the papal visits of 1459 and 1460 was the occasion for perhaps the most concerted push for the removal from palaces and houses that faced onto the main streets of *ballatoi* and other overhanging structures.[48] Again, the objective of these measures was expressed as being 'to make everything beautiful [...] particularly in view of the impending arrival of the papal court'.[49] *Ornato*-mediated renovations were carried out along the course of the *Strada Romana*, but also involved the Via di Città, which leads from the Campo to the Duomo, and the subsidiary streets that connected the mendicant complexes to the centre. Thus, to take an example I have examined elsewhere in some detail, a sequence of properties along the Via di Città was redeveloped in the years after 1459, and resulted in the construction of the new Palazzo Piccolomini 'delle Papesse', as well as the renovation of the neighbouring Palazzo Marsili and Palazzo Lolli. Land concessions made to Caterina Piccolomini in October 1459, for the construction of her palace, specified that construction should be rapid, and it was indeed the front façade on the Via di Città that was completed first, in accordance with the government's requirement that it be completed for the Feast of the Assumption, 1460.[50] This tight building schedule serves as an indication that the Sienese government had in mind the civic image that was to be on display on the occasion of the most important of the city's feast-days.

For, indeed, the common ground between *Ornato* zoning and urban renewal policies and the housing choices made by the officials 'sopra le stanze' is to be sought in those ritual occasions, when the city itself was the stage for processions and other ceremonial activity.[51] By distributing the court around Siena, the Commune was able to display the city's size, and the architectural splendour of all its parts, linking these together by the ritualized movement of the court between these various sites (Fig. 3). Moreover, since the major monastic complexes also served as residences for a number of cardinals, long-established ceremonial routes with religious ritual significance were 'reused' in the creation of new ceremonials, associated with the papal court.[52]

[48] See table in '"Ornato della città": Siena's Strada Romana', 46.

[49] ASS, *Consiglio Generale* 228, fol. 168, (4 April 1459), 'chi volesse più hedificare in quello luogo [...] facendo uno bello acconcime di quella contrada et ripararsi a tanta vergogna della città maxime avendoci ad venire la corte', (cited P. Pertici, *La città magnificata*, 66 and quoted in P. Turrini, '*Per honore et utile de la città di Siena'. Il comune e l'edilizia nel Quattrocento* (Siena 1997), 135–7). For similarly motivated urban renewal of Mantua as setting for the papal court and Council, see H. Burns, 'The Gonzaga and Renaissance Architecture', 28–9.

[50] ASS, *Consiglio Generale* 228, fol. 168 (21 October1459), 'sarebbe facta la faccia dinanzi'.

[51] The seeming overlap of tasks between the urban planning officials and those charged with organising important visits has caused some confusion in documentary studies, most notably in P. Pertici, *La città magnificata*, 64 and C. Zarrilli and S. Moscadelli, 'Domenico Beccafumi e altri artisti nelle fonti documentarie del primo cinquecento', in *Domenico Beccafumi e il suo tempo*, exh. cat. (Siena 1990), 694–6, cite ASS, *Balia* 115, fol. 1–35 (1536), who identify the eight 'spectabilissimi ominis otto ornatus pro adventu Cesare Maiestatis' elected for the festivities for Charles V (1536) as the 'Maestri dell'Ornato'.

[52] For the routes of the feast of Saint Bernardino, see my 'Cerimoniali per santi e feste a Siena a metà Quattrocento. Documenti dallo *Statuto di Siena*, 39', in *Siena ed il suo territorio nel rinascimento*, III, ed. M. Ascheri (Siena 2001), 171–84.

It would, of course, be impossible within the confines of this paper, to survey all aspects of Siena's ritual calendar during the two papal visits of 1459 and 1460, nor yet to consider all the instances where papal ceremonial was superimposed on the statutory calendar, the 'giorni nei quali la signoria esce dal palazzo,' as they are described in statute rulings.[53] Furthermore, no direct evidence for papal ceremonial practice survives for the period of Pius' stay in Siena, and tentative comparisons must be drawn with Agostino Patrizi Piccolomini's somewhat later *Pontificale Romanum.*[54] Nevertheless, some interesting evidence emerges from Table 4, which summarizes the ceremonial or ritual events that were held in Siena during the pontificate of Pius II; it records those events that were significant enough to be commented upon by diarists or required extraordinary measures by the city's ruling officials. As such, it does not include those ceremonies that formed the standard ritual calendar.[55] Although a more extensive survey would need to be made to assess the degree to which the city's ceremonial activity increased in comparison with the periods immediately before and after the pontificate, it is nevertheless evident that what might be described as a 'ceremonial culture' overtook the city during these years, and was most marked in the long papal stay of 1460.[56]

During that year, special care was made in planning the major civic religious feasts of Corpus Domini and the Assumption, with committees elected to prepare the celebrations well in advance of the usual timetable that governed those feasts.[57] Moreover, the presence of the pope and *curia* inevitably resulted in far greater emphasis being placed on the religious calendar, so that on 2 February, just two days after arriving from Mantua, Pius II officiated at the Mass for the Feast of Candlemas in the cathedral and, in the words of Allegretto Allegretti 'personally handed out the candles to every citizen of the city of Siena'.[58] Allegretti was evidently struck by the unusual observance of the feast,

---

[53] The ceremonial calendar observed by the Republic might be summarized in 'quei giorni che la signoria esce dal palazzo', ASS *Concistoro* 2357, fol. 2r (1514). The 1545 *Statuto di Siena* lists 81 feasts to be honoured, see *L'ultimo statuto della Repubblica di Siena (1545)*, ed. M. Ascheri (Siena 1993), 366–70 (4.2).

[54] M. Dykmans, *L'Oeuvre de Patrizi Piccolomini ou le cérémonial papal de la première Renaissance* (Vatican City 1982), vol. 1, 9–15 and 21–26; see also below.

[55] ASS, *Concistoro* 2357, fol. 2r (1514); listed in my 'Cerimoniali per santi e feste'.

[56] It is my impression that patterns can be traced in the quantity and lavishness of the city's ritual activity, and that these closely follow the presence of important visitors to Siena, indicating that processions and other visible rituals in some sense 'played' to temporary spectators. A political motive for ritual 'performance' as entertainment is suggested by M. Mallett, 'Horse Racing and Politics in Lorenzo's Florence', in *Lorenzo the Magnificent. Culture and Politics*, ed. M. Mallett and N. Mann (London 1996), 253–62, who also comments on Siena's *palio*, 259.

[57] For Corpus Domini, see ASS, *Concistoro*, 562 fol. 24v (10 June), committee: Caterino Adorandi, Lodovico Tondi, Bartolomeo Landucci, Iacobo di Andrea Georgii. Assumption: ASS, *Concistoro* 563, fol. 3v (4 July), the officials were: Giovanni Cerretani, Lorenzo di Ghino di Bartolomeo, Gabriele Palmieri, Cristoforo di Nanni Gabrieli. The general observance of the feast in Siena is discussed in the essay by Machtelt Israëls in this volume.

[58] A. Allegretti, 'Ephemerides Senenses', 770, 'dè le candele di sua mano a tutti cittadini della città di Siena'.

Table 4 Ceremonial or ritual events held in Siena during the pontificate of Pius II Piccolomini (1458–64), selected from ASS *Concistoro and Consiglio Generale* as well as the diaries of Allegretto Allegretti and Tommaso Fecini

Date	Event/feast	Site	Papal/curial involvement	Civic participation
20 August 1458	News of Papal election in Rome	Campo and city	–	Bell-ringing and 3 day fair
3 September 1458	Papal coronation in Rome/Siena	Campo	–	Enact coronation Ceremony, *apparato*
24 Feb 14589	Pius II arrives from Rome	Porta Romana	Pope and 6 cardinals	Ceremonial of welcoming Signori and citizens.
4 March 1459	Pius II donation of 'Rose'	Duomo	Pius II mass and procession	
16 April 1459	Pius II raises Siena to Metropolitan	Duomo	Pope invests Antonio Piccolomini da Modanella	
23 April 1459	Pius II and court leave for Mantua	Porta Camollia	–	Ambassadors accompany Pius to Florence
4 January 1460	Marriage of Papal nieces in Spoleto	–	–	Donation of gifts by Signori. Orators sent to Spoleto.
31 January 1460	Pius II and Cardinals arrive from Mantua	Porta Camollia and Strada Romana	Ceremony of keys at the gate	Signori, religious and citizens present on Prato di Camollia
2 February 1460	Candlemass	Duomo	Pius II gives candles to citizens	Signori large gift to Pius II
6 March 1460	Pius II makes four cardinals	Duomo: concistory prepared	Pius II in Duomo	Signori pay homage
16 March 1460	Pius II makes two cardinals: include Francesco Todeschini Piccolomini	Duomo: concistory prepared	Pius II in Duomo	Signori pay homage
2 May 1460	Calling the dead	Church bells and town criers	–	Ban on 'suonare al morto' during the stay of the curia Funds assigned, orators named
5 May 1460	Visit of the Marquis of Mantua	–	–	
May 1460	Pentecost: Papal plenary indulgence	Duomo	Pius II sung mass and procession	All citizens and Signoria procession and mass
10 June 1460	Corpus Domini	Duomo	?	Provisions for observation of feast

Table 4 *Continued*

Date	Event/feast	Site	Papal/curial involvement	Civic participation
9 July 1460	–	–	–	Gift to the Cardinal of S. Pietro in Vincoli
15 August 1460	Assumption	Campo spectacle and Duomo mass	Pius II and Cardinals	Special provisions
19 August 1460	Anniversary of Pius II election	Campo	?	Pay for a bonfire and other signs of joy
10 September 1460	Pius II departs from Siena for Rome	Porta Romana	Pius II and cardinals	Escorted by Signori to S. Maria degli Angeli
10 June 1461	Visit of Cardinal of Rieti			Funds fixed to honour visit
16 August 1461	Canonisation of S. Caterina celebrated	Campo 'Paradiso' and procession to Fontebranda	Pope in Rome	Signoria, guilds and people
19 March 1462	Visit of Cardinal of Mantua			Funds fixed to honour visit
8 October 1462	Procession to chapel of S. Maria delle Grazie against plague	Duomo	–	Signoria and citizens
February 1463	Visit to Siena of Antonio Piccolomini, Duke of Amalfi	great honours paid	–	
May 1463	Feast of S. Caterina	Mass and procession	Pope returns to Siena from baths	Signoria and citizens
February 1464	Pope at Pienza: visit expected			Orators sent and rooms prepared
Spring 1464	Various provisions for the Crusades			Fund raising, gifts, embassies and processions
6 May 1464	Donation of the arm of St. John the Baptist	Mass and procession to Duomo	Pius II and cardinals	Signori, also 'gift' to Despot of Morea
11 May 1464	S. Bernardino	Mass and processions		Extraordinary provisions
April–June 1464	Numerous visitors: e.g. Signore di Piombino, King of Naples, Roberto di Sanseverino		?	Appropriate honours paid and accompanied to pope at baths

and his telling observation becomes eloquent when read in conjunction with the near-contemporary papal ceremonial, which established an increased emphasis on the active role of the pope in the Feast of the Purification, or Candlemas, and the distribution ceremony, during which the 'pontifex dat candelam'.[59]

The pope's presence, and the requirements of papal ceremonial, also significantly altered local observance in certain other respects; thus in May 1460, Pius awarded a plenary indulgence to all believers who visited the cathedral on the Feast of the Pentecost.[60] This extraordinary 'plenary indulgence of all sins, and removal of guilt and punishment in perpetuity,' led to the redaction of a new ceremonial by the civic authorities, which established that all the city officials, as well as guild members and citizens, should process to the cathedral to hear mass. Four officials oversaw preparations for the feast and ordered appropriate decorations for the Piazza Duomo and the interior of the cathedral.[61] In order to further enrich the cathedral's High Altar, and as a sign of the Commune's participation in the feast, the sacristan of the Palazzo Pubblico loaned sculptures of the Virgin Mary, Siena's privileged intercessor, and Saints Peter and Paul, the Apostolic papal patrons.[62] While only a temporary measure, this reordering of the High Altar's traditional arrangement around the civic icon of Duccio's *Maestà* visibly marked the papal presence and intervention in the religious life of the city.

Of course, the Pentecost indulgence in some ways transposed the special concessions awarded in Rome during Jubilee years to a Sienese venue, and Pius II's account of visitors coming to Siena from all over Central and Northern Italy suggests that the Pentecost was observed in a similar manner by the faithful.[63] The practical consequence of the arrival of so many pilgrims to Siena was a serious shortage of accommodation, as all inns and hospices were

---

[59] M. Dykmans, *L'Oeuvre de Patrizi Piccolomini*, II, 332–9, 342–3; the participation of the pope was so important as to warrant an alternative ceremonial to be observed in his absence, 339–42, as for other major feasts.

[60] The ceremonial rules for this extraordinary feast are published in my 'Cerimoniali per santi e feste', 182–4. ASS, *Statuto di Siena* 39, fol. 80–1 (16 May 1460), for 'indulgentia plenaria di tutti li peccati, et rimossione di colpa et pena in perpetuo duratura'.

[61] The development of this new ceremonial was recorded in both the city statutes and in the volumes of the *Consiglio Generale*: ASS, *Consiglio Generale* 228, fol. 242v–243v (16 May 1460) and ASS, *Statuto di Siena* 39, fol. 80–1 (16 May 1460). The officials and their tasks are noted in ASS, *Concistoro* 561, fol. 10v, (17 May): Baldino Tolomei, Salimbeni Petroni, Andrea di Cristoforo, Antonio di M° Luca. To these were added ASS, *Concistoro* 561, fol. 11v (21 May): Giovanni Falammi, Antonio Bellanti, Nicola di Battista, Iacobo Guidini.

[62] ASS, *Concistoro* 561, fol. 17v–18 (31 May), 'pro ornatu altarii dicte ecclesie'. It is interesting to note that four decades later the High Altar was permanently reordered around a sculptural group, which also led to the removal Duccio's panel, see F. Fumi, 'Nuovi documenti per gli angeli dell'altar maggiore del Duomo di Siena', *Prospettiva* 26, (1981), 9–25.

[63] A. S. Piccolomini, *I Commentarii*, I, 260–1 (IV.16), 'Tuscia, Liguria, Gallia, Vmbria ac Pyceno'. Such indulgences awarded to churches outside Rome were not infrequent however; other Sienese cases are those awarded at the oratory of Santo Sepolcro in 1460 (see G. Cecchini, 'La Cappella di San Sepolcro', *Terra di Siena*, 1959, 31–3) and at the church of Santa Maria in Portico di Fontegiusta by Sixtus IV in 1482 (see Biblioteca Apostolica Vaticana, *Chigi*, G. I. 8, fol. 13v–14r).

full, so that the city authorities allowed citizens to take foreigners into their homes, in order to stop them sleeping in the streets.[64]

On such occasions as the Candlemas and Pentecost feasts, the presence of the pope and *curia* not only heightened the degree of attention paid to the established religious calendar, but also overlaid papal needs for the processional use of public space onto traditional ceremonial routes.[65] This situation became all the more apparent on those occasions when exclusively curial events took place, such as the 6 and 16 March 1460, when Pius II appointed a number of new cardinals.[66] These ceremonies, which made such an impact on the local population as to warrant being recorded with a commemorative *Biccherna* panel (attributed to the young Francesco di Giorgio Martini), were reported by Pius in his *Commentarii*, where he noted that 'he [Pius] called a consistory in the cathedral and summoned to it the new cardinals'.[67] The election of the five cardinals, which included the young papal nephew, Francesco Todeschini Piccolomini, was also marked by a gift-giving ceremony by the city officials.[68] As Alessandro Angelini has noted, the *Biccherna* did not show the cathedral as the setting for the event, although Pius indicates clearly that the ceremony, which involved a papal speech, the investiture with the cardinals' hat, the kissing of the papal foot and a series of sung motets, took place in that church. These were followed by a procession in which the existing cardinals accompanied the new ones to the altar of the Virgin (probably the Madonna del Voto). After this the procession left the cathedral, entering the Bishop's Palace where the new cardinals participated in a public consistory, which is almost certainly the scene represented in the *Biccherna*.[69] Again, all stages of the investiture ceremony can be identified in the papal ceremonial, transposed from Rome to a Sienese setting.

One of the consequences of Pius II's appointment of his nephew as cardinal archbishop of Siena, was that the pope handed over the Bishop's Palace to

---

[64] ASS, *Concistoro* 561, fol. 17v–18 (31 May), 'Considerantes que proximo festo prope indulgentiam plenaria in ecclesia catedrali posita que incipit hodie hora vespertina ex deliberatione Summi Pontficis hodie facta et durat usque ad vesperas diei lune proximi abundantia multitudo magna forensium adeo que nis alia provideret cum hospitia et taberne [. . .]', rooms were made available 'per civitatem vagabundi nec reperient locum ubi se reponerent'.

[65] The most comprehensive relevant source for this is M. Dykmans, *L'Oeuvre de Patrizi Piccolomini*.

[66] ASS, *Concistoro* 561, fol. 6v–7 (6 March) and fol. 15 (16 March) and ASS, *Consiglio Generale* 228, fol. 208 and fol. 214v. The procedure and ceremonial (that specifies the rooms involved in the procedure) for the election of cardinals is described in M. Dykmans, *L'Oeuvre de Patrizi Piccolomini*, 133–40 and 140–64; see also C. Eubel, *Hierarchia*, II, 13–4 and n.3, for listing of the new cardinals: Angelo Capranica (Bishop of Rieti), Bernardo Eruli (Bishop of Spoleto), Niccolò Forteguerra (Bishop of Teano), Alessandro da Sassoferrato (Prior General of Augustinians), Francesco Todeschini Piccolomini (Bishop of Siena), Burchard Weisbriach (Bishop of Saltzburg).

[67] A. S. Piccolomini, *I Commentarii*, I, 255 (IV.11): 'indicto concistoro in ecclesia cathedrali iussit pontifex cardinales nouos'; for the *Biccherna*, see A. Angelini, 'Pio consacra cardinal suo nipote', in L. Bellosi ed., *Francesco di Giorgio*, 116–7.

[68] ASS, *Concistoro* 561, fol. 6v–7 (6 March) and fol. 15 (16 March).

[69] It is noteworthy that the *Biccherna* seems to evoke the ceremonial described for the public consistory of new cardinals, as described by Agostino Patrizi Piccolomini in M. Dykmans, *L'Oeuvre de Patrizi Piccolomini*, 143–4.

Francesco as his residence, himself moving to the palace of Bartolo di Andrea, probably in the Casato di Sopra and thus not far from the 'court' precinct.[70] During the summer months, however, as both Allegretto Allegretti and Pius himself report, the pope chose to reside between the suburban hillside site of the Osservanza and the monastic complex of San Francesco, as both locations were more open to breezes and the views of the country-side, while also being well connected and close to the city centre.[71] The move helped to establish the young Cardinal Piccolomini at the centre of the city's religious and curial life, by placing him in the palace that had served briefly as the papal palace. Pius's curial officials remained around the Duomo, and as is also noted in the *Commentarii*, the pope continued in his official duties, preferring where possible to hold consistorial and private meetings, as well as public audiences in open-air venues, such as a small wood at the Osserv-anza and by a fountain built for him in the gardens of San Francesco.[72] While Pius' pastoral consistories are a far cry from the highly articulated hierarchy of architectural spaces described for the Vatican, the range of papal engagements outlined by Pius, closely resembles those described in Patrizi's manual.[73]

Such brief notices as these confirm that, although far from Rome, the life of the papal court continued to operate around the person of the pope and that political and ceremonial activity was located in the venues chosen by Pius II. Thus, as Didier Boisseuil has shown, the cardinals had to gather where Pius chose to be, even if this meant convening a consistory on the banks of the river, when the pope was at the thermal baths of Petriolo or San Filippo.[74] That such would have been the case is perhaps not surprising, particularly to scholars of the itinerant courts of Northern Europe that oper-ated on the move with a bureaucratic self-sufficiency that was also vital for the papacy during its 'itinerant' phases.[75] In Siena, this means that we should consider not only the ritualized movement of the cardinals to the cathedral

---

[70] ASS, *Concistoro*, 2480, fol. 27; ASS *Lira* 136, fol. 6.

[71] A. Allegretti, 'Ephemerides Senenses', 770; O. Malavolti, *Dell'historia di Siena*, Venice 1599, III, 64; A. S. Piccolomini, *I Commentarii*, 259–60 (IV. 15) and 262–3 (IV.18).

[72] A. S. Piccolomini, *I Commentarii*, I, 258 (IV.14), at 'la Capriola', 'non tamen aut signaturam aut secreat consistoria pretermisit neque audientiam negavit aduentantibus. in nemore, quod perpetuo uiret lauro et ilice frequenti, auditorium sibi constituit, loco aprico sub monte'. For an act of vandalism on the fountain, see ASS, *Concistoro* 562, fol. 9 (12 July), 'Destruxit ut fregat fontem de novo factam prope conventum dicti Sancti Francisci'.

[73] M. Dykmans, *L'Oeuvre de Patrizi Piccolomini*, 164–8.

[74] D. Boisseuil, *Le thermalisme en Toscane à la fin du moyen, âge: les bains siennois de la fine du XIII* au début du *XVI siècle* (Rome 2002), 181–5, with references to the *Commentarii*.

[75] Such issues of relocation of the papal court and establishment of new models of centralisation are key themes in B. Guillemain, *La cour pontificale d'Avignon*. Pius II had extensive first-hand experience of the Imperial court and chancery, and it is intersting to note that a much reduced expenditure was registered back in Rome, where a 'skeleton staff' was kept on in the absence of the pope, see ASR, *Camerale I: Spese minute di Palazzo (Spenditore cubiculario)*, 1476, fol. 1r, bis: 'Questo e lo libro tenuto per me Nastoccio Saracini, vice maestro di palazo di N S, restato in Roma. Nel quale saranno scripte tutte lo spese si faranno in detto palazo per lo governo de la famiglia restata [. . .]'.

on feast days, but also the far more regular traffic that connected the palaces appointed as cardinals' residences to the Bishop's Palace. These patterns of usage naturally created new, privileged pathways through the city. These routes had in part been prepared in advance by *Ornato*-enforced policies with this intention, and were also to result in a continued process of urban beautification.[76] It can thus be argued that the temporary presence of the pope and *curia* in Siena marked the city in a permanent fashion, redrawing or at least underlining processional routes, and providing an important catalyst for the architectural renewal of those streets.

Università degli Studi di Siena

[76] The improvements to the area between Piazza Tolomei and San Francesco would seem to have been prompted by exactly such altered usage, as women and pilgrims were forced to pass through down-at-heel streets where gamblers and prostitutes clustered; see ASS, *Concistoro* 2125, fol. 23 and ASS, *Consiglio Generale* 230, 68–9 (18 December 1463), cited by P. Pertici, *La città magnificata*, 79–80.

6
Peace-making rituals in fifteenth-century Siena

CHRISTINE SHAW

In the last decades of the fifteenth century, Siena had the reputation of being one of the most factious and divided cities in Italy. One way in which the Sienese tried to quiet factional conflict and bring the citizens together, was by the administration of solemn communal oaths to lay aside enmities and keep the peace. Such oaths were imposed on several occasions in the 1480s and in 1494, and earlier in the century as well. They were the central feature of ceremonies designed to make public demonstration of the promised reconciliation and to impress upon the participants the solemnity of the obligations they were undertaking. These were not routine ceremonies: they were used when discord and rancour had been running high. Aspirations to union among citizens, the promotion of the virtues of concord and peace in the city, were political commonplaces in Renaissance Italy, and the Sienese were scarcely unusual in their outward espousal of such values. But the frequency of the ceremonies to which they resorted in their attempts to promote and enforce these values was unusual.

Analogous oaths to make peace with rivals and enemies were taken by members of political factions in other cities, in ceremonies that were sometimes made more solemn by the celebration of a mass or by exhortations from a preacher or an oration by a representative of the government. On occasion public embraces, perhaps a kiss of peace, would be exchanged by members of the different factions.

In Lucca in 1392, for example, at a time when political divisions among the citizens ran deep, the Gonfaloniere di Giustizia and the Anziani ordered that all members of the Consiglio Generale should take an oath renouncing faction, with their hand on a crucifix held by an Augustinian, maestro Stefano d'Arezzo, who gave a sermon on the benefits of peace and concord.[1] When the Mediceans were under challenge in Florence in May 1466, it was ordered that all citizens aged twenty-four and over who had been considered eligible to hold office in the Signoria[2] should come to the chapel of the Palazzo della Signoria, and there, with their hand on the

---

[1] C. Meek, *Lucca 1369–1400: Politics and Society in an Early Renaissance City-State* (Oxford, 1978), 266; *Le croniche di Giovanni Sercambi Lucchese*, ed. Salvatore Bongi, 3 vols. (Lucca, 1892), I, 270–1.
[2] That is, the *veduti* for the 'Tre Maggiori'.

missal on which the Signori took their oath of office, should swear not to take part in any private political gatherings, to do justice impartially if they held office, to lay aside all enmities, and to be absolved from any private obligations concerning the government of Florence they had entered into.[3]

Such oaths could be imposed in subject towns and cities as well. All citizens of the city and contado of Pavia aged eighteen and over were ordered by a Milanese ducal decree in 1440 to take an oath before government officials, renouncing allegiance to the Guelf and Ghibelline factions.[4] To prepare for the return of political exiles to Assisi in 1425, Pope Martin V ordered the papal legate to organize a ceremony in his palace in Perugia in which the exiles and their rivals from Assisi swore to keep the peace.[5] A ceremony of reconciliation between the factions of Orvieto in January 1461 was ostensibly the outcome of an initiative by the leaders of the Melcorini faction, but the ground had been well prepared by a number of sermons on the virtues and benefits of peace delivered by preachers sent by Pope Pius II and by Pius himself when he visited Orvieto in 1460. He had also ordered the papal governor, the Sienese Francesco Luti, to promote reconciliation between the factions. When peace was formally proclaimed in a *parlamento* (a general meeting of the citizens), the governor gave an oration, members of the rival factions tearfully embraced, and bells were rung and bonfires lit throughout the city.[6]

Pope Julius II brought extra solemnity to his pacification of the factions of Perugia in September 1506, not only by presiding over the ceremony he ordered to be held in the church of San Francesco, but also by the consecration of two hosts, one of which was reserved after the celebration of mass. Members of the factions were brought up to the pope, a papal notary recorded their undertakings not to offend against each other in future, and they exchanged a kiss of peace. Then, in pairs composed of members of either faction, they approached the altar, took an oath together with their hands touching the reserved host which was covered by a fine cloth, and kissed the pope's foot. Julius had wanted this ceremony to begin with a thirty-minute sermon by Egidio da Viterbo exhorting the pope to bring peace to the people, but the preacher ignored his instructions and merely lauded

---

[3] N. Rubinstein, *The Government of Florence under the Medici (1434 to 1494)*, 2nd edn. (Oxford, 1997), 177–8; *Ricordi storici di Filippo di Cino Rinuccini dal 1282 al 1460 colla continuazione di Alamanno e Neri suoi figli fino al 1506*, ed. G. Aiazzi (Florence, 1840), XCIX; G. Pampaloni, 'Il giuramento pubblico in Palazzo Vecchio a Firenze e un patto giurato degli antimedicei (maggio 1466)', *Bullettino Senese di Storia Patria* (hereafter BSSP), 71 (1964), 212–38.

[4] L. Osio (ed.), *Documenti diplomatici tratti dagli archivi milanesi*, 3 vols. (Milan, 1864–72), III, 222.

[5] F. Guardabassi, 'La pace fra gli "Extrinseci" e gli "Intrinseci" di Assisi dell' 11 febbraio del 1425', *Bollettino della R. Deputazione di Storia Patria per l'Umbria*, 32 (1935), 233–53.

[6] The peace agreement contained detailed provisions about the structure of the civic government as well as clauses concerning the relations between the factions. L. Fumi, 'Pio II (Enea Silvio Piccolomini) e la pace di Orvieto', *Studi e documenti di storia e diritto*, 6 (1885), 249–72.

the pope. A similar ceremony had been held by Julius in Viterbo a year before.[7]

These examples show that the rituals surrounding and solemnizing the communal oath-takings that will be analyzed here were by no means peculiar to Siena. The Sienese rituals brought together elements that belonged to a common tradition.[8] But while the ceremonies in other cities were isolated episodes, in fifteenth-century Siena they were staged repeatedly. Consequently, they provide an unusual – perhaps unique – opportunity to examine a series of such rituals in one city, one political community, and to compare them. No set pattern emerges. Like those who organized the rituals in other cities, the Sienese chose different elements each time from the repertoire associated with such events. The heart of the ritual, the oath, also varied each time, with the terms of each oath arising out of the immediate political circumstances.

The oaths were imposed on all *riseduti*. As members for life of the Consiglio del Popolo, *riseduti* could be said to have constituted the political elite of Siena, although one which numbered several hundred men. If the *riseduti* were united, the government was secure. The oath was usually taken in the palace of the Signoria in a meeting of the Consiglio del Popolo, and taken individually. Rather than signify assent as members of an assembly, each man swore singly to abide by its terms.

The principal focus here will be the ceremony of 6 November 1482, a particularly elaborate one. In it, members of the *monti* of the *Riformatori* and the *Nove* swore to forgive past injuries and not to offend or attack one another in future, while the members of the *Monte del Popolo* swore to act as guarantors of this pact. The ceremony took place during the period between the return to the city in the summer of 1482 of exiled members of the *Monte dei Riformatori* and the readmission of their *monte* to the regime (from which they had been expelled in June 1480), and the expulsion of the *Monte dei Nove* from the regime in February 1483 and the exile of many of its members.[9] This was the period when the *Monte del Popolo* was becoming increasingly influential. Many of the returning *Riformatori* blamed the *Noveschi* for

---

[7] L. Frati (ed.), *Le due spedizioni militari di Giulio II tratte dal Diario di Paride Grassi bolognese* (Bologna, 1886), 47; C. Pinzi, *Storia della Città di Viterbo lungo il medioevo*, 4 vols. (Rome, 1889–1913), IV, 405–11; C. Shaw, *Julius II: The Warrior Pope* (Oxford, 1993), 153–4, 157.

[8] I do not know of any general survey of these rituals in Renaissance Italy. C. L. Polecritti, *Preaching Peace in Renaissance Italy: Bernardino of Siena and His Audience* (Washington DC, 2000), has a chapter (84–124) on 'Peacemaking: Community and Coercion', but she does not distinguish clearly between the pacification of political factions and the pacification of private feuds and quarrels en masse, and is mostly concerned with the latter. She comments that 'Analysis of the collective peacemaking ritual is difficult, given that few sources provide more than a brief synopsis of what actually took place' (95), but she does not consider the Sienese rituals analysed here.

[9] For summaries of these events, see C. Shaw, *The Politics of Exile in Renaissance Italy* (Cambridge, 2000), 42–6; A. K. Isaacs, 'Cardinali e "spalagrembi". Sulla vita politica a Siena fra il 1480 e il 1487', in *La Toscana al tempo di Lorenzo il Magnifico: Politica, Economia, Cultura, Arte*, 3 vols (Pisa, 1996), III, 1018–33; for a detailed account, see C. Shaw, 'Politics and institutional innovation in Siena, 1480–1498', *BSSP*, 103 (1996), 45–82.

their troubles, the *Noveschi* felt threatened, and some *Popolari* were using this opportunity to give their *monte* a greater share in the regime.

The ceremony of November 1482 will be compared with others that took place in February 1429 and July 1439, though the political context of these two is not clear; in March 1480, a couple of months before the expulsion of the *Monte dei Riformatori*, and in September 1480, just after the consequent reorganization of the regime; and in September 1484, when the drive for dominance of some members of the *Monte del Popolo* was causing increasing unease and tension in the city. Comparison will also be made with analogous ceremonies.[10] The first was in April 1457, when there had been an experiment with largely replacing the Consiglio del Popolo with a more restricted council, the Balia Maggiore, which had proved an unpopular move. This oath was taken by all members of the Balia Maggiore just before they agreed provisions to enlarge the membership of their council to take in nearly all those members of the Consiglio del Popolo who had been excluded from it.[11] The second took place in April 1459, when the *Monte dei Gentiluomini* were being admitted, under pressure from the Sienese Pope Pius II, to what was defined as a popular government.[12] The third analogous ceremony took place in the cathedral, in December 1494, when members of the *Monti dei Nove* and *del Popolo*, unhappy with recent developments in the government, made a written agreement (which apparently ran to eight pages) and took an oath to observe it.[13]

The ceremony of 6 November 1482 marked a significant stage in the gradual dominance of Sienese politics by the *Monte del Popolo*. In late July 1482 it had already been declared that, because of the benevolence and sincerity of the *Monte del Popolo* in seeking the peace and tranquillity of all citizens, in future they were to be given precedence when, for instance, offices were listed by *monti*, to be followed by the Nove and Riformatori. The previous, traditional order had been *Nove, Riformatori, Popolo*. At the same time, the *Monte del Popolo* were to be given an extra prior in the Concistoro. Whereas by long-established practice the three government *monti* had three priors each, in future the *Monte del Popolo* were to have four to the three each of the *Nove* and *Riformatori*.[14] Rather than unite to resist this assumption of superiority by the *Monte del Popolo*, the *Noveschi* and *Riformatori* continued to regard each other with suspicion and resentment. Problems over the

---

[10] For a private oath, taken by 144 men ostensibly for the preservation of the *reggimento*, in the early 1450s, see P. Pertici, 'Una "coniuratio" del reggimento di Siena nel 1450', *BSSP*, 99 (1992), 9–47.

[11] See C. Shaw, *Popular Government and Oligarchy in Renaissance Italy* (forthcoming); for the Balia maggiore, see G. Prunai and S. De'Colli, 'La Balia dagli inizi del XIII secolo fino alla invasione francese (1789)', *BSSP*, 65 (1958), 59–61.

[12] I. Polverini Fosi, '"La comune, dolcissima patria": Siena e Pio II', in *I ceti dirigenti nella Toscana del Quattrocento* (Impruneta, 1987), 509–21; Shaw, *Popular Government and Oligarchy*.

[13] Shaw, 'Politics and institutional innovation', *BSSP*, 104 (1997), 275–7; A. Allegretti, 'Diarii delle cose sanesi del suo tempo', *Rerum Italicarum Scriptores*, 23 (1733), cols. 836–7.

[14] Archivio di Stato di Siena (hereafter ASS), *Balia* 26, fol. 53v: 27 July 1482.

restitution of property to former exiles were also generating bad blood, and there was trouble when the time came, in late October, for the Consiglio del Popolo to decide on the appointment of a new Balia.[15] *Popolari riseduti* meeting alone on 29 October decided that there should be a Balia of *Popolari* only, and that the *Monte del Popolo* should act as peacemakers between the *Riformatori* and the *Noveschi*.[16]

It was this Balia that devised the form of the oath and the ceremony that took place on 6 November, which were approved unanimously by a very full meeting of the Consiglio del Popolo (390 members were present), before the *riseduti* proceeded to take the oath.[17] The proceedings began with a solemn mass of the Holy Spirit. When the mass was over, the host was left in the tabernacle on the altar. Then came a sermon, long and fervent, by an Augustinian friar, Mariano di Ghinazzo, a theologian and renowned preacher, who had been brought to Siena from San Gimigniano the day before expressly to deliver this. According to the official account, he moved his audience to tears. The diarist Cristoforo Cantoni recorded that he reminded the audience of 'very many examples of the ancient Romans, the Carthaginians and others worthy of memory'.[18] His sermon was followed by an 'elegant oration' ('elegantem orationem') by Gianbattista de' Caccialupi, who was lecturing on civil law at the university, and by some 'fine words' ('aliquibus verbis ornate dictis') from the Capitano del Popolo, Guidantonio Buoninsegni. All the speakers urged the members of the council to make and keep the peace.[19] This sermon and the speeches all came before the form of the oath was read out – an unusual amount of preparation to put the councillors in the right frame of mind.

The ceremony for the oath taken in February 1429 was also preceded by a mass of the Holy Spirit, 'so that the Lord God should be favourable to all our acts',[20] as was the oath before the vote on the expansion of the Balia maggiore in April 1457.[21] No mass was celebrated before the oath taken in July 1439, although the Bishop of Siena was present in the Consiglio del Popolo, and exhorted the members to union and concord.[22] Gianbattista de' Caccialupi, then a judge in Siena, made a speech before the oath of 25 September 1480, eloquently urging the 420 councillors who had been

---

[15] Balie acting as the major executive committee were not yet a permanent feature of Sienese government. They were elected for limited periods, generally three to six months, and had to be agreed by the Consiglio del Popolo.

[16] Isaacs, 'Cardinali e "spalagrembi"', 1025–9; Shaw, 'Politics and institutional innovation', 103 (1996), 57–68.

[17] ASS, *Concistoro* 697, fol. 4r–v.

[18] 'reducendo ad memoria alli astanti moltissimi esempli delli antiqui Romani, Cartaginesi et altri degni di memoria': C. Cantoni, *Frammento di un diario senese (1479–1483)*, ed. A. Lisini and F. Jacometti, *RR.II.SS.*, 15, part 6 (Bologna, 1939), 926.

[19] ASS, *Concistoro* 697, fol. 5r–v.

[20] 'accioche misser Domenendio sia favorevole a ogni nostro acto': ASS, Concistoro 377, fol. 27v.

[21] ASS, *Statuti di Siena* 40, fol. 44v.

[22] ASS, *Concistoro* 441, fol. 23v.

assembled to live virtuously and to have a care for the welfare of the republic.[23] Eloquence from the Capitano del Popolo, Tone di Francesco Salvi, was
used to prepare the members of the Consiglio del Popolo to take the oath
on 8 September 1484, calling on the citizens to live in concord, observing
justice, and in fear of God: this was the way to keep the republic in *libertà*.[24]

Not only was the preparation for the oath in November 1482 unusually
complex, the terms of the oath were too. Generally all those present would
take the same oath. Those who took part in the ceremonies in 1429 and 1439
swore to put aside, pardon and forget all injuries and enmities that had
arisen for political reasons.[25] In 1457, 1459, and March and September 1480
the primary clause of the oath was a pledge of loyalty to the current regime.
The members of the Balia Maggiore were to swear not to form any cabals,
but to attend to the conservation of the existing government and union of
the citizens,[26] while the *Gentiluomini* in 1459 swore obedience and reverence
to 'the present popular government'.[27] In March 1480 those present swore to
preserve the regime of the three *monti*, the *Nove*, *Popolo* and *Riformatori*.[28]
Many of the same men would have been among those taking the oath in
September 1480 to be faithful to the new popular regime (from which the
Riformatori had been excluded), to keep its secrets, and to reveal any plots
against it that came to their knowledge.[29] The oath of September 1484 had
three parts: not to do or say anything against the decrees that had been
passed against the *Monte dei Nove* and those who had been exiled; not to do
or say anything against the present regime; and not to form any cabals.[30]

In November 1482, different forms of oath were prescribed for the *Nove*
and *Riformatori*, and for the *Monte del Popolo*. The *Noveschi* were to swear to
put aside all offences and grievances, public or private, general or particular,
against the *Monte dei Riformatori* as a body or against individual *Riformatori*.
Reciprocally, the *Riformatori* were to foreswear all grievances against the *Noveschi*. Members of both *monti* were to pledge to put aside any resentment they
might feel against the *Popolari* for any interventions they had made between
them, any protection offered to one against the other, or any opposition to

---

[23] 'exortando omnes ad bene beateque vivendum et ad consulendum tuendum et manutenendum reipublicae
Senensium cum suis ornatissimis verbis et amplo sermone': ASS, *Concistoro* 684, fol. 13v.

[24] ASS, *Concistoro* 708, fols. 4v–5r.

[25] 'dimenticare, rimettere et perdonare ogni ingiuria hinc inde intervenuta et nata fra essi cittadini
popolari da ogi indrieto per qualunche ragone o cagone di regimento, et di quelle dimenticare, et più non
ricordarsi né per alcuno modo segreto o palese attendare ad alcuna vendetta né perseghuitare perlo innanzi
alcuna passione overo setta, ma con perfectissima charita amarsi et abracarsi': ASS, *Concistoro* 377, fol. 27v.
The actual text of the oath taken in July 1439 was not recorded in the deliberations of the Concistoro, but it
had been decided that the oath would be along these lines. (ASS *Concistoro* 441, fol. 21v.: 24 July 1439)

[26] 'rectum et bonum statum presentis regiminis et ad conservationem presentis status et unionem civium':
ASS, *Balia* 4, fol. 6v.

[27] 'presenti regimini populari': ASS, *Concistoro* 555, fol. 38r–v.

[28] 'ad defensionem manutentionem et conservationem montium predictorum et presentis regiminis': ASS,
Concistoro 681, fol. 6r.

[29] ASS, *Concistoro* 684, fol. 13v.

[30] ASS, *Concistoro* 708, fol. 5r–v.

their actions or desires. The *Noveschi* and *Riformatori* were also to swear never to do anything against the members of the other *monti*, prompted by public or private rancour. For their part, the *Popolari* were to swear to go to the assistance of the *Nove* or *Riformatori* if they came under attack, and to use weapons in their defence if need be. All the *riseduti* of all the *monti* were to swear to be faithful to one another, and to the present, newly-restored regime of three *monti*. They were not to form any conspiracies or cabals, or to create any disturbances or cause any trouble to the new regime.[31]

After the terms of the oath had been read out to the assembled *riseduti*, the doors of the council chamber were closed, and all the members of the council who were present moved from the upper part of the chamber towards the door, took the oath and then moved to the lower end of the chamber.[32] Members of the Concistoro took the oath first, followed by the other councillors according to their office and status.[33] Each knelt before the altar bearing the consecrated host and a missal open at the picture of the Crucified Christ, placing their hand on the missal as they took the oath.[34]

It was the usual practice for those taking such oaths to place their hand on the missal as they did so; the presence of the consecrated host on the altar in 1482 gave the gesture added solemnity. In 1429, the missal was to be held by the Capitano del Popolo: in essence, the oath was to be taken 'in the hands' of the Capitano, who was to hold the missal 'for greater devotion'.[35] The original plan for the oath of July 1439 stipulated that the oath was to be taken in the hands of the prior of the Concistoro (the chairman for the day) holding the missal, although in the account of the ceremony itself, the missal was said to be held by the bishop.[36] It was 'in the hands' of the prior of the Concistoro that those taking the oath on September 1480 were to swear; on this occasion he held a copy of the gospels, open at the page depicting the Crucified Christ.[37] Gentiluomini taking the oath of loyalty to the popular government in 1459 swore on the gospels as well as a missal, either open at the depiction of the crucifixion or with a crucifix placed on it,[38] and each

---

[31] ASS, *Concistoro* 697, fols. 5v–6v. Members of the *Monte dei Gentiluomini* and *Monte dei Dodici* who had been assigned to the *Nove* or *Riformatori* at that time took the oath with the members of their assigned *monte*. Thus, for example, Agnolo d'Azolino Ugurgieri, a Gentiluomo admitted to the *reggimento* in 1480, took the oath with the Nove (*ibid.*, fol. 12r), and Alessandro Sozzini, son of the renowned jurist Mariano Sozzini and a member of the *Monte dei Dodici* first admitted to the *reggimento* that year, took the oath with the *Riformatori*, as did the *Dodicino* doctor, Maestro Francesco di Ser Nino Nini (*ibid.*, fol. 15v).

[32] 'iverunt a medio supra dictae sale versus dictam portam . . . euntes exinde versus partem inferiorem dictae salae' (*ibid.*, fols. 6v–7r).

[33] 'secundum dignitates officiorum, graduum et personarum' (*ibid.*, fol. 6v).

[34] *ibid.*, fols. 5v, 6v–7r.

[35] 'giurare nelle mani del Magnifico Capitano del Popolo, in sul messale per più divotione': ASS, *Concistoro* 377, fol. 27v.

[36] ASS, *Concistoro* 441, fols. 21v, 23v.

[37] 'iurando . . . in manibus Magnifici prioris super figuram crucifixi nostri salvatoris et super sacris litteris' (specified earlier in the account as the gospels): ASS, *Concistoro* 684, fol. 13v.

[38] 'cum crucefisso Domino Nostro super messali': ASS, *Concistoro* 555, fol. 38r–v.

received a kiss of peace from the Capitano del Popolo.[39] The oath of 1429 was to be followed by the exchange of a kiss of peace with the priest present, as a sign of true peace and concord and in demonstration of the wish to observe the promises made.[40]

An oath taken on a picture of the crucifix in the missal and a kiss also featured in the ceremony of reconciliation between the *Noveschi* and *Popolari* in 1494, although the ceremony differed from the usual pattern in some important respects. To begin with, it took place in the cathedral, not in the palace of the Signoria. The *Noveschi* assembled in the bishop's palace next to the cathedral and the *Popolari* assembled in the hospital of Santa Maria della Scala facing the west end. Articles of agreement which had been worked out in discussions between them were read out and approved, and then as night fell, the two groups made their way to the cathedral, where the *Nove* stood on the sacristy side of the altar up to the choir, and the *Popolari* ranged themselves on the opposite side. Cardinal Francesco Piccolomini, Archbishop of Siena, who had helped to facilitate the discussions, entered from the sacristy and sat in the middle, before the altar. After a short homily by the cardinal (mostly in Italian but also citing in Latin the texts 'This is the day the Lord has made . . .', and 'Glory to God in the highest, and on earth peace . . .'), expressing his pleasure at the assembly, and at the goodwill he saw between the two *monti*, the terms of the agreement were read out, and then the oath. As notaries from the *Nove* and the *Popolari* made a note of their names, pairs of men, *Novesco* and *Popolare*, took the oath on the crucifix in the missal, before exchanging a kiss of peace. While this was proceeding, the bells rang, a Te Deum was sung and the organs played. To add to the effect, all this was taking place at night, by torchlight.[41]

Generally, there was no further ceremony after the oath. In 1459, the Gentiluomini went with the Concistoro to the cathedral, where Pius II, who was in Siena at that time, was receiving ambassadors from the emperor. In his memoirs, Pius makes no mention of this, and in fact rather plays down the whole episode, perhaps because, as he wrote, he had not got all that he wanted concerning the admission of the *Gentiluomini* to full participation in the regime.[42]

In November 1482, the ritual of oath-taking was followed by further, dramatic, ceremonies. After the Concistoro and all the councillors accompanied Fra Mariano as he took the tabernacle containing the host to the sacristy of the palace, they then processed to the cathedral three by three, each trio including a Popolare placed between a *Novesco* and a *Riformatore*. By then it was nightfall, so presumably this procession would have taken place by

[39] *ibid.*

[40] 'in segno di vera pace et concordia et in demonstratione di volere observare le chose predecte il baco et obsculo dela Santa Pace': ASS, *Concistoro* 377, fols. 27v–28r.

[41] Allegretti, 'Diarii delle cose sanesi', cols. 836–7.

[42] E. S. Piccolomini (Pius II), *I Commentarii*, ed. L. Totaro, 2 vols (Milan, 1984), I, 329–31.

torchlight, and spectators followed the councillors to the cathedral. There all knelt before the main altar, praying that God and Christ would keep them in peace, before moving to the altar of the Virgin where the councillors, 'and many others, who had come there following them for joy', knelt again. A Te Deum was sung, accompanied by the organ, and there was an oration ('oratio') in praise of the Virgin. Then the Concistoro and all the councillors returned to the palace, while the bells of the palace and of all the churches of Siena were rung for joy.[43]

At the suggestion of Fra Mariano, the Concistoro ordered further processions to be held on three consecutive days: one on Friday, in honour of the Holy Cross, in which the relic of a nail from the Cross kept by the hospital of Santa Maria della Scala was carried; the second on Saturday in honour of the Virgin in which the painting of the *Madonna delle Grazie* ('degli Occhi Grossi') was carried from the cathedral; and the third, on the Sunday, in honour of the Trinity, bearing a consecrated host. All the clergy, almost all the citizens – especially those who were qualified for political office ('regentibus') – and many women took part in these processions, and everyone said that they had never seen the like, it was noted.[44]

The notary who compiled the official record of these ceremonies and processions for the registers of the Concistoro emphasized the devotion with which the oath had been taken, and the joy of those who witnessed the public demonstration of reconciliation between the *Nove* and *Riformatori*, and the mediating role of the *Popolari*. But how seriously were these and the other, similar, ceremonies taken? What effect can they be perceived to have had? They were clearly meant to be more than a theatrical reminder of the traditional civic values of unity and concord among the citizens, and of injunctions against conspiracies and cabals.

Even though hundreds of men took part in the swearing of the oaths in these ceremonies, on every occasion each man took the oath individually, with a religious sanction to bind his conscience. Sometimes the oaths were also to be taken by those who were not present at the ceremony. In 1429 and 1439, all *riseduti* were to take the oath; in 1484, all citizens, *riseduti* or not; in 1482, all 'popolari', which meant, apparently, all members of the *popolo*, not just members of the *Monte del Popolo*. Lists of those who took the oaths survive for 1439, 1482 and 1484,[45] and presumably a list would have had to be drawn up in 1429, too, if there was to be a check on who took the oath. Particular care was taken in 1482 to enforce the order. On 8 November, the Balìa decreed that any members of the Consiglio del Popolo who had not taken part in 'the council of reconciliation' ('in consilio reconciliationis') and had not taken the

[43] ASS, *Concistoro* 697, fol. 7r–v.

[44] *ibid.*, fol. 7v; ASS, MS D58, 'Diario senese del 1479 al 1500, scritto da uno contemporaneo', fol. 38v. According to the diarist Cantoni, the procession on the Sunday was in honour of the Holy Spirit (Cantoni, *Frammento di un diario senese*, 926).

[45] ASS, *Concistoro* 441, fols. 24r–25v (1439); *Concistoro* 697, fols. 8r–17v (1482); *Concistoro* 708, fols. 33r–41r.

oath could not be included in the scrutiny of names to be placed in the electoral purses, unless they could demonstrate good cause why they had not done so. A placard was to be displayed in the chamber of the Concistoro, giving the words of the oath, and any new *riseduto* could not take up his office in the Concistoro unless he took the oath first.[46] A week later, on 15 November, the Balìa decreed that the Concistoro should order those who had not yet taken the oath to come to the council on Sunday morning, and swear it after hearing mass in the chapel; and on 20 November ordered that the Concistoro should arrange the administration of the oath to the *Popolari*, again after the celebration of mass.[47] Perhaps because the numbers involved in this extension of the oath were too great, three days later the Balìa decided that the *Popolari* of the different *terzi* should take the oath on different days.[48] A month after the original ceremony, the Balìa was still ordering the Concistoro to pursue those who had not yet complied. If the recalcitrant were members of the Consiglio Generale they could not participate in it, or hold any office, until they had sworn.[49]

Spiritual sanctions could also be invoked, by stressing the penalties that would be incurred by those who broke an oath that they had taken before God. The kiss of peace exchanged with the priest during the ceremony in 1429 was included, it was specifically stated, so that 'if anyone is acting in a spirit of insincerity, he will know he is cheating not only the world, but God and his own conscience.'[50] Terrible curses were called down on the heads of anyone who might break his oath in 1482, 1484 and 1494. The same curse was used in 1482 and 1484: contravention would bring down 'the wrath of God and of the Holy Trinity and of all the court of Paradise'; the oathbreaker would be in the hands of the devil, and he and his descendants would be subject to the ills God inflicted on malefactors, including the curse of Dathan and Abiram,[51] and the punishment of Judas – as well as the penalties ordained against seditious, pernicious and pestilential citizens, who disturbed peaceful government.[52] This oath, one diarist commented in 1482, was 'truly very dangerous for the welfare of souls and of all the city, and unworthy of grave and mature government, especially because of the nature of the hatreds and dissensions between the factions'.[53] Clearly, he was

---

[46] ASS, *Balìa* 26, fol. 139r.

[47] *ibid.*, fols. 149v, 153r.

[48] *ibid.*, fol. 153r.

[49] *ibid.*, fol. 159v.

[50] 'se niuno colo animo meno che schietto venisse a tale acto congnoscha non aver inganato solo il mondo ma idio et la propria conscientia': ASS, *Concistoro* 377, fol. 28r.

[51] Dathan and Abiram challenged the authority of Moses and Aaron; the earth opened and swallowed them up (Numbers 16: 1–30).

[52] ASS, *Concistoro* 697, fol. 6v; *Concistoro* 708, fol. 5v.

[53] V. Nuscis, 'Una nuova cronaca senese sulla crisi degli anni ottanta', in *La Toscana al tempo di Lorenzo il Magnifico: Politica, Economia, Cultura, Arte*, 3 vols (Pisa, 1996), III, 1142: 'veramente pericolosissima per la salute dell' anime et di tucta la città, né degna di grave et maturo governo, ateso potissime la natura di tali odii et dissentioni delle parti'.

impressed by its force, but pessimistic about its chances of success. The terms of the curses attached to the oath in 1494 seem to have been even more terrific, including that no spiritual benefit could save the soul of any transgressor, even at the moment of his death. Allegretto Allegretti, who was present as an observer – he was a *Dodicino* and so would not have taken part in the ceremony – said that he had never heard, and did not believe that there had ever been, a more stupendous and horrible oath. Nevertheless, like the other diarist, he was doubtful whether the ceremony would bring peace to the city.[54]

Cantoni also commented on the impression made by the curses, while indicating the practical inefficacy of the oaths. Not only the curse connected with the oath in November 1482, but also the maledictions called down on the heads of those who might transgress it by Fra Mariano in his sermon, terrified those present at the ceremony, he wrote. Yet the three processions ordered were, according to his account, in part intended as expiation for failures to keep previous oaths. Thus the first procession was to be in honour of the Holy Cross, offended by the breaking of the oath of March 1480 to defend and maintain all three government *monti*, the *Nove, Popolari* and *Riformatori*, which had been followed three months later by the expulsion of the *Riformatori* from the regime. The Virgin, the dedicatee of the second procession, had been offended by the plots against the welfare of her city, while the Holy Spirit – according to Cantoni, the dedicatee of the third procession – had been offended by how previous oaths had been observed, or rather, not observed.[55]

In fact, for all the emotional impact these processions and ceremonies in November 1482 were said to have had, they did little to bring about better relations between the *monti*. Only a few months later, many *Noveschi* would be subjected to a terrifying ordeal, detained in the council chamber for days – ostensibly for their own safety, although at one point they barricaded the doors fearing they would be assaulted – and then their *monte* was expelled from the *reggimento*.[56] There is too little evidence to judge how efficacious the ceremonies of 1429 and 1439 were. Those in 1480, 1484 and 1494 had no lasting effect, and did not bring any noticeable diminution in tension or rancour. No oath, it seems, however impressive the ceremony surrounding it, could bind together the factious citizens of Siena in the late fifteenth century.[57]

THE GABELLA PANEL OF 1483: AN IMAGE OF CIVIC UNION?

The famous *Biccherna* panel for the cover of the accounts of the *Gabella* of 1483 (Fig. 1) has nothing to do with the ceremony of November 1482, although one

---

[54] Allegretti, 'Diarii delle cose sanesi', col. 837.
[55] Cantoni, *Frammento di un diario senese*, 926.
[56] *ibid.*, 931–5; Allegretti, 'Diarii delle cose sanesi', cols. 811–13.
[57] The ceremonies in other cities outlined above (pp. 224–6) were no more effective.

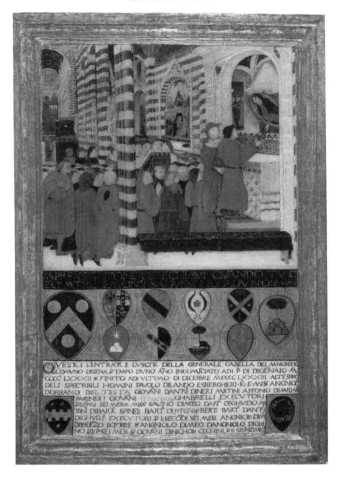

Fig. 1　Pietro Orioli *Dedication of the City to the Virgin in the Duomo,* (1483), Museo delle Biccherne, (Archivio di Stato, Siena)

of the ceremonies it commemorated – it will be argued here that it is, in fact, a conflation of two ceremonies – was supposed to be a celebration of unity.

The panel has attracted much attention both because it illustrates the interior of the cathedral of Siena, and because of its depiction of the most famous of Sienese civic rituals, the dedication of the city to the Virgin.[58] Those commenting on the picture seem to have accepted the implication of the inscription, that it depicts a single ceremony, associating the rededication of

[58] See D. Norman, *Siena and the Virgin: Art and Politics in a Late Medieval City State* (New Haven and London, 1999), for the association of Siena with the cult of the Virgin. For ceremonies of the dedication of the city to the Virgin, and of the images of the Virgin which were their focus, see 28–34.

the city to the Virgin with the reconciliation of the *monti* and their union into a single *monte*. In the catalogue of *Biccherna* panels published in 1984, for example, this 1483 panel is described as 'The union of the classes and the offer of the keys of the city to the Virgin'.[59] Recently, the panel has been described as 'a precise and quasi-documentary depiction of the ceremony and of the place in which it was celebrated'.[60] It seems to have escaped attention that the ceremony of rededication was not in fact associated with the unification of the *monti*, which took place some months earlier and was celebrated by a separate ceremony in the cathedral.[61]

According to the inscription on the panel, the ceremony depicted was 'the presentation of the keys [to the Virgin] when all four *monti* were brought together into one'. The provisions for the unification of the *monti* were passed by the Consiglio del Popolo on 22 March 1483, with much play being made in the text about the ill-effects of having several *monti*, and how now one, now another had been expelled from the *reggimento* in the past.[62] The irony of the inscription on the *Biccherna* panel is that this was described as the unification of 'all four *monti*' because one of the five *monti*, the *Monte dei Nove*, had just been expelled from the *reggimento*.[63] At least the provisions made some allowance for those *Noveschi* who had not in some way been punished to be considered 'abilitati al reggimento' – that is, eligible to be considered for political office – provided they had first formally forgiven anyone who might have offended them during the recent troubles in the city.[64]

After the Consiglio del Popolo had agreed these provisions, unanimous consent was given to a proposal by Andrea Piccolomini that the entire council should accompany the Concistoro to the cathedral, and there 'at the altar of

[59] 'L'unione delle classi e l'offerta delle chiavi della città alla Virgine'. L. Borgia, E. Carli, M. A. Cappari et al. (eds), *Le Biccherne. Tavole dipinte delle magistrature senesi (Secoli XIII–XVIII)* (Rome, 1984), 184.

[60] '. . . una rappresentazione precisa e quasi documentaria della cerimonia e del luogo in cui si è svolta'. V. Ascanio, 'Siena, Archivio di Stato, 41', in A. Tomei (ed.), *Le Biccherne di Siena. Arte e finanza all'alba dell'economia moderna* (Azzano San Paolo (Bergamo) and Rome, 2002), 218.

[61] In Bram Kempers' essay 'Icons, altarpieces and civic ritual in Siena cathedral 1100–1530', in B. A. Hanawalt and K. L. Reyerson, *City and Spectacle in Medieval Europe* (Minneapolis and London, 1994), 89–136, the 1483 panel is discussed as an important example of the depiction of civic ritual in the cathedral, but his account of the political background to the ceremony of 24 August is confused (121–3). He cites Cantoni's account of a stage in the reorganization of the *monti* in June 1482 after the *Riformatori* exiles had been allowed to return (Cantoni, 896–900), as a response to a threat of war in mid-September, and describes the processions following the ceremonies of 6 November 1482 as 'thanksgiving processions' for 'success in the battle' (the Sienese were not engaged in a war and there had not been any battle). Describing the ceremony of 22 March (misdating it to 21 March) as 'the cardinal, speaking on behalf of the pope, proclaimed an indulgence in the Cappella delle Grazie', he makes no reference to why the ceremony took place, or its relevance to the inscription on the panel. His explanation of the ceremony of 24 August is that 'internal and external threats inspired the civic authorities with a desire to reinforce internal cohesion and peace.'

[62] ASS, *Consiglio Generale* 239, fols. 77v–78r; Isaacs, 'Cardinali e 'spalagrembi', 1034–5.

[63] The four *monti* would thus be the *Popolo* and *Riformatori* together with the *Gentiluomini* and *Dodici*, who were then admitted to the regime after having been excluded for most of the fifteenth century.

[64] ASS, *Consiglio Generale* 239, fol. 78r. For the troubles, see Shaw, 'Politics and institutional innovation', 103 (1996), 74–83.

the Madonna of the cathedral, together with Cardinal Malfetta, pray and give thanks, and a Te Deum Laudamus should be sung.'[65] Cardinal Malfetta (Molfetta) was Cardinal Giovanni Battista Cibo, who was to be elected as Pope Innocent VIII the following year. He was in Siena as a papal legate, sent by Sixtus IV as a mediator to try to pacify the internal dissensions of Siena.

Prayers and thanks were offered at the altar, it should be noted, not the keys of the city. It was at another ceremony later that year, in August, at which the keys were presented to the Virgin. On the suggestion of Andrea Capacci, after the Consiglio del Popolo had been considering what to do about the threat from the Noveschi exiles on 7 August, they agreed to give the city and contado of Siena to the Virgin. The ceremony did not take place until 24 August. On that day, a procession led by the civic officials, followed by a large crowd of citizens, made its way from the Palace of the Signoria to the cathedral, where Cardinal Francesco Piccolomini, Archbishop of Siena, said mass at the high altar. After hearing an Italian oration by Mariano da Ghinazzo in praise of the Virgin, they then moved to the chapel of the Madonna delle Grazie, where the keys were placed on the altar by the Prior of the Concistoro, Andrea Sani. In the painting, the Madonna leans forward to receive the keys. A formal contract recording the presentation of the keys and the dedication of the city was drawn up by the notary of the Concistoro, and then Andrea Sani took the keys back. The singing of a Te Deum and a benediction from the cardinal concluded the ceremony.[66]

It is interesting that this instance of the ceremony of the dedication of the city to the Virgin, a ceremony that has always been considered of great significance to the Sienese, did not attract the attention of Allegretti or of the diarist edited by Nuscis. Allegretti did, however, note a procession a few days earlier, on 20 August, in honour of a league with the pope that had just been concluded. A prime motive for this league had been fear of the exiles,[67] and some said, he noted, that because of it the Nove would never return to Siena.[68] In the official record of the ceremony of the donation of the city to the Virgin, it was explicitly declared that this did not signify the subjection of Siena to any other power, temporal or ecclesiastical.[69] Another anonymous diarist did record it, noting that the dominion over the city that had been given to the Madonna in the past had been taken from her, for example, when Siena had become 'raccomandata' to the Duke of Milan,[70] and that 'today it is 223 years to the day that this was done another time, when the

---

[65] 'tutto il consiglio dovesse andare a far compagnia a' Signori a Duomo. E all'altare della Madonna di Duomo, insieme col Cardinale Malfetta ferono orazione, e renderono grazie, e cantossi Te Deum Laudamus': Allegretti, 'Diarii delle cose sanesi', col. 813.

[66] ASS, *Concistoro* 701, fols. 19v–20r.

[67] Shaw, 'Politics and institutional innovation', 103 (1996), 95–8.

[68] Allegretti, 'Diarii delle cose sanesi', col. 815.

[69] ASS, *Concistoro* 701, fol. 19v.

[70] Siena was subject to the Visconti from 1390 to 1404.

Florentines came to besiege us, which is called the defeat of Montaperti'.[71] The ceremony could be seen as an affirmation of Sienese independence as well as a plea for protection against the exiles, but it may have been regarded as a partisan gesture, by a regime concerned about the threat from its enemies, rather than an invocation of divine protection for the city by a government acting on behalf of all the citizens.

The *Biccherna* panel thus brings together elements of both ceremonies, that of 22 March and that of 24 August. Both involved the Concistoro and a large number of citizens, both involved prayers at the altar of the Virgin. On each occasion, a Te Deum was sung. (In the panel, the singers are shown gathered around the stand on which their music book – like those displayed today in the Piccolomini Library of the cathedral – is placed.) A cardinal was present on both occasions, but a different one each time, Cardinal Cibo in March and Cardinal Piccolomini in August. There is not enough of the portrait about the depiction of the cardinal to provide any clue as to which the painter may have had in mind. The image of the dedication of the keys points to the August ceremony; the inscription to the ceremony in March. Both ceremonies could be seen as an attempt to invoke divine protection for a partisan regime, rather than as a celebration of the unity of purpose and of spirit of the citizens of Siena.

Darwin College, University of Cambridge

---

[71] 'La Signoria di Siena ordinò e vensesi in conseglio di dar le chiavi de la Città di Siena a la Nostra Donna, a la quale altre volte si gl'eran date, e perché per i tempi passati si trova che l'era stato tolto il dominio e massime quando le fu raccomandata al Duca di Milano . . . hoggi questo dì si fa 223 anni che quest' atto fu fatto un' altra volta quando e' Fiorentini ci vennero a campo, che si chiama la sconfitta di Montaperto.': ASS, MS D58, fol. 42v. The Sienese defeated the Florentines at Montaperti on 4 September 1260.

7

Pomp or piety? The funeral of Pandolfo Petrucci

PHILIPPA JACKSON

'TIRANNUS ISTE TANDEM MORTUUS EST.'[1]

With these words, the canon and chronicler, Sigismondo Tizio, described the death of Pandolfo Petrucci, the so-called tyrant of Siena, who died on Friday, 21 May 1512, at the age of sixty, in San Quirico d'Orcia.[2] He was returning home from a trip to the baths of San Filippo, begun in mid-April, which was probably aimed to cure the asthma, from which he had been suffering for some time. It is not clear why Pandolfo chose to go to these baths, rather than to his own house at the baths of Caldanelle near Petriolo, another place famous for its healing waters, although presumably the decision was made on medical advice.[3] His body was carried back to Siena where it was left, in accordance with normal custom, outside the city walls, in this case in the Olivetan monastery of San Benedetto outside Porta Tufi, to await the start of the formal funeral ceremonies. This was the end of a man whose grip on power had grown until he was indisputably the leader of the city, but who had constantly to appease his supporters and control the endemic factionalism from which the Sienese state had suffered for so long.[4] During his lifetime, he seems to have been careful not to indulge in too overt personal celebration, choosing instead to act as part of a close-knit oligarchy and to cloak his patronage powers with the promotion of the city itself. It is his funeral that most clearly displayed his position as head of government, and glorified him as an individual, as well as exalting the power of his family and the regime he represented.[5] State spectacle was important for the exercise and transfer of power, and an impression of political stability was clearly

---

[1] S. Tizio, *Historiae Senenses*, VII, Biblioteca Comunale di Siena (hereafter BCS), Ms. B.III.12, fol. 305; G. A. Pecci, *Memorie storico-critiche della città di Siena*, 2 vols. (Siena, 1755–1760), I, (i), 273 n. (a).

[2] Pecci, *Memorie storico-critiche* I, (i), 265–6; G. Gigli, *Diario sanese*, 2 vols. (Siena, 1723) I, 206–8; Archivio di Stato di Siena (hereafter ASS), Balìa, 59, fols. 4v–6v; Tizio, VII, fols. 304–305.

[3] D. Boisseuil, *Le thermalisme en Toscane à la fin du Moyen Âge* (Rome, 2002) 262–4 (Caldanelle), 274–7 (Petriolo), 284–91 (San Filippo); D. S. Chambers, 'Spas in the Italian Renaissance', in *Reconsidering the Renaissance*, ed. M.A. di Cesare (Binghamton, 1992) 3–27.

[4] C. Shaw, *The Politics of Exile in Renaissance Italy* (Cambridge, 2000) 40–54; idem, 'Politics and Institutional Innovation in Siena 1480–1498', (1) in *Bullettino Senese di Storia Patria* (hereafter *BSSP*), CIII (1996) 9–102 and (II) in *BSSP*, CIV (1997) 194–307.

[5] A useful contemporary comparison of a grand funeral for a public figure prominent in a Tuscan republican state, is that of Giuliano de' Medici, Duke of Nemours, in Florence, in 1515: S. Strocchia, *Death and Ritual in Renaissance Florence* (Baltimore and London, 1992) 21–23.

given by this funeral.[6] Although he never destroyed the republican structure of the Sienese state, by the time of his death, Pandolfo controlled every aspect of the government in a way that is reflected in the civic honours paid to him.

Before examining this particular event, it is important to consider what constituted a Sienese public funeral in this period.[7] What were the similarities to, or differences from, the honours given to other important figures of the late fifteenth and early sixteenth centuries and how did Pandolfo's rites differ in terms of space, participants, and ritual? Accounts of Sienese public funerals can be found, such as that of the famous *condottiere*, Guidoriccio da Fogliano, in 1352, or of the *capitano del popolo*, Bernardino Benassai, in 1476, but no detailed analysis exists.[8] The republic, in the late fifteenth century, did not give funeral honours to foreigners and only rarely honoured the deaths of Sienese permanently residing abroad. An exception, in January 1493, was Antonio, Duke of Amalfi and nephew of Pope Pius II, in whose honour a ceremony was held on the Piccolomini loggia to which the government sent wax and standards. The Balìa, the main executive magistracy during this period, appointed two of their number to provide for this on the grounds of his support for the city.[9] The most important comparisons for Pandolfo's funeral ceremonies are those of the priors who died in office, and of other leading citizens, such as Andrea Piccolomini in 1505, and Bartolomeo Sozzini in 1506. The descriptions of the rituals surrounding their deaths also reveals the increased importance of the Balìa in state rites during the early sixteenth century.

Sienese public figures, that is to say priors, rectors of the hospital of Santa Maria della Scala, and eminent men such as former chancellors of the republic, were given special recognition by the government on their deaths. These honours primarily took the form of gifts of wax torches, suitably embellished with the black and white city symbol of the *balzana*, supplied for the funeral procession, or for the vigil;[10] the carrying of the city's banners in the procession, showing the *balzana* and the coat of arms of the *popolo* of Siena, a white lion on red ground; and finally, for the most important individuals, the attendance of the funeral rites, by the city's leading magistrates. The *balzana*

[6] Pandolfo had already made steps to ensure the succession of his son Borghese as the *primus inter pares* in the Sienese state, but the funeral was an important moment for the orderly transfer of power. See n.5 and also E. Muir, *Civic Ritual in Renaissance Venice* (Princeton, 1981) 263–77 on the funeral of the doge of Venice.

[7] On death and burial in Siena more generally see S. J. Cohn, Jr., *The Cult of Remembrance and the Black Death. Six Renaissance Cities in Central Italy* (Baltimore and London, 1992), idem, *Death and Property in Siena, 1205–1800* (Baltimore and London, 1988).

[8] W. S. Bowsky, *A Medieval Italian Commune. Siena under the Nine, 1287–1355* (Berkeley-Los Angeles-London), 49 and n.81; A. Liberati, 'Un funerale a Siena nel XV secolo', *BSSP*, XLVI (1939) 53–58; P. Turrini, 'Le ceremonie funebri a Siena nel basso medio evo: norme e rituale', *BSSP*, CX (2003) 53–102, 84–91.

[9] 'Pro ipsius benemeritis erga rempublicam senensem': ASS, Balia, 38, fol. 35v; Turrini, 'Ceremonie', 90.

[10] ASS, *Concistoro*, 793, fol. 5r when the government provided wax candles 'cum balzanis in dictis staggiuolis affixis expensas comunis Senarum' for the funeral of the prior Pietro Sansedoni.

and *popolo* symbols can be clearly seen in a procession shown on a maiolica plate now in Rouen.[11] It seems that the amount of wax sent was carefully considered and depended partly on one's social status, as well as one's service to the republic. Thus, on the death of Angelo Fondi, the former chancellor, in August 1505, the Balìa decided he should be honoured with five *doppieri* (double-branched candles), as he was also a palatine count.[12]

A particularly good description is that of the funeral, on 9 November 1498, of the prior Pietro Sansedoni, who died in office and was awarded full public honours.[13] Where the person was of considerable importance, or died while residing as a prior, the Captain of the People, all of the priors who comprised the Concistoro, other magistrates, and their officials would attend, accompanied by the state musicians, and members of the palace staff who acted as pallbearers.[14] There appears to have been no legal restriction on the attendance of funerals by the Balìa until the decision, on 28 November 1510, that the members of the Balìa could accompany the dead for a funeral only when the deceased was actually one of their number.[15] The priors of the city were forbidden by law to leave the Palazzo Pubblico during their tenure, other than for official ceremonies, one of which was the attendance of a funeral of one of their number, or of another eminent figure.[16] If someone of lesser stature died, such as a relative of a residing magistrate, then a smaller sub-committee would be given special permission to attend the funeral ceremonies.[17] There were variations depending on the office held by the deceased. In the case of rectors of the hospital, their bodies were normally dressed in their rectors' robes for the funeral, and they were carried to their final resting place by the friars of the hospital.[18] These rectors were wealthy men of knightly status who had sumptuous tombs in prominent churches of the city, sometimes in the clothes of their office, such as that of Giovanbattista Tondi shown in his rectors' robes on a tomb slab in the hospital of Santa Maria della Scala.[19]

---

[11] M. Luccarelli, 'Contributo alla conoscenza della maiolica senese', in *Ceramica Antica* 10 (131), xii (Novembre 2002), 32–61, 43.

[12] ASS, *Balìa*, 51, fol. 49v.

[13] ASS, *Concistoro*, 793, fols. 4v–5r; see too ASS, Concistoro, 794, fol. 8r for the funeral of the prior Girolamo di Antonio Orlandi on 15 January 1499.

[14] ASS, *Concistoro*, 793, fol. 5r: 'portatum est corpus in feretro locatum super humeros domicellorum palatii'. On the state musicians see F. D'Accone, *The Civic Muse. Music and Musicians in Siena during the Middle Ages and the Renaissance* (Chicago and London, 1997) especially 413–4 and 466–8.

[15] ASS, *Balìa*, 56, fol. 65r.

[16] M. S. Elscheikh ed., *Il Costituto del Comune di Siena volgarizzato nel MCCCIX–MCCCX*, 3 vols. (Città di Castello, 2002) II, 539–41, Dist. VI. 12.

[17] ASS, *Concistoro*, 775, fol. 14r: six priors were chosen to attend the funeral of Giovanni Finetti, brother of one of their number, on 16 December 1495; ASS, Concistoro, 794, fol. 18r: six priors attended the funeral of Giovanni Colombini, uncle of the prior Alessandro Colombini, on 15 February 1499.

[18] Most rectors were buried in the hospital during the fifteenth century: see L. Banchi, *I Rettori dello Spedale di Santa Maria della Scala* (Bologna, 1877).

[19] R. Munman, *Sienese Renaissance Tomb Monuments* (Philadelphia, 1993), 82–89, 150–1; S. Colucci, *Sepolcri a Siena tra Medioevo e Rinascimento* (Florence, 2003), 361–3.

Funeral ceremonies in general were governed by the social norms of the day, sumptuary legislation which controlled numbers, clothing, and dining, the deceased's status and official position, as well as his personal requests for his death rites if they were expressed in his will.[20] As public funerals were normally for the highest class of citizen, many of the sumptuary law restrictions did not apply, but sometimes there had to be accommodation between public ritual and the private wishes of the testators. There were relatively few Sienese in this period who made express provisions for their funerals, although it was common to state a preferred place of burial.[21] When these provisions were particularly precise, this was normally when wealthy testators were especially pious, had no sons to take charge of such an important event, or they were residing abroad. An example of the latter is the will, dated 1 August 1510, of Galeazzo Saracini, a wealthy Sienese merchant and brother-in-law of Agostino Chigi, who was residing in Bruges.[22] He wanted to be buried in the Saracini chapel in the Osservanza, but, as he was living in another country, he had to make special testamentary provisions for his burial. He arranged that his body should be placed in an 'archa plumbea', a lead coffin, and buried temporarily in a chapel in the Augustinian monastery of Bruges, to be transferred back to Siena at a later date.[23]

Pandolfo's wishes for his burial, which he laid down in his will dated 2 October 1511, were simple. He wanted to be buried in the tomb he had commissioned in the church of the observant Franciscans, commonly known as the Osservanza, which was at Capriola, outside the city.[24] Unlike some testators who were of a particularly pious disposition, such as Niccolò Ricoveri, the rector of the hospital, who was buried in the Osservanza in 1477, he did not request that his corpse be dressed in the habit of an observant Franciscan friar.[25] The interrelation of public custom and private wishes can

[20] On sumptuary legislation see C. Mazzi, 'Alcune leggi suntuarie senese del secolo XIII', *Archivio Storico Italiano*, ser. 4, V (1880) 133–44; C. Bonelli Gandolfo, 'La legislazione suntuaria senese negli ultimi cento-cinquant'anni della Repubblica' in *Studi senesi*, XXXV (1920), fasc. 3–4, 243–75; fasc. 5, 334–98 especially 355–59; D. Owen Hughes, 'Mourning Rites, Memory, and Civilization in Premodern Italy', *Riti e rituali nelle società medievali*, ed. J. Chiffoleau et al. (Spoleto, 1994) 23–38; M. A. Ceppari Ridolfi and P. Turrini, *Il mulino della vanità. Lusso e cerimonie nella Siena medievale*, (Siena, 1998) 56–75.

[21] For testamentary wishes more generally see n.7 above and U. Morandi, 'Il sentire religioso dei Senesi dinanzi alla morte (secc. XII–XV)', in *Chiesa e vita religiosa a Siena dalle origini al grande giubileo*, eds. A. Mirizio and P. Nardi (Siena, 2002) 179–190.

[22] Biblioteca Apostolica Vaticana, Archivio Chigi, 3666 (8). His death is recorded by Agostino Chigi in a letter to his brother, Sigismondo, on 15 August 1510: I. D. Rowland, *The Correspondence of Agostino Chigi (1466–1520) in Cod. Chigi R.V.c.* (Vatican City, 2001) 84–5.

[23] On the division, transportation and secondary burial of bodies, see E.A.R. Brown, 'Death and the Human Body in the Later Middle Ages: the Legislation of Boniface VIII on the Division of the Corpse', *Viator*, 12 (1981) 221–70.

[24] ASS, *Notarile ante-cosimiano*, 1080, 382, 'in sepulcro condito et ordinato a dicto testatore'. M. Bertagna, *L'Osservanza di Siena. Studi storici*, 3 vols. (Siena, 1963–4), III, especially 70–74; *Restauro di una terracotta del Quattrocento. Il 'Compianto' di Giacomo Cozzarelli* (Modena, 1984); *L'Osservanza di Siena. La basilica e i suoi codici miniati* (Siena, 1984).

[25] This was also the wish of Giovanni Martinozzi in 1473: see Bertagna, *L'Osservanza di Siena*, II, 92, n.46, and was most commonly requested by Franciscan tertiaries.

most clearly be seen in the funeral of Ricoveri.[26] The vigil was held at the
church of the hospital, with his body dressed in rector's clothes, attended by
many relatives, knights, doctors, priests and the whole cathedral chapter.[27]
The following day, in accordance with his testamentary request, his body
was dressed in the habit of an observant Franciscan friar and carried by the
hospital friars to the Porta Ovile, from which four brothers of the confraternity of Santa Lucia carried it to his tomb in the middle of the Osservanza's
church.[28]

This choice of burial place was one of the most popular for the pious and
wealthy citizens of Siena during the late fifteenth and early sixteenth centuries.[29]
The famous lawyer, Bartolomeo Sozzini, chose the Capriola in his will of 1506,
despite having a family chapel in S. Domenico, which would have been the
natural choice for his tomb.[30] This popularity was related to the cult of San
Bernardino, who had founded the Osservanza, and the need for financial
subsidies to build a larger church and friary to house the growing numbers of
friars.[31] Even where burial itself did not take place there, it is clear from
Sienese wills of the late fifteenth and early sixteenth centuries that observant
prayers were deemed of greater value than those of other congregations,
particularly as a remedy for one's sins.[32] It was common for a testator to
request either, or both, Franciscan and Dominican observant friars to pray for
his soul, even in cases where he had a burial chapel or tomb elsewhere.[33]

Various members of the Petrucci family, including Pandolfo's own
father, Bartolomeo, in his will of 24 September 1485, requested burial in the
Osservanza in their testaments.[34] It may well have been his father's choice
that influenced Pandolfo to become a patron there and to choose this site.

[26] See Banchi, *I Rettori*, 119–30; M. Martellucci, '"Dio li perdoni ch'egli è stato buono rettore": I testamenti,
i funerali e le eredità dei rettori dell'ospedale di Santa Maria della Scala nel Quattrocento', *BSSP*, CX (2003)
452–88, 473–5.
[27] ASS, *Santa Maria della Scala*, 24, fols. 258r–259v. Agostino Dati gave the funeral oration: *Augustini Dathi
Funebris Oratio altera habita ab eo in hospitali ede pro Nicolao Recupero de laudibus eius & vita* in A. Dati, *Augustini
Dati Senensis Opera* (Siena, 1503) xcvii r–v; Banchi, *I Rettori*, 128–30.
[28] ASS, *Santa Maria della Scala*, 25, fol. 259v.
[29] Eminent foreigners also sought burial there, such as Dionora Orsini, widow of Paulo Savelli, in her will
of 14 January 1514 (dated 1513 according to the Sienese style): ASS, *Notarile ante-cosimiano*, 816, 263.
[30] R. Bargagli, 'Documenti senesi per la biografia di Bartolomeo Sozzini', *BSSP*, IC (1992) 266–323, 322–3.
[31] See Bertagna, *L'Osservanza di Siena*, III.
[32] During this period testamentary gifts in Siena relating to masses for the dead, and for the marriage of
poor girls, were nearly always expressed in terms of being a remedy for sins, or for the soul of the deceased.
On prayers for the dead more generally see M. McLaughlin, *Consorting with Saints: Prayers for the Dead in Early
Medieval France* (Ithaca and London, 1994) especially 3–9.
[33] The painter, Girolamo di Domenico, requested burial in S. Giovanni, in his will, dated 6 November 1474,
and Gregorian masses in the Osservanza (ASS, *Notarile ante-cosimiano*, 660, 42); Mariana di Berto Berti, whose
will of 16 November 1477 stipulated burial in S. Domenico, left 25 florins to the friars of Capriola for masses
for the soul of herself and of her husband (ASS, *Notarile ante-cosimiano*, 605, 27); Matteo di Paulo Biringucci
requested thirty Gregorian masses for his soul from the observant Franciscans despite choosing burial in S.
Agostino (ASS, *Notarile ante-cosimiano*, 829, fols. 68v–71r); and Paulo Venturi, who was also to be buried in the
latter, requested in his testament of February 1505, that offices of the dead be said for his soul by both the
observant Franciscans and Dominicans (ASS, *Notarile ante-cosimiano*, 816, 97).
[34] See ASS, *Notarile ante-cosimiano*, 525 for the will of Bartolomeo di Giacoppo Petrucci.

Yet, there was another reason to seek such a holy and revered place of burial, as this tomb monument, constructed in simple materials appropriate for an observant institution, would be situated in the friary founded by one of the most famous saints of his day, a place of pilgrimage and sanctity for Sienese and non-Sienese alike. Cardinals and dignitaries visited the Osservanza, and those visiting in the early sixteenth century would have seen both the friary, adorned with the Petrucci coat of arms, and Pandolfo's tomb, near to the relics of San Bernardino, which must have enhanced his reputation as a patron of pious causes.[35] His wish, however, to establish a family tomb for his descendants to rival the traditional Petrucci choice of S. Domenico was less successful.[36] This preference is made particularly clear in the will of Iuditta Bulgarini, the widow of Pandolfo's nephew, Girolamo di Camillo Petrucci, of 11 April 1534. She requested burial in S. Domenico in the tomb of her husband, referring to his body in deposit at the Osservanza, and made arrangements for the transfer of both of their bodies to S. Domenico when the tomb there had been completed.[37]

In order to assess the grandeur of Pandolfo's funeral it is helpful to consider the quantity of wax assigned by the state for this occasion, the types and costs of processional banners, as well as the rites, participants and ritual route taken for the funeral procession.

The quantity of the wax torches that the state granted in honour of a public figure on his death was directly related to his status.[38] It was extremely rare for any public recognition to be given to a woman, and so the gift of wax, on 14 July 1512, to honour the widow of Pandolfo, Aurelia Borghese, who died less than two months after her husband, was quite exceptional, and reflects the pre-eminent position that the Petrucci family had gained.[39] Government records contain the information that reveal the wax so assigned and incidentally contain a useful death record for prominent members of the regime. The average amount of wax provided by the government at the start of the sixteenth century cost 14 lire and 6 soldi (£14 s.6), with greater amounts awarded to honour the deceased chancellor, Angelo Fondi (£22 s.5), and far more for leading figures such as Andrea Piccolomini, the nephew of Pius II, (£304 s.1) and Antonio Bichi (£276 s.13).[40] The wax

[35] For example, Pius II, with other clerics, stayed there from 22 March–4 April 1460: Bertagna, *L'Osservanza di Siena*, I, 128–9; and Cardinal Francesco Borgia made a visit in 1510: Tizio, VII, fol. 79.

[36] Archivio Osservanza, J.1, lists various members of the Petrucci family who were buried there, yet S. Domenico remained the preferred choice if the necrology of S. Domenico is examined: BCS, C.III.2. For Petrucci burials before the sixteenth century see too M.-H. Laurent ed., *I necrologi di San Domenico in Camporegio*, in *Fontes vitae S. Catharinae Senensis historici*, vol. 20, eds. M.-H. Laurent and F. Valli (Florence, 1937).

[37] ASS, *Notarile ante-cosimiano*, 1525(8).

[38] ASS, *Concistoro*, 770, fol. 5v, 8 January 1495: the Concistoro deliberated to provide four *doppieri* 'cum armis comunis Senarum' for the funeral of Giovanni Gabriele, a former chancellor of the republic.

[39] See ASS, *Balia*, 59, fol. 14r when it was decided to honour her with 'quinque paria doplerioum consueta aliis morientibus de collegio, et unum par dopleriorum grossorum retortorum'.

[40] ASS, *Balia*, 51, fol. 70v for these payments for wax candles by the state, save that for honouring Antonio Bichi in ASS, *Balia*, 52, fol. 21r.

ordered for Pandolfo's funeral was greater, however, costing £389 s.9, and there was a grant of forty torches to the confraternity of Santa Croce and ten *doppieri* for the friars of San Francesco, with the proviso that they kept them alight around the body of Pandolfo during the time his body lay in their church.[41] The hospital of Santa Maria della Scala also sent eight *staggioli* for the funeral, each painted with its own coat of arms.[42] The Balìa, in an extraordinary measure and which reflects the importance of Pandolfo's death for the regime, ordered that all the subject cities and communities, including those of the *Masse*, the area on the outskirts of the city, should be represented at the funeral, and they attended with their own candles and standards.[43]

Although the government sometimes ordered banners to be made for less important funeral processions, it is clear from the deliberations and the sumptuous standards commissioned that they were keen to make this event a particularly grand affair.[44] When the death of Pandolfo was announced, the Balìa immediately started making plans for the funeral by appointing, on 22 May 1512, a sub-committee, which included Pandolfo's close associate, Antonmaria Cinughi, to organize the state rites.[45] The event was evidently considered of great significance by the regime, as it involved the closure of all shops and businesses until the funeral ceremonies were over, a decision that was only taken for particularly special occasions. The first consideration was the quantity of money to be assigned by the government to pay for the event, which was set at 700 ducats, with an understanding that this sum might not adequately cover all the expenses.[46] The Balìa decided to order magnificent fabrics to make the banners for the funeral, including damasks, brocade, velvet and various types of taffeta.[47] The largest cloth was to be of gold brocade of twenty-six *braccia* trimmed with red velvet displayed during the funeral mass and later granted to the cathedral.

The government accounts for the funeral, dated 8 July 1512, show the types of materials, as well as the companies involved in providing these luxury items.[48] There were various silk merchants in the city, who could supply expensive fabrics. The company of Agniolo Tancredi and partners, received

[41] ASS, *Balia*, 59, 13v; Pecci, *Memorie storico-critiche*, I (i) 268–9.

[42] ASS, *Santa Maria della Scala*, 889, 36r: G. Fattorini, 'Le copertine dipinte dell'ospedale: note di cronologia, iconografia e stile', in *Arte e Assistenza a Siena*, exh.cat. (Siena, 2003) 47–55, 55, n.20.

[43] ASS, *Balia*, 59, 5r–v; Pecci, *Memorie storico-critiche*, I (i) 268–9.

[44] The silk provided for the funeral of Bartolomeo Sozzini cost the government £319 s.10: Bargagli, 'Documenti senesi per la biografia di Bartolomeo Sozzini', 322, yet this was far less than that spent on the funeral of Pandolfo.

[45] ASS, *Balia*, 59, 4v. By this time the Balia was more important than the Concistoro and Pandolfo was its leading member.

[46] *Ibid.*, 5r; Gigli, *Diario sanese*, 206.

[47] On fabrics and the silk trade see L. Banchi, *L'arte della seta in Siena nei secoli XV e XVI. Statuti e documenti*, (Siena, 1881); M. Ciatti, 'Note sulla storia del tessuti a Siena', in *Drappi, velluti, taffettà et altre cose. Antichi tessuti a Siena e nel suo territorio*, ed. idem (Siena, 1994) 16–49, and L Molà, *The Silk Industry of Renaissance Venice* (Baltimore and London, 2000) 9–10, 33, 45.

[48] ASS, *Balia*, 59, fols. 12v–14r.

over £304 for fifty-seven *braccia* of black and white damask to make three
banners, presumably showing the *balzana*, while one of Pandolfo's own
companies, Giovanni Marretti and partners, which was based in a shop on the
Campo, provided a wide range of fabrics, including ornamental caparisons,
and various Venetian materials.[49] This company also supplied a large number
of wax torches for the funeral ceremonies so that, even in death, Pandolfo's
business interests were making substantial profits for the Petrucci family. The
most luxurious materials of gold brocade and red velvet were imported from
Florence, which indicates an acknowledgement that superior quality had to
be sought outside the city. Local Sienese painters, however, were employed
to decorate the funeral banners. Giacomo Pacchiarotti and his company, were
hired to paint the standards and the small banners, and Guidoccio Cozzarelli
to paint a plaque.[50] The quantity and quality of the materials ordered for
Pandolfo's procession makes clear that the government wished to present a
sumptuous display that was far greater than any other Sienese public funeral
of the time.

The first part of the ritual, the night before the funeral, was the vigil,
usually held either in the deceased's parish church, or in a religious place
with which he was associated, due to his office. For instance, when a rector
of the hospital died, this ceremony took place in the church of Santa Maria
della Scala, and his body laid in the chapel of relics to await the funeral
service.[51] In Pandolfo's case, his vigil was held on the night of 23 May in the
cathedral, a place that was large enough to hold all the leading citizens, their
wives, relatives and friends. It was appropriate, too, that this should have been
chosen as a place of official mourning as Pandolfo had been one of the three
Operai, or overseers, of the cathedral.

Normally, when the priors attended a public funeral they would put on
appropriate mourning apparel of 'panni pavonazi', clothing of a purplish
colour, and would process to the house of the deceased where the other
mourners would have also assembled for the start of the ritual. Often, on the
occasion of the death of a political figure, the first stage involved the funeral
oration by a prominent scholar. The collected works of the fifteenth-century
Sienese chancellor Agostino Dati, published in 1503, contain a section
devoted to his funeral orations for leading members of Sienese society.[52] It
was usual for this part of the ceremony to be held outside the home of the
deceased, but in the case of the funeral of Andrea Piccolomini, nephew of
Pius II, in 1505, the body was brought from his parish church of San Martino
to the Piccolomini loggia, which was situated near his palace.[53] Apparently the

[49] *Ibid.*, fols. 13r–v.

[50] ASS, *Balìa*, 59, fols. 13v–14r; Borghesi and Banchi, 442.

[51] See Banchi, *I Rettori*, and M. Martellucci, '"Dio li perdoni ch'egli è stato buono rettore"', 470–88 for the
deaths and funerals of the rectors of the hospital.

[52] A. Dati, *Opera* (Siena, 1503) libro quinto, lxxxxvi–ci.

[53] A. L. Jenkens, 'Pius II and His Loggia in Siena', in *Pratum Romanum: Richard Krautheimer zum 100. Geburtstag*,
R. L. Colella et al. eds. (Wiesbaden, 1997) 199–214, 203; Biblioteca Angelica, Ang. Lat., 1077, fol. 53v.

Fig. 1   Vecchietta Studio (Francesco di Giorgio) *St Bernardino Preaching* Walker Art Gallery, National Museums Liverpool

normal custom was for most of those attending to sit on the ground while listening to the oration, but owing to their status, the priors were seated on benches, sometimes described as being of two tiers, opposite the heirs of the deceased.[54] A temporary pulpit was sometimes set up for the orator, as was the case for both Bartolomeo Benassai's and Andrea Piccolomini's funeral ceremonies.[55] The practice of important people sitting on wooden benches facing each other to hear an orator or preacher in a pulpit, while others stand or kneel on the ground, can clearly be seen in a painting of a sermon by San Bernardino, now in the Walker Gallery in Liverpool. (Fig. 1).[56]

On Monday, 24 May 1512, twenty of the magistrates of the Balìa, with their standards and wax, dressed in their mourning clothes, processed to San Desiderio, Pandolfo's parish church, and on to his home, the Palazzo del Magnifico.[57] There, with the heirs, relatives, and other citizens, they listened to the funeral oration of Piermarino Gori of Foligno. This humanist, who was closely associated with the Petrucci family, taught the art of rhetoric at the University of Siena.[58] He arrived in the city in the 1490s and, together with his brother Vincenzo, a cleric who later became a canon of the cathedral of Siena, he acted as tutor to Enea Piccolomini.[59] His oration, which has not

[54] As occurred for the funeral of Pietro Sansedoni when the priors 'in loco eminenti constitutus hoc est in una banca super aliam bancam locata: et ipsis sedentibus contra filios veste lucubri indutos et alios consanguineos dicti Pietri': ASS, *Concistoro*, 793, fol. 4v.

[55] Simple wooden pulpits were often set up for preachers during this period as one can see from the illumination of San Bernardino in P. Palladino, *Treasures of a Lost Art. Italian Manuscript Painting of the Middle Ages and Renaissance* (New Haven and London, 2003) 154–155, 155.

[56] L. Bellosi ed., *Francesco di Giorgio e il Rinascimento a Siena 1450–1500* (Milan, 1993) 110–1.

[57] Gigli, *Diario Sanese*, 207; ASS, Balia, 59, fol. 6r; Pecci, *Memorie storico-critiche*, 1 (i) 272.

[58] Tizio, VII, fol. 305: 'Petrus Marinus Fulginas familiaris vir alioquin doctus orationem habuit'; On Piermarino Gori see M. Faloci Fulignani, 'Siena e Foligno', *Bollettino della Regia Deputazione di Storia Patria per l'Umbria*, XXIII (1918) 115–206.

[59] P. Piccolomini, 'Istruzioni di Giacomo Todeschini-Piccolomini al figlio Enea (1499–1500) e Calendario dello Studio Senese nel 1510', *BSSP*, X (1903) 107–16.

yet been traced, probably followed the classical form of epideictic oratory, similar to those of Agostino Dati.

After the oration, the magistrates, and other dignitaries including prelates such as Angiolo Petrucci, the Bishop of Bertinoro, the college of lawyers and doctors and university representatives, all went to the Porta Tufi to await the body, which was carried into the city under a baldachin adorned with the Petrucci coats of arms. There is no description of how the body was dressed, although the garments were likely to have been of silk, velvet, or another expensive material.[60] When Pius II's nephew, Andrea Piccolomini died, in September 1505, his body was dressed in a brocade jacket and velvet robe with a golden necklace, sword and spurs.[61] Thus the clothes adorning Pandolfo could have been of sumptuous gold brocade, as he was both a knight and a palatine count, or of black to indicate that he was a simple citizen, as occurred for the funeral of Agostino Chigi in 1520.[62]

The funeral cortege contained the most eminent representatives of the government and subject cities and, according to the chronicler, Tizio, all the population of Siena.[63] First, came the banners showing the symbols of Siena, which included the *lupa*, the Sienese she-wolf and her twins, alluding to the Roman foundation legend of the city, as well as those showing the Petrucci family coat of arms. Then came representatives of the subject cities, the guilds, the canons of the cathedral and many other officials, as well as all the religious of the city carrying wax torches. Behind these, but in front of the body, marched the members of the government, and after the baldachin, the sons and relatives would have processed with the rest of the populace making up the rear. They must have walked up from the Porta Tufi to the Piazza Postierla and then the cortege is recorded as having crossed the piazza of the hospital (Fig. 2). It is not clear what route they then took, but they probably then went down the via dei Fusari to the Piazza of San Giovanni, and then on to the door of the Palazzo del Magnifico, where Pandolfo's female relatives, in accordance with normal custom, awaited to pay their last respects.[64] Sienese women from 1262 onwards were legally prohibited from taking part in the procession and their lamentation at the entrance to the home of the deceased was a well-established ritual.[65] The cortege then proceeded to the

---

[60] For the importance of funeral clothing, focussing on Arezzo in 1510, see L. Berti, 'La normativa sui panni funebri della fraternita di Arezzo. Autodelimitazione di un ceto dirigente del primo cinquecento ed esorcizzazione delle conseguenze sociali della morte', *Annali Aretini* III (1995) 5–50.

[61] See n.53.

[62] J Shearman, *Raphael in Early Modern Sources*, 2 vols. (New Haven and London, 2003) I, 579–80.

[63] Tizio, VII, fol. 305: 'Sociavit Pandulphum universa civitas'. For the order of the procession see Gigli, *Diario Sanese*, 207–8 and Pecci, *Memorie storico-critiche*, 1 (i) 272.

[64] It was customary for women to make extravagant grief stricken gestures such as tearing their hair and wailing, which the Petrucci women did too when the procession arrived at the door. See Gigli, *Diario sanese*, 208: 'transiverunt ad Ostium domus defuncti, ubi erant Uxor, Filia, Nepotes et Consanguinei sparsis capillis, percutientibus manibus cum magno fletu ipsorum'.

[65] Owen Hughes, 'Mourning Rites', 31; F Casanova, 'La donna senese del Quattrocento nella vita privata', *BSSP*, 8 (1901) 54–57.

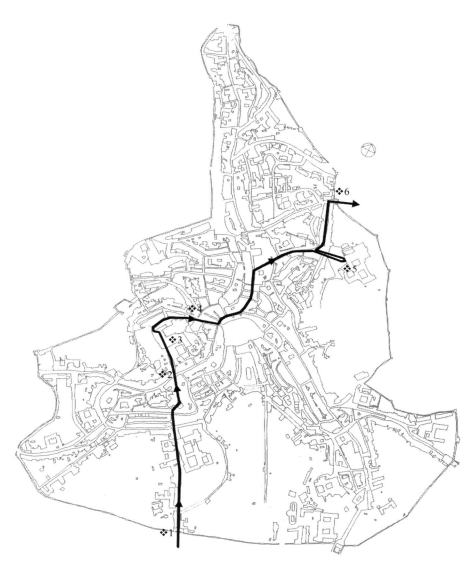

Fig. 2   Map showing funeral route for the cortege of Pandolfo Petrucci. The numbers mark the major sites involved in the procession: (1) Porta Tufi (2) Piazza Postierla (3) Piazza Duomo (4) Palazzo del Magnifico (5) San Francesco (6) Porta Ovile leading to the Osservanza (map: F. Nevola)

croce del travaglio, and finally on to the church of San Francesco where the body of Pandolfo was laid, and the crowds of mourners left.

After sunset, the body was carried by the observant Franciscan friars, through the Porta Ovile, to the Capriola to be laid in his tomb. Burials in the Osservanza, in keeping, with Franciscan concepts of simplicity, were usually not grand affairs. For example, when the wealthy Bernardino Francesconi set out his own burial wishes in his will of 1518, he requested a simple burial, stating that his body should not be accompanied by friends and family to the friary, and that only six priests would be allowed to go to his tomb.[66]

On Tuesday 25 May, the final ceremony to honour Pandolfo was held when a funeral mass was celebrated in the cathedral, the place where he had taken a leading role in the modernizing plans for the restructuring of the interior. The university professor and Franciscan friar Giovanni of Lucignano gave the sermon in praise of the deceased. Normally this ceremony would have taken place in the parish church, in Pandolfo's case, San Desiderio, but according to Tizio it was too small to hold the number of mourners.[67] A 'castello', a wooden structure of ephemeral funeral display, lit with many candles, presumably similar to those used to honour prominent figures such as rectors of the hospital, was constructed in the cathedral to honour him.[68] Although no drawing survives, designs exist for the grand Sienese catafalques of the later sixteenth century and such structures were common for Renaissance rulers during this period.[69] With this ceremony, after three days of religious and state rites the funeral of the tyrant of Siena was over.

Every public funeral ceremony in Siena during this period seems to have been governed by a combination of factors: the individual's testamentary wishes, the office he held (or had held) within the city, his social status, the place where he lived, and his standing in the eyes of the regime on the date of his death. There do seem to have been some basic similarities between the funerals, such as the awards of wax, the commissioning and carrying of banners with the republic's symbols, the site of the funeral oration, and processional activity involving a visit to the female relatives at the house of the deceased. There was some flexibility also, particularly as most funerals took place within a day of death of the individual so not allowing much time for organization, and there could be a clash between personal wishes and official customs, as in the case of the hospital rector, Niccolò Ricoveri.

---

[66] ASS, *Notarile ante-cosimiano*, 1404, 27 September 1518.

[67] 'Desiderii templum incapax erat': Tizio, VII, fol. 305.

[68] The accounts of the *Opera del Duomo* of 1512 reveal the wax provided by this institution for the funeral: Archivio dell'Opera della Metropolitana di Siena, 511, 21 Left for 26 May 1512: 'E a dì detto £cinquantacinque s.6 di cera di falcole della sepoltura del magnifico Pandolfo' and idem, on 9 June, for £101 paid out for the wax, 'la quale fu di quella del castello del magnifico Pandolfo'.

[69] On later drawings see M. Ascheri ed., *I Libri dei Leoni. La nobiltà di Siena in età medicea (1557–1737)* (Siena, 1996) 358–61 and, for comparison, R. Signorini, 'Gonzaga Tombs and Catafalques' in D. Chambers and J. Martineau eds, *Splendours of the Gonzaga*, exh. cat. (Cinisello B. (Milan), 1981) 3–13.

By this time, it was common for eminent Sienese men to have funerals where their bodies lay on silk cloths, dressed in sumptuous brocades, and velvets, accompanied by the insignia of their status, and at this period in the city, no-one was considered more important than Pandolfo Petrucci. His exequies were not only a personal celebration, but a glorification of the regime governing Siena, and the honouring of his death helped legitimize the continuation of Petruccian hegemony. The republican values of the state were exalted at the same time as the honouring of the individual and his family. In the numbers of participants, particularly of those representatives from outside the city walls, in the extensive awards of wax candles, the sumptuousness of the materials for the banners, and the length of time of the ceremonies, no other public funeral in Siena of this time matched the grandeur of this one. The total government expenditure on banners and wax amounted to £2,292 and that does not take into account the sums spent directly by the Petrucci family and its supporters, the subject cities, the cathedral chapter, the hospital, guilds or other religious institutions.[70] Thus it was clearly pomp that was the guiding principle of the funeral honours granted to the deceased tyrant by his city. The pious element of this event, if there was one, lay in Pandolfo's choice of burial in the Osservanza, and his wish to be associated with the religious values of the observant Franciscans.

London

---

[70] ASS, Balia, 59, fol. 14r.

8

The rise of the new civic ritual of the Immaculate Conception of the Virgin in sixteenth-century Siena*

MAURO MUSSOLIN

In his *Diario Sanese*, Girolamo Gigli proudly proclaims that 'it is, in conclusion, not to be overlooked that the Sienese were the first in Italy to venerate this [the Immaculate Conception] mystery, and that through the centuries they were its unvanquished defenders'.[1] While the Sienese were not the first to venerate the Immaculate Conception, nonetheless their support for the cult from 1526 was spectacular and long-lasting. Prior to the fifteenth century, the feast had received only a scant following.[2] As in other cities, it was only during the Quattrocento that the cult of the conception was promoted through the activity of Franciscan and Servite friars, who gave the feast an unequivocal interpretation in terms of the Virgin's immaculacy.[3] By contrast,

* My warmest thanks to Mario Ascheri, Philippa Jackson and Fabrizio Nevola; Fabrizio is also responsible for the fine translation of my text into English. For reasons of space, the notes that follow are limited to the most important and recent bibliographic references as well as to archival material. An extended study of the same subject is forthcoming by the author in *Quaderni dell'Opera della Metropolitana di Siena*. In the meantime, see M. Mussolin, 'Il convento di Santo Spirito a Siena e i regolari osservanti di San Domenico', *Bullettino Senese di Storia Patria* (hereafter *BSSP*) CIV, (1987), 138–57, that can be considered in relation with G. Bosco, 'Intorno a un carteggio inedito di Ambrogio Caterino', *Memorie Domenicane*, 1950, 103–20, 137–66, 233–66. On the history of the Immaculate Conception in Tuscany, see M. Bertagna, 'Episodi toscani riguardanti la controversia e il culto dell'Immacolata Concezione', in *Virgo Immaculata. Acta Congressus mariologici-mariani Romae anno MCMLIV*, vol. XIV: *De Immaculata Conceptione apud varias nationes* (Rome, 1957), 360–84; M. Bertagna, 'L'Immacolata nella predicazione di S. Bernardino da Siena', in *Virgo Immaculata*, vol. VII: *De immaculata Conceptione in Ordine S. Francisci*, fasc. II: *Doctrina auctorum inde a saec. XV usque ad nostram aetatem* (Rome, 1957), 20–1; R. M. Dessì, 'La controversia sull'Immacolata Concezione e la propaganda per il culto in Italia nel XV secolo', *Cristianesimo nella storia*, 12 (1991), 265–93. For the iconography and history of the cult in Lucca and Florence, see especially: M. Tazartes, 'Nouvelles perspectives sur la peinture lucquoise du Quattrocento', *Revue de l'art*, 75, (1987), 29–36; L. Dal Prà, 'Publica disputatio peracta est'. Esiti iconografici della controversia dell'Immacolata Concezione a Firenze', *Medioevo e Rinascimento*, II (1988), 267–81; M. T. Filieri, 'Il rinnovamento delle chiese lucchesi alla fine del Quattrocento', in *Matteo Civitali e il suo tempo: pittori, scultori e orafi a Lucca nel tardo Quattrocento* (Milan, 2004), 222–4, 546–9, with an ample and up to date bibliography.

[1] G. Gigli, *Diario sanese* (Siena, 1854), vol. 2, 620.

[2] The Immaculate Conception became dogma only on 8 December 1854. It was then established as a revealed truth that Mary, foreshadowing the merits of Christ, was preserved from Original Sin from the beginning of her existence. The subject is still competently covered by the monumental *Virgo Immacolata*, 18 vols. (Rome, 1955–8). See also: X. Le Bachelet, 'Immaculée Conception', in *Dictionnaire de Théologie catholique*, VII (Paris, 1927), 845–1218; *Bibliographia mariana*, ed. G. M. Besutti, 6 vols. (Rome, 1950–80); *The Dogma of the Immaculate Conception. History and Signifiance*, ed. E. D. O'Connors (Notre Dame, 1958).

[3] F. Nevola, 'Cerimoniali per santi e feste a Siena a metà Quattrocento. Documenti dallo Statuto di Siena 39', in *Siena e il suo territorio nel Rinascimento 3*, ed. M. Ascheri (Siena, 2000), 171–84.

the Dominicans had always been strongly opposed to the feast, manifesting their opposition by celebrating instead the 'Sanctification of Mary,' on the same date of 8 December. Thus, the Franciscan Saint Bernardino, in a sermon on the theme of the annunciation to the Virgin, held on Siena's Piazza del Campo in 1427, expressed his enthusiasm for Mary's original purity. The friar was, however quite cautious when instructing his fellow friars, not wishing to fuel the controversy that was characteristic between preachers, and often remarked that 'in those places where there are Dominican friars, do not preach about the Immaculate Conception'.[4]

By the beginning of the sixteenth century, the debate around the Immaculate Conception evidently tormented the souls of the Sienese, much as it did those of the faithful of the rest of Western Europe.[5] That conflict was not confined to the pulpit; the lecture halls of the *Studium Urbis*, populated by doctors of theology from diverse and opposing religious backgrounds, were also the setting for heated debates. Francesco Sanson, who had promoted the Immaculate Conception during its public disputation, ordered by Pope Sixtus IV in Rome in 1477, had lectured in the Sienese *Studium* in 1473 and from 1476 had become the Master General of the Franciscan order.[6] The local chronicler, Sigismondo Tizio, reported direct conflict between Franciscans and Dominicans in Siena. An emblematic incident was that of the expulsion of Dominicans from the cathedral at the hands of the enraged populace, reacting to a sermon given on the eve of the feast (7 December) in 1510, by the Franciscan Giovan Gualberto Rovai. Again, a protracted disputation that lasted from 4–5 July 1517, took place in the *curia arcivescovile*, revealing the cathedral canons' interest in the cult of the Immaculate Conception.[7]

THE IMMACULATE CONCEPTION AND THE BATTLE OF PORTA CAMOLLIA

When they were faced with the demand that they should celebrate the feast of the Immaculate Conception during the period 1526–32, the two Dominican monasteries in Siena responded in different ways. Two distinct communities occupied these monasteries: the so-called Conventuals resided in San

---

[4] Bernardino da Siena, *Prediche volgari sul Campo di Siena 1427*, ed. C. Del Corno, II (Milan, 1989), 824 ff.; A. Emmen, 'S. Bernardino e l'Immacolata Concezione di Maria. Nuova luce su un vecchio problema', *Studi francescani*, 61, (1964), 7ff.; D. Pacetti, *De sancti Bernardini senensi operibus. Ratio criticae editionis* (Quaracchi, 1947), 56 and 223, 'in locis ubi sunt fratres sancti Dominici non praedices de Conceptione' and 'melius est tacere, quam de talibus praedicare [. . .] sicut in conceptione Virginis et similibus'.

[5] R. Di Segni, '"Colei che non ha mai visto il sangue". Alla ricerca delle radici ebraiche dell'idea della concezione verginale di Maria', *Quaderni storici*, 75, (1990), 757–89. The subject is also object of an important forthcoming study by Adriano Prosperi, outlined in his, 'Scienza e immaginazione teologica nel Seicento: il battesimo e le origini dell'individuo', *Quaderni storici*, 100, (1999), 173–98.

[6] Dal Prà, '"Publica disputatio peracta est"', 280, n. 30; A. Zanelli, 'Maestro Francesco Sanson. Notizie e documenti (1414–1499), *Bullettino Senese di Storia Patria* (hereafter 'BSSP'), IV, (1879), 83–100.

[7] Bertagna, 'Episodi toscani', 362–363.

Domenico in Camporegio, while Santo Spirito was home to the Observant friars of the reformed Tusco-Roman congregation, that in their Florentine house of San Marco had produced Saint Antoninus Pierozzi and Girolamo Savonarola. The historical trigger to these events dates to the days leading up to the Sack of Rome, following the French defeat at Pavia in 1525, which had weakened the papal authority of Clement VII. In Siena, the anti-Medicean faction had toppled the *Nove* government, killing their leader, Alessandro Bichi and imposing a new government, which went under the name of the *libertini*. Relations between this government and the pope broke down, while the exiled Sienese turned to the pope for support in their revenge. Florentine and papal troops soon prepared a siege outside the walls of Porta Camollia, while within the walls popular resentment against the Medici, the Florentines, and the *Novesco* exiles, grew to a head.[8]

In early July 1526, the city government decided to appeal for divine assistance, on the advice of Margherita Bichi Buonsignori, a widowed noblewoman who had become a Franciscan Tertiary. Margherita was recognised to have the gift of prophecy, and many considered her to be living in an odour of sanctity, one of the many 'sante vive' that amounted to a typical and widespread phenomenon of those years. In Siena, as in other centres, these women were invested with a social function resembling that of state councillor. Bichi was related to many members of the government, and this seems to have assured her easy access to the authorities, although her spiritual director, Giovan Battista Pecci, mediated all contact between her and her public.[9]

At the first sign of the imminent siege, the city magistracies sought Bichi's advice. She advised a pacification process between all the Sienese, by means of a general penance, in honour of the Immaculate Conception. This new civic ritual was to have been opened with a procession, led by a large banner (*gonfalone*) dedicated to the Immaculate Conception. The banner requested by Bichi was prepared on 17 July, utilizing a work that had recently been completed by Giovanni di Lorenzo, a painter who specialized in the production of such objects.[10] While we shall return to the image and author of this

[8] G. B. Pecci, *Memorie storico-critiche della città di Siena* (Siena, 1755; repr. Siena, 1988), I, 167ff. More recently M. Ascheri, *Siena nella storia* (Siena, 2000), 162–79; R. Terziani, *Il governo di Siena dal Medioevo all'età Moderna. La continuità repubblicana al tempo dei Petrucci (1487–1525)* (Siena, 2002), 218ff.

[9] On 'sante vive,' G. Zarri, *Le sante vive. Cultura e religiosità femminile nella prima età moderna* (Turin, 1990). On Margherita Bichi, *Fasti Senenses* (I edition, Siena, ante 1669), 165–173, G. B. Luti, *Vita della venerabile serva di Dio Margherita Bichi [. . .]* (Siena, 1699); P. Misciattelli, *Misticismo senese*, ed. A. Lusini (Siena, 1966), 163–71; S. Menchi, *ad vocem* 'Bichi, Margherita', in *Dizionario Biografico degli Italiani*, X (Rome, 1968), 351–3; R. Argenziano, 'L'iconografia dei santi e beati senesi: un Medioevo ininterrotto', in *Santi e beati senesi. Testi e immagini a stampa* (Siena, 2000), 21 and 125.

[10] On Giovanni di Lorenzo, see A. Bagnoli, in *Domenico Beccafumi e il suo tempo* (Siena, 1990), 330–343; C. Zarrilli and S. Moscadelli, 'Appendice documentaria. Parte III: Altri documenti su Giovanni di Lorenzo', in *Ibid.*, 704–6; *Giovanni di Lorenzo dipentore*, ed. M. Ciampolini (Siena, 1997); G. Fattorini, *Considerazioni su Giovanni di Lorenzo ed altri 'comprimari' della maniera moderna a Siena* (unpublished thesis; Univ. di Siena, 1999), with documents and rigorous analysis.

now-lost banner, it is important to note the original subject depicted on it was a traditional *Madonna della misericordia* hovering above a view of the city of Siena. The figure of the Virgin resembled that of an Assumption, surrounded by angels 'on account of the fact that above all the other solemn feasts, the most solemn (*solennissima*) for the Sienese is the Assumption of Mary, so it should reasonably be this figure of the Virgin that should be represented on the banner'.[11] In order to execute Bichi's wishes, the banner was thus modified with the addition of texts dedicated to the Immaculate Conception that made explicit reference to the donation of the city keys: on the front was written 'Immaculatae Conceptioni Virginis Mariae dicatum,' while the back was inscribed 'Donasti claves/ claves et moenia servo funde preces nato libera facta meo'.[12] The following day, 18 July, the Bishop of Pienza, Girolamo Piccolomini, assisted by another canon of the cathedral, Giovanni Pecci, consecrated the banner to the Immaculate Conception in the cathedral. The secular and regular clergy, who had been summoned for the occasion some days in advance, subsequently took it in procession through the city. The friars of the two Dominican monasteries made a point of disobeying the Republic's general request for attendance.

Subsequently, on Friday 20 July, Margherita Bichi dictated to the Balia a famous deposition that was believed to have been directly inspired in her by the Virgin. The two canons from the Pecci family were her spokespersons and somewhat tendentiously pronounced that 'on account of the fact that Siena was the first city in Italy to sacrifice, with humility in their hearts, the magnificence of the times and of the holy altars to the name of the purest Conception, so she demanded that that fervour should persevere in her citizens on the strength of that proud claim'.[13] Bichi touched on many points, but there were three key issues in her deposition that were supposed to occur in sequence. The first demanded that the next Sunday the city should renew its votive offering of the keys of the city to the specific honour of the Immaculate Conception. The second required that 'the day that this city is freed from so much misery, a very solemn feast, beyond all the others, will be held to honour her very Immaculate Conception,' for the centuries to follow. The third prescribed that 'all the clergy and others that do not accept and honour that feast, will not be allowed to live in the city, or have any residence there'. In spite of some uncertainties, the deposition was

---

[11] Quoted from A. M. Orlandini, *La gloriosa vittoria de sanesi per mirabile maniera conseguita nel mese di luglio del anno MDXXVI* (Siena, 1527), c. 9r. For the Assumption, F. Glenisson-Delaunée, 'Fête et société: l'Assomption à Sienne et son évolution au cours du XVIe siècle', in *Les fêtes urbaines en Italie a l'époque de la Renaissance. Verone, Florence, Sienne, Naples*, F. Decroisette and M. Plaisance eds. (Paris, 1993) 65–129. Sienese devotion to the Virgin is comprehensively covered by D. Norman, *Siena and the Virgin: art and politics in a late medieval city state* (New Haven-London, 1999); A. Toti, *Atti di votazione della città di Siena e del Senese alla Santissima Vergine Maria* (Siena, 1870). On the issue of the city's votive promise to the Virgin, see the essay by C. Shaw in this collection.

[12] Orlandini, *La gloriosa vittoria dei Senesi*, 9.

[13] Luti, *Vita della venerabile serva*, 26.

ratified as law on Saturday 21 July 1526.[14] The next day, which coincided with Pentecost Sunday, the ritual offering of the keys to the Madonna delle Grazie in the cathedral was renewed.[15] The day also coincided with the feast of Mary Magdalene, and it may be that there was also the desire to eradicate the memory of a feast that had been associated with the Petrucci family, thus replacing races and *palios* with processions and fasting.[16]

Why was the Sienese government so willing to accept Bichi's requests and alter the traditional ritual practice of the donation of the keys to the Virgin, by introducing a new dedication? Almost certainly the decision to choose the Immaculate Conception as a new civic cult was made in a bid to re-establish the ancient image of *Sena civitas Virginis*, by means of investing Mary with a new and clearly defined role as protectress of republican liberties. As Gigli put it, 'Mary, the mystic Judith liberator of the Sienese people.'[17]

It is well known how the ritual offering of the keys of the city to the Virgin before the 1260 Battle of Montaperti marked the beginning of the civic patronage of the Virgin as *Advocata senensis*.[18] Bichi's ritual not only evoked an ancient ceremony, but it systematically repeated each of its parts. The city had renewed its vow through a pacification ceremony and the donation of the keys, which underlined the exile of the *Noveschi* faction as a threat to the peace, and introduced the total abolition of the earlier *Monti*, or political factions.[19] The repetition of this sequence for a third time in 1526 could not but evoke a series of political messages, to which was added the investiture of the Immaculate Conception as guarantor of Sienese liberty.

Even the manner in which these events were described was based upon the chronicles of the Montaperti myth, a number of which had been written in the fifteenth century with revisionist intentions.[20] Additional variants introduced by Bichi to the ceremony of the citizens' oath to the Virgin reveal how the political function of the events was gauged to satisfy the requirements of circumstances. The new government's need for legitimation resulted in the daring and difficult decision to rededicate the ancient ritual to the spiritual sovereignty of the Immaculate Conception, erasing decades of ceremonial

---

[14] Archivio di Stato di Siena (hereafter ASS), *Balia 85*, cc. 60–4 [20–21 July 1526]; Pecci, *Memorie storico-critiche*, 213; G. Bosco, 'Intorno a un carteggio inedito', 108–9.

[15] Perhaps the scene represented by Domenico Beccafumi in the Devonshire collection panel at Chatsworth, showing a 'Ceremony of thanks in the Cathedral', for which see *Domenico Beccafumi e il suo tempo*, 131, Fig. 9.

[16] A. Bardi, Biblioteca Comunale di Siena (hereafter *BCS*), ms A.VI.51, c. 31.

[17] G. Gigli, *La città diletta di Maria* (Siena, 1716), 58.

[18] R. Argenziano, 'Le origini e lo sviluppo dell'iconografia della Madonna a Siena', in *L'immagine del Palio. Storia, cultura e rappresentazione del rito di Siena*, ed. M. A. Ceppari Ridolfi, M. Ciampolini, P. Turrini (Siena, 2001), 92–7.

[19] A. Allegretti, 'Ephemerides Senenses . . . [Diari . . . delle cose sanesi]', in *Rerum Italicarum Scriptores*, tomo XXIII (Milan, 1733), 815.

[20] D. L. Kawsky, *The Survival, Revival, and Reappraisal of Artistic Tradition: Civic Art and Civic Identity in Quattrocento Siena*, Ph.D. thesis Princeton Univ. 1995 (Ann Arbor, 1995), 122–6 and 'Appendix II', 245–60; G. Parsons, *Siena, Civil Religion and the Sienese* (Aldershot, 2004), 1–31.

practices associated with the *Nove* in one stroke. The oath was structured according to the antique *ordalia*. The victory that was assured to the Sienese by way of Bichi's prophecies, invested the new government with authority. Furthermore, the long-lasting conflict between the Sienese and the community of the reformed Dominicans of Santo Spirito, who were subject to the Florentine house of San Marco, served to polarize the population's xenophobic feelings against their traditional enemies.[21]

Three days later, providence seemed to have been on the side of the Sienese. The feast of St James (25 July), is still remembered by the Sienese for the glorious victory of Porta Camollia; endless ceremonies of thanks followed in the city and the countryside, and further innumerable miraculous events were recorded and ascribed to the Immaculate Virgin On 5 August, the sceptical Francesco Vettori reported the unexpected Sienese victory to Machiavelli as an event of quasi-biblical significance.[22] Almost all the sources are silent with regard to the Dominicans, although Gigli refers to the fact that the victory 'closed the mouths of the opponents of the mystery of the Immaculate Conception of the Blessed Virgin'.[23] (Fig. 1)

Margherita Bichi had also followed in the footsteps of the ancient myth on another point, inspired by the victorious cart and banner of Montaperti, and the uniforms of the soldiers. A fourteenth-century chronicle of the battle reports that after the conflict of 1260, the huge white banner had been brought back into the city as a symbol of victory, and had become in the eyes of the Sienese the concrete expression of the luminous mantle of protection that the Virgin had, according to the legend, cast over Montaperti and the city of Siena. The same chronicle states 'the said banner was white as a symbol of the Virgin Mary and had at the top a verse written along a band, which said "Sena vetus civitas Virginis, alpha et omega, principium et finis"'.[24] Bichi had also requested that the army should follow the two banners bearing the symbols of the 'crucified God' and 'the white banner of Mary [...] shouting out no name other than that of the God the Saviour and Mary [...] and so that everyone could freely see for whom they were to be victorious, the captains and others wishing to do so, should wear an inscription on their breast that recited *Per Immaculatam Virginis Conceptionem de inimicis nostris libera nos Deus noster*'.[25]

[21] On the Sienese and Girolamo Savonarola in the community of Santo Spirito in 1494, see Mussolin, 'Il convento di Santo Spirito', 52–70.
[22] N. Machiavelli, *Opere. II: Lettere, legazioni e commissarie*, ed. C. Vivanti (Turin, 1999), 436ff.; A. Liberati, 'Battaglia di Camullia', *Miscellanea storica senese*, 5, (1898), 96–7, Idem, 'Battaglia di Camullia', *BSSP*, XIII (1906), 220–1; M. Callegari, 'Il fatto d'armi di Porta Camollia nel 1526', *BSSP*, XV, (1908), 319–320; J. C. D'Amico, 'Margherita Bichi et la bataille de Porta Camollia', in *Les guerres d'Italie. Histoire, pratiques, représentations*, Actes du Colloque International, Paris 1999, ed. D. Boillet and M. F. Piejus (Paris, 2002), 73–87, whom I thank for stimulating conversations on the subject.
[23] Gigli, *Città diletta*, 15.
[24] 'Cronaca senese d'autore anonimo', in *Rerum Italicarum Scriptores [...]*, vol. XV, part VI, [*Cronache senesi*, ed. A. Lisini and F. Iacometti] (Bologna, 1931), 58.
[25] Orlandini, *La gloriosa vittoria dei Senesi*, fol. 18 v.

Fig. 1   Giovanni di Lorenzo, *The victory of Porta Camollia in 1526*, 1526, tempera on panel, Museo delle Biccherne, Archivio di Stato, Siena (photo reproduced with permission of Archivio di Stato, Siena)

According to a number of the sources, Bichi was repeatedly consulted in the prelude to the battle by Alessandro Politi, and his son Camillo, for instructions regarding the order of the attack. Alessandro had allegedly been chosen by the Virgin herself to lead the army into battle. A first contingent led by the banner of Crucifixion, a symbol of the Terzo di Città, left the city from Fontebranda, while a second group wearing white shirts followed the white banner of the Terzo di Camollia. The latter were the 'lady Margherita's youths' that were the first to raise the white banner in the enemy camp, contributing to that image of the battle that Gabriele Fattorini felicitously described as suspended between 'mysticism and heroic classicism'.[26] (Fig. 2)

Every church in Siena rapidly and spontaneously united in the festivities of 8 December (Fig. 3), in accordance with the terms prescribed in Bichi's deposition, with the sole exception of the two Dominican communities. The city's long-lasting diffidence with respect to the friars of Santo Spirito was thus rekindled with unprecedented vigour and violence. On account of the

---

[26] Gabriele Fattorini notes that military-political exploits had rarely been accompanied by mystic sentiments during the *novesco* government of Pandolfo Petrucci, see Fattorini, *Considerazioni su Giovanni di Lorenzo*, 11. My warm thanks to the author for allowing me to read the unpublished thesis and for his valuable suggestions.

Fig. 2   Giovanni di Lorenzo, *The Immaculate Conception protects the Sienese at the Battle of Camollia*, 1528, tempera on panel, Siena, Church of San Martino (photo: author)

Fig. 3   Antonio Gregori, *The Senate pays homage to the Virgin after the battle of Camollia*, 1619, fresco (Sala del Capitano del Popolo, today the Aula consiliare, Siena, Palazzo Pubblico)

fact that the monastery community was made up of a majority of Florentine friars, and that it was located in the vicinity of the city walls and the gate of San Viene, it became the object of the citizens' compulsive and irrational resentment, directed at Florence as a whole. For their part, the friars who were renowned for their intransigence, refused any form of compromise solution, and put their reputation and personal safety on the line. Sigismondo Tizio, one-time confessor of Margherita Bichi, is again an exceptional witness to events. He unsparingly attacked her prophecies, judging her a 'futilis mulier', while at the same time he considered the tormented Sienese Dominicans, and particularly those of Santo Spirito, unjustly considered by many to be traitors, especially on account of the many Florentines in the community, and the proximity of their convent to the city walls.[27]

SITE AND IMAGERY OF THE NEW CIVIC CULT OF THE IMMACULATE CONCEPTION

Within a short space of time, in Siena the feast of the Immaculate Conception became a matter of state, and all eyes turned on the Dominicans. Meanwhile, the government passed laws that set the feast on the same level as that of the Assumption.[28] In mid November 1526, the prior and all the Florentine friars of Santo Spirito were expelled from the city. By 1527, as the tragedy of the Sack of Rome was in progress, the remaining non-Florentine friars of Santo Spirito continued firm in their refusal to observe the feast, supported in their intent by the general chapter of the Congregation of San Marco.

The Sienese preacher Ambrogio Catarino Politi was called back to the city by his brethren to replace the expelled Florentine friars, and thus returned to Siena in this tense climate. Catarino was remarkable among Dominicans for his acknowledged devotion to the Immaculate Conception, on account of the fact that he believed that he had benefited from a miraculous cure at her hands in his youth.[29] It seems likely that this led to his superiors in the Order deciding that he was the best person able to mediate what had become an unmanageable situation.[30] As has been mentioned, a number of his relatives had been interlocutors for Margherita Bichi, and the fact that his brother Giovanbattista Politi held office as prior in the Concistoro, augured well for a solution being found, in part through these family

---

[27] S. Tizio, *Historiarum Senensium*, BCS, ms. B. III. 15 (vol. X), 293–6; cited in Pecci, *Memorie storico-critiche*, II, 212 note.

[28] ASS, Balìa 92, fol. 217 (28 November 1527), 'Item che il dì di dicta festività de la Inmaculata Conceptione sia feria [. . .] come supra la festa di Sancta Maria di Agosto, e questo s'intenda per la città et contado.'

[29] Dessì, *La controversia sull'Immacolata Concezione*, 284–7; U. Horst, *Die Diskussion um die Immaculata Conceptio im Domenikanerorden* (Paderborn, 1987).

[30] Baptised Lancelloto Politi (1484–1553), he took the name Ambrogio Catarino in honour of the local Dominican saints, Catherine of Siena and Ambrogio Sansedoni; he was consistorial advocate in Leo X's Rome and became a Dominican in 1517 at the Florentine house of San Marco. I. Schweizer, *Ambrosius Catharinus Politus* (1484–1553), ein Theologe des Reformationszeitalters (Münster i. W., 1910), 43–63; V. Criscuolo, *Ambrogio Caterino Politi teologo e padre al Concilio di Trento* (Rome, 1987).

connections. As things turned out however, the choice was particularly disadvantageous for the entire Order. Catarino immediately set to work to find a peaceful settlement; he was elected prior of Santo Spirito in 1528 and obtained the right to postpone the celebration of the feast until such time as the papal authority had been decreed on the matter. Nonetheless, the status quo was short lived, as in the autumn of 1528 a papal brief was issued to the effect that every priest was free to celebrate the feast according to the dictates of his individual convictions.

The Conventual friars at San Domenico immediately accepted the celebration. Likewise for Catarino the matter was resolved, and from that moment onward he became the most outspoken supporter of the Immaculate Conception in the Dominican order. By contrast, the friars of the reformed Observant community of Santo Spirito remained firm in their opposition to the feast. Catarino's response caused a scandal: on 8 December 1528 he donned his prior's insignia and recited the office for the feast of the Immaculate Conception in the church of Santo Spirito, before his shocked brethren. Tizio reports that this resulted in the formation of a city faction that supported Politi (the so-called *catarinotti*), who was in turn removed from the position of prior. An epistolary battle ensued, whose complex web involved the highest church authorities in Florence, Siena and Rome.

The turn of events that saw the institution of the second Florentine republic and the siege of Florence in 1530 resulted in further widespread criticism of the San Marco congregation's active involvement in politics, and it is clear that the Sienese criticism of the friars was far from being an isolated case. This situation was to be further aggravated by a dramatic occurrence on the night of 4 December 1531, when a fire broke out in the church of San Domenico in Camporegio. The relic of the skull of Saint Catherine was miraculously saved, while the body of the Blessed Ambrogio Sansedoni was virtually consumed by the flames. The fire was almost immediately turned into an event of portentous significance, considering the outbreak of a fire in the Dominican monastery so soon before the feast of 8 December. While the cause of the fire remained unidentified, each side in the dispute blamed their opponents for arson, and the city magistracies once again used the fire as an opportunity to denounce the obstinate stand of the friars at Santo Spirito to their superiors in the order. This final turn of the screw forced the *Curia Generale* of the Dominican Order to remove any residual prejudicial judgement from the cult of the Immaculate Conception in the city of Siena, and on 19 June 1532 a definitive disposition was issued in favour of the celebration of the feast in the two Sienese convents.

The period between the battle of 1526 and 1532, when it became possible for the feast of the Immaculate Conception to be celebrated at Santo Spirito, thus coincides with the length of time required by the republic of Siena to elaborate and define all the aspects of the new cult. In 1532, the pope absolved Politi from all connections with the Dominican order, and the latter published the *Disputatio pro veritate Immaculatae Conceptionis Beatae Virginis Mariae* in Siena. In it, the author resumed the polemic that had raged through the previous years. For Politi, the publication of the book amounted to a belated victory, and in the years that followed he continued to publish his thesis, and as papal theologian at the Council of Trent, chose that international forum as the opportunity to advance his personal campaign for the definitive doctrinal definition of the mystery of the Immaculate Conception.

Catarino's intellectual standing in Siena and the weight of his political thought stood him in high regard among the Sienese intelligentsia already many years prior to the events here outlined. Indeed, in the same year as he was nominated a professor in the city *Studium* (1502), Politi had published *La sconficta di Monte Aperto*, using his secular name Lancellotto; this was the first book to have been produced by the Sienese publisher Simone di Niccolò Nardi.[31] In this work, dedicated to Pandolfo Petrucci, Politi added a classicising tone to the more ancient chronicles of the battle of Montaperti, and the text constitutes a fundamental precedent for the events of 1526.[32]

While there is no direct proof that Margherita Bichi knew the book, it seems highly likely that her knowledge of that victorious battle was drawn from this easily accessed and recently published source. More importantly, the woodcut illustration on the frontispiece constitutes the first instance of the traditional iconography of the *Madonna della Misericordia* as protectress of Siena being combined with a city view, showing the fortifications of Porta Camollia. The print also included an invocation to the Virgin, 'Salva nos ne pereamus' and the text 'Sena vetus'.[33] In view of the book's publication date, the print predates the well-known view of Siena, painted in the Piccolomini Library fresco by Pinturicchio, in the scene in which 'Aeneas Silvius Piccolomini introduces Frederick III to Eleonora of Portugal'.[34] The decision to represent the exterior of Camollia was not purely coincidental. Rather, it shows the author's conscious desire to update by means of a realistic city-portrait, the more generic images of the Madonna as protectress of the city, a well-known example of which is the *Biccherna* panel painted 'al tenpo de' tremuoti' ('at the time of the earthquakes') by Francesco di Giorgio Martini, in 1467–8.[35]

Porta Camollia was not only the first view of the city glimpsed by pilgrims on their way to Rome, but it was also the departure point of the road to

---

[31] F. Iacometti, 'Simone di Niccolò Nardi', *La Diana. Rassegna d'arte e vita senese*, I (1926), 184–202; N. Pallecchi, 'Una tipografia a Siena nel XVI secolo. Bibliografia delle edizioni stampate da Simone di Niccolò Nardi (1502–1539)', *BSSP*, CIX, 2002, 184–233.

[32] L. Politi, *La sconficta di Monte Aperto*, reprinted A. Leoncini (Siena, 2002) lacks the dedicatory page to Pandolfo Petrucci *signore* of Siena.

[33] E. Pellegrini, *L'iconografia di Siena nelle opere a stampa [. . .]* (Siena, 1986), 31–2 and *L'immagine di Siena. Le due città [. . .]* (Siena, 1999), 26–7.

[34] P. Scarpellini and M. R. Silvestrelli, *Pintoricchio* (Milan, 2003), 265–269.

[35] M. C. Paoluzzi in *Le Biccherne di Siena. Arte e Finanza all'alba dell'economia moderna*, ed. A. Tomei (Rome, 2002), 198–200.

Florence. The area just outside the gate, at Santa Petronilla, had been the theatre for the first skirmishes between the Florentine troops encamped in the environs, and the Sienese, in the days preceding the battle of Montaperti, on the 13 and 14 May 1260.[36] Furthermore, the fourteenth-century chronicles confirm that the company of soldiers from the district of Camollia had distinguished itself particularly in the battle, and this fact is emphasized in Politi's *Sconficta*.[37] The nearby Fonte Becci, which was used as the hand-over site for the ransomed Florentine prisoners, also served as a reminder of the shame inflicted by the Sienese on the Florentines. It was thus natural that it should be around this area that signs of the Virgin's protection should be most evident, guarding the liberty of the Sienese state, so that with time the area came to be layered with images and chapels dedicated to Her.

Perhaps the most significant of these iconic images was the *Assumption of the Virgin*, painted on the so-called Antiporto di Camollia, in the early fourteenth century. The fresco, which is usually attributed to Simone Martini, and is now entirely lost and replaced by much more recent paintings of the same subject, must have constituted one of the most frequently imitated models of the image of the Assumption in Siena.[38] That Madonna seemed spontaneously to interact with passers-by: for San Bernardino the *Assumption* at Porta Camollia was *par excellence* the image of the 'Vergine bella', and added value to a site that was in many respects considered holy (Fig. 4).[39] In 1460, when Pope Pius II made his entry to the city, a grandiose theatrical apparatus was erected in front of the Virgin of Camollia, where a chorus of angels in movement turned to the pope and the image of the Madonna, asking both for their help and protection. A cult sprang up around that image of the *Assumption*, and it is known that from as early as 1466, the *Biccherna* tax office made an annual offering of 12 *lire* of wax on the 2 July.[40] It is, moreover interesting to note, that one of the first legislative acts of the

---

[36] G. Merlotti, *Memorie storiche delle parrocchie suburbane della Diocesi di Siena*, ed. M. Marchetti (Siena, 1995), 355–66; P. Brogini, 'Presenze ecclesiastiche e dinamiche sociali nello sviluppo del borgo di Camollia (secc. XI–XIV)', in *La chiesa di San Pietro alla Magione nel Terzo di San Martino*, ed. M. Ascheri (Siena, 2001), 7–102; *Porta Camollia. Da baluardo di difesa a simbolo di accoglienza* (Siena, 2004); *Santa Petronilla, eventi storici e vicende dalle origini alla Parrocchia dei nostri giorni*, ed. B. Chiantini and P. Staderini (Grosseto, 1995), 25–44.

[37] L. Politi, *La sconficta*, 82.

[38] P. Leone de Castris, *Simone Martini* (Milan, 2003), 286–92. On the Sienese iconography of the Virgin, N. Fargnoli, *Vecchietta's Assumption of the Virgin at Montemerano. Restoration and new keys for interpretation* (Asciano, 2004); A. Gianni, 'Iconografia della Madonna della Misericordia nell'arte senese', in *La Misericordia di Siena attraverso i secoli dalla Domus Misericordiae all'Arciconfraternita di Misericordia*, ed. M. Ascheri and P. Turrini (Siena, 2004), 95–111; G. Fattorini, 'Le copertine dell'Ospedale: note di cronologia, iconografia e stile', in *Arte e assistenza a Siena. Le copertine dipinte dell'Ospedale di Santa Maria della Scala* (Pisa, 2003), 47–55.

[39] Bernardino da Siena, *Prediche volgari* (Milan, 1989), 69; V. Lusini, 'La Madonna dell'Antiporto di Camollia detta la Madonna di San Bernardino', in *Miscellanea storica senese*, a. II, n.1 (January 1894; reprinted, Siena 2004), 3–8; E. Carli, 'Luoghi e opere d'arte senesi nelle prediche di Bernardino del 1427', in *Bernardino predicatore nella società del suo tempo* (Todi, 1975), 155–71; an image showing 'The young San Bernardino praying before the image of the Virgin at Porta Camollia' was frescoed in the present Sala del Consiglio of the Palazzo Pubblico (1598), see entry by G. Borghini, in *Il Palazzo Pubblico di Siena. Vicende, costruzione e decorazione*, ed. C. Brandi (Siena, 1983), 293–4, Fig. 382.

[40] Merlotti, *Memorie storiche*, 360.

Fig. 4   Ventura Salimbeni, *The young Saint Bernardino praying in front of the 'Virgin of Porta Camollia'*, 1598, fresco (Sala del Capitano del Popolo, today the Aula consiliare, Siena, Palazzo Pubblico)

new government of the *libertini* in 1525 was to decree that 'above those gates to the city where up to this time an image of the most holy Mary had not been completed, it should be painted', so as to conform every gate to the undisputed venerability of the Antiporto di Camollia.[41]

The victory at Camollia in 1526 thus confirmed all earlier beliefs associated with that site, with the force of a fully revealed truth. The effect can be summarised using the words of the nineteenth-century memorial of the suburban parish priest Giuseppe Merlotti, who declared that 'the environs of this parish of Santa Petronilla have always been the theatre for wars and triumphs that the ancient Sienese have always achieved against their enemies'.[42] The view of Camollia in Politi's *Sconficta* thus consciously anticipated and defined one of the principal *topoi* of the city's myth-making and collective memory. From that moment and for many years to follow, Camollia became the 'postcard' view of the city of Siena.

The battle of 1526 can be reconstructed through a number of sources.[43] Among these, the most interesting are those written with a particular bias, which later formed the basis for hagiographic and celebratory narratives.

---

[41] Pecci, *Memorie storico-critiche*, vol. I, 176; Gigli, *Città diletta*, 45. Machtelt Israëls has recently shed light on the Marian subject of frescoes on city gates, in 'Al cospetto della città. Il Sodoma a Porta Pispini, culmine di una tradizione civica' presented at the conference *Siena nel Rinascimento: l'ultimo secolo della Repubblica* (Siena, 16–18 September 2004); I thank the author for allowing me to consult her forthcoming article.

[42] Merlotti, *Memorie storiche*, 364.

[43] See manuscript sources in BCS: S. Tizio (above note 26); A. Bardi, *Storie senesi* [1512–1526], ms. A.VI.51, fol. 18–31v; G. Tommasi, *La seconda parte inedita delle Historia di Siena*, BCS, ms. A. X. 74; U. Benvoglienti, BCS, ms. C. IV. 21, fol. 244r–v. Also, M. Guazzo, *Historie . . . di tutti i fatti degni di memoria . . . dall'anno 1524 al 1546* (Venezia, 1552), 43–73; A. Sozzini, *Diario delle cose avvenute in Siena dal 20 luglio 1550 al 28 giugno 1555* (Firenze, 1842), 20; O. Malavolti, *Dell'historia di Siena. Prima parte* (Venezia, 1599), fol. 128v–31v.

Achille Maria Orlandini's, *La gloriosa vittoria de sanesi per mirabil maniera conseguita*, was printed on 16 February 1527 by the same publisher as Politi's text, Simone di Niccolò Nardi.[44] A rhyming poetic version of that text soon followed with the title *Vittoria gloriosissima deli Sanesi, contro ali Fiorentini*, an anonymous work, undated and with no reference to its publisher; it was almost certainly published by Simone di Niccolò soon after the other text, and it seems probable that its authorship should be attributed to Orlandini.[45] In the first description of the battle of Porta Camollia, Orlandini borrowed wholesale from chronicle histories of Montaperti. The text was evidently intended to legitimate recent political events through the agency of the Immaculate Conception and the work of Margherita Bichi. While many of the narrative turns are inspired by the 'widely respected style of the Greek and Roman writers', an overwhelming mystic theme pervades the text, since every event is shown to corroborate the Virgin's intercession. Furthermore, the publisher Simone di Niccolò Nardi played an important role in establishing continuity between Orlandini's composition and Politi's, as he inserted also a woodcut image of the first banner of the Immaculate Conception, painted by Giovanni di Lorenzo, half way through Orlandini's text. Thus, if Orlandini might be described as the historian of the events, Giovanni di Lorenzo was their official artist. Indeed, as Ettore Pellegrini has noted, the image in Orlandini's text constitutes the natural evolution of the frontispiece image of Politi's book.[46] The standing figure of the Madonna appears with one arm pointing towards the ground and the other towards the sky, in a gesture of mediation, suspended among the heads of cherubim and clouds, and surrounded by rays and angels that are crowning her, and two putti at her feet, offering her olive branches. A scroll beneath the feet of the Virgin, placed above the city view seen from Camollia, should ideally be read in conjunction with the text that appears outside the frame 'You, Lady of the Heavens/ You it was that freed us/ there are cohorts of your faithful here below, that believe the Father did not sin in you, that are always favoured and beautiful'. (Fig. 5)

Similarly interesting is the second work here considered. It is certainly no accident that this rare verse text attributed to Orlandini should have reused the same woodblock for the frontispiece, as that of Politi's *Sconficta di Monte Aperto*, showing the view of Siena. (Fig. 6) Another small woodcut in the text shows a scene of the battle of Camollia in front of the second gate – the so-called Torrazzo di Mezzo – that had been damaged by enemy artillery. In this

[44] Orlandini, *La gloriosa vittoria dei Senesi*, motivates the enthusiasm for Margherita shown by: Luti, *Vita della Venerabile serva*; S. Conti, *Vittoria maravigliosa per intercessione della Venerabile Madre Margherita Bichi terziaria di S. Francesco ottenuta a 25 di luglio del 1526*. See also BCS, ms. A.VI.15 [seventeenth century].

[45] *Vittoria gloriosissima deli Sanesi, contro ali Fiorentini, nel Piano di Camollia adì XXV di Luglio anno MDXXVI [. . .]* ([Simone di Niccolò Nardi?], Siena post 1526), reprinted in *La guerra di Camollia e la presa di Roma. Rime del secolo XVI*, ed. F. Mango, in *Scelta di curiosità letterarie inedite o rare dal secolo XIII al XIX*, Bologna 1886 [reprinted Bologna 1969], 1–116 with an attribution to Orlandini.

[46] E. Pellegrini, *L'iconografia di Siena*, 31–8 and *L'immagine di Siena*, 26–31.

VOI VOI DONNA DEL CIEL I VOI FVSTE QVELLA
CHE LIBERASTE NOI I NON POCHE SQVADRE
PER FAR FEDE QVAGGIV CHEL PRIMO PADRE
NON PECCO IN VOI SEMPRE GRADITA ET BELLA.

Fig. 5   Achille Maria Orlandini, *La vittoria de sanesi per mirabile maniera conseguita nel mese di luglio del anno MDXXVI*, Simone di Niccolò, Siena 1526, woodcut frontispiece to book II, unpaginated but fol. 10v (Siena, private collection)

war scene, Siena is shown in the distance, with its many towers (Fig. 7). There can be no doubt that the design was provided by Giovanni di Lorenzo. It is also possible that the publisher was an ardent supporter of the Immaculate Conception, since many of his later publications bear the invocation 'Laus Deo onnipotenti et semper Immaculatae Virgini Mariae'.[47]

Certainly, the painter was one of the youths that fought beneath the white banner of Camollia on the 25 July 1526. This artist's devotion, intense social and political activity, and particular style, have recently been the object of study. He was known as Giovanni Bianco on account of the fact that he continued to wear that colour for many years, as a mark of his devotion to the Virgin. He became an oblate of the Ospedale di Santa Maria della Scala from 1552, held the post of captain and standard-bearer for the district of Salicotto in the 1540, and is said to have died in 1562, having preserved his virginity in honour of the Virgin. It seems he even went so far as to have the young Ignatius of Loyola as a guest in his house, when he came through Siena.[48] The Immaculate Virgin as he portrays her, is always shown in a white robe decorated with gold gilt that shimmers with bluish metallic tinges. Simone di Niccolò Nardi and Giovanni di Lorenzo, together with Orlandini, were thus the image-makers that forged the iconography and defined the new rituals associated with the Immaculate

---

[47] P. Turrini, 'La costruzione dell'oratorio della contrada della Torre [. . .]', in *Giovanni di Lorenzo dipentore*, 58.
[48] Fattorini, *Considerazioni su Giovanni di Lorenzo*, 45.

Fig. 6   Anonymous, *Vittoria gloriosissima deli Sanesi, contro ali Fiorentini, nel Piano di Camollia adì XXV di Luglio anno MDXXVI [. . .]*, [Simone di Niccolò Nardi?], Siena post 1526, woodcut frontispiece that reuses the woodcut from L. Politi, *La Sconficta di Monte Aperto*, Siena 1502 (Siena, Archivio di Stato)

Conception. The government Balia of twenty-one *conservatori della Libertà* were their virtual patrons, and from behind the scenes, the influence of the works and opinions of Lancellotto/Ambrogio Catarino Politi can be felt.

The fame of the what came to be known as the 'Banner of the Immaculate' afforded its painter great renown, so that his Assumption/Immaculate Conceptions came to be identified as the icon of that victory, that was frequently reproposed over the century that followed.[49] Giovanni di Lorenzo's most

Fig. 7 Anonymous, *Vittoria gloriosissima deli Sanesi, contro ali Fiorentini, nel Piano di Camollia adì XXV di Luglio anno MDXXVI [. . .]*, [Simone di Niccolò Nardi?], Siena post 1526, woodcut (Siena, Archivio di Stato)

famous work that has always hung in the church of San Martino, the *Virgin of the Immaculate Conception protecting Siena during the Battle of Camollia* (Fig. 1), confirms this impression, as it was commissioned by the Balìa themselves.[50] The painting is signed and dated 1528, but payments for it begin in 1526, and there are few variations in the design with respect to the print in Orlandini's book. The detail of the painting shows how the banner of the Immaculate Conception had been raised up on the gate of Camollia, flanked by that of the Emperor, represented by the Imperial banner with an eagle. The Torrazzo di Mezzo is shown in a derelict state, much as is it appears in the second woodcut, while the Antiporto is shown in sufficient detail that the frescoed image of the Assumption can be discerned, above the she-wolf symbol of the city, on the gate. Again, in 1526, Giovanni di Lorenzo had painted a *Biccherna* panel showing the same battle scene, although in this instance the image is confined to representing the moment of the conflict, repeating the details visible in the San Martino altarpiece.

[50] See note 10; Gianni, 'Iconografia della Madonna della Misericordia', 107–8.

In this period, while Ambrogio Catarino Politi was intent on resolving the issue of the celebration of the feast in the monastery of Santo Spirito, the city government was actively legislating in favour of rendering the feast increasingly solemn, so that the memory of the battle of Camollia would remain alive. In November 1527, the end of a bout of plague was attributed to the intercession of the Virgin Immaculate, and the Balia does not appear to have tired of making offerings and creating new altars and churches dedicated to the feast.[51] Just as the battle of Montaperti had been celebrated in the victory-church of San Giorgio in Pantaneto, so too it was decided that a church should be offered to the victory of Camollia, and the confraternity of San Giovanni Battista took up the charge of constructing a new building. Very little is known of the patrons' intentions, although the involvement of the architect Baldassarre Peruzzi in the project underlines its importance.[52] Nonetheless, there is a certain irony in the fact that the site identified for the construction of the new building coincided with the old church of San Giovanni Battista (now the oratory of the Contrada del Liocorno), which had belonged to the monastery of Santo Spirito since 1362. A drawn-out dispute between the city government and the community of Santo Spirito is documented from October 1528, and reveals the Dominicans' reluctance to cede the necessary site, so that the Balia eventually turned their attention to other projects instead.[53]

Among these was the construction of a new church in the street of Salicotto, dedicated to the titular saints of the 25 July anniversary of the Camollia victory, Saints Christopher and James the Great. Documents indicate that construction began in 1531, and a stone inscription placed at the completion of work, underlines the motives for the church's construction as 'IM(macu-late) MAR(iae) OB VICT(oriam) 1526–1536 F(ecit) P(opulus)'. The history of the church of Santi Giacomo e Cristoforo, which is now the oratory of the Contrada della Torre, has recently been written in some detail.[54] While the government authorities took part in the project through considerable subventions, the true patrons of the church were the 'populus' of the district of Salicotto that had fought among the 'youths of Donna Margherita [Bichi]'.

---

[51] For other dedications to the Immaculate Conception in the city: Bertagna, 'L'Immacolata nella predicazione', 365; Israëls, 'Al cospetto della città', notes 22 and 27.

[52] Mussolin, 'Il convento di Santo Spirito', 150–2.

[53] G. Milanesi, *Documenti per la storia dell'arte senese* (Siena, 1856), vol. III, 107, 'li magnifici signori Conservatori della libertà hanno procurato che si edifichi un tempio ad honore et laude della Inmaculata Conceptione della Madonna, vera patrona di questa alma città'; A. Liberati, 'Chiesa di San Giovannino in Pantaneto', *BSSP*, LX (1953), 255; D. Ceccherini, *Gli oratori delle Contrade di Siena. Storia, architettura, arte* (Siena, 1995), 88–97.

[54] Turrini, 'La costruzione dell'oratorio', 37–75; P. Turrini, 'La chiesa dei santi Giacomo e Cristoforo in Salicotto: il profilo storico', in *L'oratorio della Contrada della Torre San Giacomo maggiore. Restauri, storia e testimonianze* (Siena, 2003), 28–39; Ceccherini, *Gli oratori delle Contrade*, 166–173.

Fig. 8   Giovanni di Lorenzo, *Immaculate Conception between Saints James and Christopher*, post 1532, tempera on panel (Siena, Oratory of San Giacomo e Cristoforo)

Giovanni di Lorenzo was again a vital force and protagonist in the project, serving from the beginning as master of works, accountant and in the end, also artist for the church, since the high altarpiece showing the *Immaculate Virgin between the Saints James and Christopher* was in place by 1535 (Fig. 8).

From 1526, another site attracted the attention of the city's governors, the hugely important church of Santa Maria dei Servi, to which the Balìa had a long history of financial aid to its slow construction. Towards the end of construction, the high altar was dedicated to the Immaculate Conception on 18 May 1533, by the same Girolamo Piccolomini, Bishop of Pienza, who had blessed the banner of the Immaculate Conception in 1526.[55]

In 1535, Margherita Bichi arranged for her tomb to be set up before the new altar dedicated to the Immaculate Conception in the church of San Francesco. That chapel had belonged for many years to the Politi family, and was later also decorated with a new monument to Ambrogio Catarino. For indeed, that church had been the first proponent of the mystery of the Immaculate Conception, and following the funerals held there for the

---

[55] Gigli, *Città diletta*, 49; G. Cecchini, 'Dedicata nel 1533 alla Immacolata Concezione la chiesa di Santa Maria dei Servi', *Ausonia. Rivista di lettere e arti*, IX, (1954), 58–62; Bertagna, 'Episodi toscani', 365; Israëls, 'Al cospetto della città', note 23.

Fig. 9   *Grosso da 40 quattrini,* recto with portrait bust of the Madonna, above a city-view of Siena, 1528–31 or
1536–39 (Siena, Museo Civico)

noblemen that had fallen in the battle of Camollia, the church was chosen
for many of the government's official religious ceremonies.[56]

Another feature of the events confirms a narrative of crossed destinies
between the battles of Montaperti and Camollia. As early as 1279 a series of
Sienese coins had been introduced that added to the traditional inscriptions
of 'Sena Vetus' and 'alpha et omega', the new text of 'Civitas Virginis'
and 'principium et finis', as an evident gesture of honour towards the new
dedication of the city to the Virgin after Montaperti. A similar intention lay
behind the coining of three series of *grossi* during the 1530s, whose obverse
was decorated with an image of the Virgin (Fig. 9). No government decision
explains the production of these prototypes, although it is possible that they
were celebratory medals with an apotropaic function, which might explain
the reason for which all surviving examples have a hole bored through them.
The Madonna is shown with her cloak outstretched over a view of the city
of Siena seen from Porta Camollia, unquestionably re-evoking the print
contained in Politi's *Sconficta di Monte Aperto.* Again, therefore, the image can

[56] Luti, *Vita della venerabile serva,* 47–8; Ugurgeri Azzolini, *Pompe Sanesi,* vol. I, 141–6 e 155; V. Lusini, *Storia della basilica di San Francesco in Siena* (Siena, 1894), 147–56.

be seen to derive from the iconographic workshop that emerged in the aftermath of the victory of Camollia around Giovanni di Lorenzo and Simone di Niccolò Nardi. The image of the Virgin that the coin circulated, acquire such a strong symbolic value that it even survived the conquest of Siena on the part of Cosimo de' Medici, as is evidenced by the so-called 'Testone' of 1557, the first coin made after the fall of the republic (1555). Here, the obverse shows the profile of the city's new ruler, while for obvious reasons of political expedience; the reverse shows the traditional image of the Virgin, shown above the city view from Camollia.[57]

Once the Dominicans had consented to celebrate the feast in 1532, it seemed that nothing could interfere with the course of the celebration. Nonetheless, in spite of the great efforts that had been made to establish the feast as one of civic and popular devotion, following the definitive political split with Spain, the subsequent return of the *Nove*, and eventual Florentine dominion, the city's fragile political climate meant that the observance of the feast was challenged, on account of the fact that it was so closely bound with issues of civic pride and liberty. The first step in this direction was the suppression of the *palio* race of 25 July dedicated to St. James from 1557, and its replacement with 19 July, in commemoration of Siena's becoming part of the Medici state.[58] Even so, Camollia remained an area imbued with civic memories. It was decided in 1623 that the new monastery of the Cappuccins should be built outside the gate, near the church of Santa Petronilla; the foundation stone of the church was laid the following year, and work was completed by 1627. When the monastic complex was completed in 1632, the church was dedicated on 19 September to the Immaculate Conception of the Virgin Mary, as ancient protectress of Siena and that part of the city.[59]

Throughout the seventeenth century, the cult of the Immaculate Conception appears to have flourished in Siena, much as it did in the rest of Catholic Europe.[60] As the political significance of the feast was gradually lost, so the antiquity of Sienese devotion to the cult came to be emphasized, as Girolamo Gigli so clearly testified. Indeed, the bull *Sollicitudo omnium ecclesiarum*, issued by the Sienese Pope Alexander VII Chigi, was extraordinarily important for the diffusion and observance of the cult during the Baroque era, and is directly linked to the papal patronage of the newly-constructed

---

[57] For the coins which were worth 40 and 20 *quattrini*, see B. Paolozzi Strozzi, 'Qualche riflessione sull'iconografia monetale senese', in *Le monete della Repubblica senese* (Siena, 1992), 73–169; G. Toderi and F. Vannel Toderi, 'Collezioni pubbliche e private. Le falsificazioni', in *ibidem*, 231–5; G. Toderi, 'Le monete della Repubblica di Siena (1180–1559)', in *ibidem*, 348–87.

[58] Gigli, *Diario sanese*, vol. II, 31 and 134; Ascheri, *Siena nella storia*, 165–79.

[59] *Santa Petronilla, eventi storici*, 53 ff. For the forgotten monastery of the Immaculate Conception, see G. Gigli, *Città diletta*, 50; Idem, *Diario Sanese*, 618; G. Macchi, ASS, ms. D. 107, fol. 421 (210/73), 42 (24), D. 111, fol. 221, 307.

[60] A catalogue of Sienese sixteenth-century images of the Immaculate Conception is R. Argenziano, 'La beata nobiltà. Itinerario iconografico', in *I Libri dei Leoni. La nobiltà di Siena in età medicea (1557–1737)* (Siena, 1996), 289 and note 16; Argenziano, 'Le origini e lo sviluppo', 109. Many thanks to the author for his valuable help.

Cappella della Madonna delle Grazie in Siena's cathedral from 1659, whose altar was rededicated to the Immaculate Conception.[61] To this can also be added the papal commission of a new chapel in the church of Sant'Agostino in Siena, whose altar was adorned with Carlo Maratta's masterpiece of 1671, showing 'The Virgin Immaculate between the Saints Thomas of Villanova and Francis de Sales.'[62] In this image, the Immaculately Conceived Virgin is seen for the first time with her most common attributes: seated in a *contrapposto* pose on the moon, her foot crushing a snake, her hands clasped, and her head crowned with twelve stars. It was only the arrival in Siena of these unquestionably cosmopolitan masterpieces that rendered obsolete the design derived from Giovanni di Lorenzo's banner.

It is precisely in this respect that the development of the representation of the Immaculate Conception as it occurred in Siena, differed from the varied and complex typologies that had emerged under distinct iconographic and ideological conditions elsewhere in Italy. In every other case, a theological, not a political, debate had underpinned the evolution of the form, so that the images are often described in secondary studies as showing 'debate over the Immaculate Conception.'[63] However, only one example of this type is known in the environs of Siena, an altarpiece attributed to Bartolomeo di David, now in the Buonconvento Museum.[64] By contrast, the iconographic typology that was most widely adopted in Siena resulted from a marked lack of interest in

---

[61] The bull specifically declared for the first time that Mary's soul was immune from Original Sin from the instant of its conception. On the chapel see M. Butzek, *Alessandro VII Chigi (1599–1667): il papa senese di Roma moderna*, ed. A. Angelini, M. Butzek, B. Sani (Siena, 2000), 409–12; M. Butzek, *Il Duomo di Siena al tempo di Alessandro VII. Carteggio e disegni (1658–1667)* (Munich, 1996), 31–4. Thanks to Maarten Delbeke who sent me his essays (one of which is still unpublished) on the diffusion of the cult of the Immaculate Conception and its diffusion in the Netherlands, sponsored by Alexander VII: M. Delbeke, 'A Note on the Immaculist Patronage of Alexander VII Chigi and the Pilgrimage Church of Scherpenheuven in the Low Countries', *Bulletin de l'Institut historique belge de Rome*, LXXI, (2001), 167–200 and 'Alexander VII Chigi and the Immaculate Conception in Siena, Scherpenheuvel and Rome', in *Scherpenheuvel Anthology* (Brepols, forthcoming 2005).

[62] For Maratta in Siena, A. Angelini, 'Giuseppe Mazzuoli, la bottega dei fratelli e la committenza della famiglia De' Vecchi', *Prospettiva*, 79, (1995), 81–6 and *Alessandro VII Chigi*, 481–2.

[63] On the problem of the representation of the Immaculate Conception during the early sixteenth century, examples of which are Leonardo's *Madonna of the Rocks*, Titian's *Pesaro Altarpiece* and '*Assumption*' at the Frari, see G. Vasari, *Le vite dei più eccellenti pittori, scultori e architettori*, ed. G. Milanesi (Florence, 1906), VII, 667–9; also R. Stefaniak, 'On Looking into the Abiss: Leonardo's *Vergin of the Rocks*', *Konsthistorisk Tidskrift*, LXVI, (1997), 1–36; R. Goffen, *Devozione e committenza. Bellini, Tiziano e i Frari* (Venezia, 1991), 53 and ff. Classic studies of the Immaculate Conception iconography remain M. Carmichael, *Francia's Masterpiece. An Essay on the Beginnings of the Immaculate Conception in Art* (London, 1909); A. M. Lépicier, *L'Immaculée Conception dans l'art et l'iconographie* (Spa, 1956); A. Pigler, *Barockthemen. Eine Auswalth von Verzeichnissen zur Ikonogrphie des 17. Und 18. Jahrunderts* (Budapest, 1956), I, 497–505; M. Levi d'Ancona, *The Iconography of the Immaculate Conception in the Middle Ages and Early Renaissance* (New York, 1957); M. Vloberg, 'The Iconography of the Immaculate Conception', in *The Dogma of the Immaculate Conception*, 463–512; also, *Virgo Immaculata*, XV, *De Immaculata Conceptione in litteratura et in arte christiana* (Rome, 1957). Useful comparisons with Siena are the case studies: A. Galizzi Kroegel, 'Una sant'Anna problematica: l'invenzione immacolista per la pala del Pordenone a Cortemaggiore', in *Studi di Storia dell'arte in onore di Maria Luisa Gatti Perer*, ed. M. Rossi e A. Rovetta (Milano, 1999), 223–32.

[64] B. Santi, in *Buonconvento, Museo d'arte sacra della Val d'Arbia* (Genova, 1981), 48–50; F. Bisogni, 'Del cataletto di Sant'Onofrio ossia di Bartolomeo di David', in *Scritti di storia dell'arte in onore di Federico Zeri* (Milano, 1984), 379–87; A. Bagnoli, 'Bartolomeo di David', in *Domenico Beccafumi*, 312, Fig. 307.

theological issues. Rather, as has been shown, a casual invention that was repeated time and again, as in the spectacular example of the Immaculate Virgin shown in the 'Paradiso Senese' that crowns Francesco Vanni's well-known city view of 1596, offered constant homage to Giovanni di Lorenzo's lost banner of the 'childless' Assumption/*Madonna della misericordia* that bore the explanatory inscription 'Immaculatae Conceptioni Virginis Mariae dicatum'.

New York University in Florence

Index

Printed and bound by CPI Group (UK) Ltd, Croydon, CR0 4YY